PADRAIC COLUM

was born in 1881 in the center of Ireland and grew up in the midst of the Celtic Revival. His first poems were published in the early 1900's and his first play was produced when he was twenty. In 1916 he founded, with several colleagues, the Irish Review *which contributed greatly to the renascence of Irish letters.*

Mr. Colum is perhaps best known for his ability to retell folk-stories with freshness and simplicity. He has produced several volumes of folk-stories for children as well as for adults. L. A. Strong has said that he "has brought to mature manhood a curious innocence of vision, a power of seeing familiar things as if he had only just come across them." It is with this same vision and power that Mr. Colum has written this celebrated volume of stories, MYTHS OF THE WORLD.

In 1952 Mr. Colum received the award of the American Academy of Poets and in 1953 he was awarded the Gregory Medal of the Irish Academy of Letters for distinguished work in Irish literature. In 1958 Mr. Colum received the degree of Doctor of Literature from Dublin University. Yeats is the only other writer so honored by the university.

For other UNIVERSAL LIBRARY *titles see the list at the end of this book.*

MYTHS
OF THE
WORLD

PADRAIC COLUM

MYTHS OF THE WORLD

ORIGINAL TITLE: ORPHEUS

TWENTY ENGRAVINGS BY BORIS ARTZYBASHEFF

The Universal Library

GROSSET & DUNLAP

NEW YORK

THE SIGNIFICANCE OF MYTHOLOGY

Not until late centuries did reflective minds see in mythology any of the significance that we have come to see in it. The Italian philosopher of the seventeenth century, Vico, knew that the heroes of myth—Hercules, whose arms could rend the mountains, Lycurgus and Romulus, law-givers, who in a man's lifetime accomplished the long work of centuries—were creations of the collective mind. When man craved for men-like gods he had his way, Vico showed us, by combining in an individual, by incarnating in a single hero, the ideas of a whole cycle of centuries.[1] Then came Goethe who maintained that "the earlier centuries had their ideas in intuitions of the fancy, but ours bring them into notions. Then the great views of life were brought into shapes, into gods; to-day they are brought into notions."[2] In our day, one who loved and studied the mythologies of diverse peoples, wrote:

There are two nouns in the Greek language which have a long and interesting history behind them; these are *mythos* and *logos*. Originally they had the same power in ordinary speech; for in Homer's time they were used indifferently, sometimes one being taken, and sometimes the other, with the same meaning that *Word* has in our language. . . . *Logos* grew to mean the inward constitution as well as the outward form of thought, and consequently became the expression of exact thought—which is exact because it corresponds to universal and unchanging principles—and reached its highest exaltation in becoming not only the reason in man, but the reason in the universe—the Divine Logos, the Son of God, God Himself. . . . *Mythos* meant, in the widest sense, anything uttered by the mouth of man—a word, an account of something, a story understood by the narrator. . . . In Attic Greek, *Mythos* signified a prehistoric story of the Greeks. The application of the word *Myth* among scholars is plain enough up to a certain point; for from being a myth of Greece only, it is now used to mean a myth of any tribe of people on earth. . . . The reason is of ancient date why myths have come, in vulgar estimation, to be synonymous with lies; though true myths—and there are

[1] Michelet's Introduction to *La Scienza Nuova*.   [2] Letter to Reimer.

many such—are the most comprehensive and splendid statements of truth known to man. A myth, even when it contains a universal principle, expresses it in special form, using with its peculiar personages the language and accessories of a particular people, time, and place; persons to whom this particular people, with the connected accidents of time and place, are familiar and dear, receive the highest enjoyment from the myth, and the truth goes with it as the soul with the body.[3]

From these sayings of Vico's, of Goethe's, of Jeremiah Curtin's, we learn something of the inner significance of mythology. Then we may turn to a specialist who can show us how to distinguish myths from fables and from incidents in romance and epic narrative. "I maintain," writes Bronislaw Malinowski, "that there exists:

"A special class of stories, regarded as sacred, embodied in rituals, morals, and social organization, and which form an integral and active part of primitive culture. These stories live not by idle interest, not as fictitious or even as true narrative, but are to the natives a statement of a primeval, greater, and more relevant reality, by which the present life, fates, and activities of mankind are determined, the knowledge of which supplies man with the motive for ritual and moral actions, as well as indications of how to perform them." [4]

This statement gives us a definition: mythology is made up of stories regarded as sacred that form an integral and active part of a culture. The stories in this collection will be such, or they will have the marks of having been at one time such. . . . However, the sacred stories of only a few of the tribes of mankind can be of interest to us who read books. An Australian, African, or South American group may have a sacred story about the world being made by a beetle, and it may form an integral and active part of their culture. But we should not know how to tell such a story. "The primitive forms of civilization, so gross and so barbaric, lay forgotten, or but little regarded, or misunderstood, until that new phase of the European spirit, which was known as romanticism or restoration, 'sympathized' with them— that is to say, recognized them as its own proper present interest." [5] So Benedetto Croce writes, and I use his sentence to indicate the limits of our reach with regard to stories from the mythologies of the world;

[3] Jeremiah Curtin: Myths and Folklore of Ireland. Boston, Little, Brown & Co.
[4] *Ibid.*   [5] On History.

they shall be stories in which there is matter that can be "sympathized" with—recognized as being of proper present interest—by readers of to-day.

EGYPTIAN MYTHOLOGY

It is natural to begin with things Egyptian. But the stories that we have from the mythology of that great civilization are all fragmentary; for the most famous of them we have to go to a Greek work—to Plutarch's treatise on Isis and Osiris. In the story as given here the outline is Plutarch's. But included in it is the story of the Creation which is from Egyptian sources; the names of the deities are not as in Plutarch, but are given in forms sanctioned by Egyptian scholars. The second story is mythological in all that deals with the course of the Sun. The greater part of Egyptian mythology dealt with the appearance, disappearance, and reappearance of the Sun, and with descriptions of the World of the Dead. But no piece of mythology extant gives us in narrative form the Egyptian ideas on these subjects. To provide an outline in which this mythology could be given in story form, the tale about the brothers and their dying father has been invented. The hymn given in this story is from Adolf Leman's *"La religion Egyptienne."*

How greatly the story of Osiris and Isis influenced the ancient world outside of Egypt can be understood from the speculation which Plutarch commits himself to:

This thing that our priests to-day, with prayer for mercy and in dim revelation, most reverently do hint, even that Osiris is King and Lord among the dead, bewilders the minds of most men who know not how the truth of this thing is. For they fancy that Osiris, in whom most surely is all holiness of God and nature, is thus said to be in the earth and beneath the earth, where are hidden the bodies of those who seem to have had their end. But Osiris's self is far indeed from the earth, untouched, undefiled, immaculate of all substance that admits of corruption and death. And souls of men, here in the embrace of bodies and of passions, have no communion with the God save as in a dream, a dim touch of knowledge through philosophy. But when they are set free, and shift their homes into that Formless and Invisible and Pure, then in truth is God their leader and their king, even this God, so that fastened unto him, and insatiably contemplating and desiring that Beauty ineffable and indescribable of man—whereof the old legend would have it that Isis was in love, and did ever pursue and with it consort—all beings there are fulfilled of all the good and fair things that have share in creation.

Plutarch's interpretation of the Osiris-Isis story is not necessarily an Egyptian one. Nor can we be sure that the prayer that Apuleius's hero, Lucius, makes to Isis is one that an Egyptian at any period might make:

O thou most holy and eternal saviour of the human race, and ever most munificent in thy tender care of mankind, unto the hazard of our sorrow thou givest the sweet affection of a mother. Nor doth any day or any night's repose, nay, not a tiny moment, vanish past empty of benefits, but ever on earth and sea thou art protecting men, driving aside life's tempests, stretching forth thy right hand of salvation. The threads of our life, by us inextricably entangled, thou dost untwine; thou stillest storms of fate, thou holdest the evil goings of the stars. Thee Heaven doth worship; the shades are thy servants; 'tis thou dost spin the world, and lightest up the sun, and governest the universe, and tramplest upon hell. To thee the stars make answer, for thee the seasons return, heaven's powers exult, the elements obey. At thy nod blow the breezes, clouds give fertility; thine is the germing of the seed and the growth of the germ. Before thy majesty the birds do tremble whose goings are in the air, and the beasts that haunt the hills, and the serpents lurking in the dust, and the monsters that swim in the ocean. But I, scant of soul for the offering of thy praise, poor of patrimony for the celebrating thy sacrifices, feeble of voice for the telling out my heart's knowledge of thy Majesty—nay, nor would one thousand mouths, one thousand tongues suffice, nor the long utterance of an eternal lauds,—I, what (in my poverty) my worship, at least, can do, that will I care to effect. Thy divine countenance and most holy godhead, stored within my heart of hearts, will I forever keep, and there will watch and picture it.

BABYLONIAN

The Babylonian religion was on a higher level than the Egyptian, which, according to Maspero, one of the greatest of Egyptologists, was close to the animism and fetichism of the African tribes. Yet the Sumerians and Babylonians, compared with the Egyptians, had a very faint conception of a life beyond the grave. "They imagined the lower world to be a place of darkness, where the departed, retaining their consciousness, were condemned to lie motionless for ages, under the stern rule of a goddess who reigned in that world." Then Professor Rostovtzeff goes on to say:

The hymns and prayers addressed to the gods of Babylon and Assyria are full of religious inspiration and unfeigned religious feeling. The Babylonians in their epic poetry sought to explain the mighty secrets of nature, connected with the life of gods and men.[6]

Their stories of the struggles of the gods against Chaos and the monsters produced by Chaos, of Gilgamish's adventures, of Ishtar's descent into the World of the Dead, are comparable to nothing else but their sculptures—those carvings in which kings and soldiers, horses and lions, chariots and spears, are rendered with such power as seems to us terrifying.

> Marvels that showed a mighty will,
> Huge power and hundred-handed skill,
> That seek prostration and not praise
> Too faint such lofty ears to fill![7]

We owe the preservation of the Babylonian and Sumerian stories, in a large measure, to an Assyrian king of the neo-Babylonian epoch, to Ashur-bani-pal, who reigned in Nineveh B.C. 668. Says a pamphlet published by the British Museum:

Having determined to form a Library in his palace he set to work in a systematic manner to collect literary works. He sent scribes to ancient seats of learning, *e.g.*, Ashur, Babylon, Cutah, Nippur, Akkad, Erech, to make copies of the ancient works that were preserved there, and when the copies came to Nineveh he either made transcripts of them himself, or caused his scribes to do so for the Palace Library. In any case he collated the texts himself and revised them before placing them in his Library. The appearance of the tablets from his Library suggests that he established a factory in which the clay was cleaned and kneaded and made into homogeneous, well-shaped tablets, and a kiln in which they were baked, after they had been inscribed. The uniformity of the script upon them is very remarkable, and texts with mistakes in them are rarely found. . . . Ashur-bani-pal was greatly interested in the literature of the Sumerians, *i.e.*, the non-Semitic people who occupied Lower Babylonia about B.C. 3500 and later. He and his scribes made bilingual lists of signs and words and objects of all classes and kinds, all of which are of priceless value to the modern student of the Sumerian and Assyrian languages.[8]

The Greeks borrowed one myth from the Babylonians—the myth of Adonis who is Tammuz. "Every year," says Frazer in "The Golden

[6] A History of the Ancient World, Vol. I.   [7] George Darley, *Nepenthe.*
[8] The Babylonian Story of the Deluge and the Epic Gilgamish: 1920.

Bough," "Tammuz was believed to die, passing away from the cheerful earth to the gloomy subterranean world, and every year his divine mistress journeyed in quest of him." Tammuz's death was mourned by men and women at midsummer. The story of Ishtar's descent into the World of the Dead was probably made up from the hymns chanted during the mourning ceremonies. Like Osiris, Tammuz personified the vegetable life that dies and rises up again.

PERSIAN

At the time when the Assyrian kings of the neo-Babylonian epoch were publishing the Babylonian mythological cycles, and when Egyptian and Greek mythologies were flourishing, the original Persian or Iranian mythology was being stopped in its growth; afterwards nearly all records of it were destroyed. This happened in the reign of Darius (sixth century B.C.), through the rise of the Mazdean or Zoroastrian dualism which, accepted by the king and the governing classes, had the effect of depriving the old mythology of all value and significance.

The Zoroastrian dualism represented a religion that was on a higher level than the religions of Egypt and Babylon. Says Professor Rostovtzeff:

Like the Hebrew prophets, Zoroaster reached the conception of a single spiritual god, Ormuzd or Ahura Mazda, in whom the principle of good is personified, while the evil principle is embodied in Ariman or Angra Mainyu. The two principles strive eternally in life and nature, and in the struggle men take part. Man is responsible for his actions, good and bad; he is the master of his fate; his will determines his line of conduct. If he struggles against evil, confesses God, and cares for the purity of his body and soul, then, after four periods, of three thousand years each, in the world's history, when the time shall arrive for final victory of good over evil and of Ormuzd over Ariman—the general resurrection of the dead and the last judgment will assure him his place among the saved and the righteous.[9]

The Persian religion had strong influence upon both Judaism and early Christianity: a king who was the champion of early Zoroastrianism ended the Babylonian captivity and enabled the Jews to reconstitute themselves as a religious body; the star of the Nativity was hailed by

[9] A History of the Ancient World, Vol. I.

the Magi who were Persians and Zoroastrians. This religion in the form of the worship of one of the angelic powers of Zoroastrian theology, Mithra, spread through the West during the late Roman Empire, and made itself a powerful rival of young Christianity. Mithra, who was identified with the Sun, had a cult that was fostered by the Roman military guild; it is known that as far west as Britain there was a temple built to him. Present-day Christianity, on the side of ceremony and ritual, has elements that have come into it from its one-time closeness to Mithraism. If we read Francis Thompson's "Orient Ode" we shall know something of the fervours of Mithraism; it is significant that the metaphors in the opening verse are from the sacred ritual of the Mass:

> Lo, in the sanctuaried East,
> Day, a dedicated priest
> In all his robes pontifical exprest,
> Lifteth slowly, lifteth sweetly,
> From out its Orient tabernacle drawn,
> Yon orbéd sacrament confest
> Which sprinkles benediction through the dawn.

Mithraic feeling is stronger in another verse:

> Thou art the incarnated Light
> Whose Sire is aboriginal, and beyond
> Death and resurgence of our day and night;
> From his is thy vicegerent wand
> With double potence of the black and white.
> Giver of Love, and Beauty, and Desire,
> The terror, and the loveliness, and purging,
> The deathfulness and lifefulness of fire!

The original mythology of Iran or Persia is supposed to have been of the type that existed in Aryan India around 1000 B.C.—the mythology of the Vedic Hymns. Many names out of the oldest strata of Iranian tradition can be equated with names in the Vedic Hymns. One of these names is Yima which in later Persian becomes Jamshīd. Yima is the same as the Vedic god Yama: Yama, in India, was the god of the dead. "The evidence concerning Yama-Yima," writes Albert J. Carnoy, "is, on the whole, that he is the setting sun. He follows the path of the sun to go to a remote recess, whither he leads all men with him. . . . In Iran the solar nature of Yima is rather more accentuated than in India, and the old epithets of Yima are striking in this respect. He is commonly called *Khshaēta* ('brilliant'), an adjective which is at the same time a regular epithet of the sun." [10] The story of Jamshīd is the most explicit piece of mythology that has come down to us from ancient Iran—it is preserved in a very late work—in the Shāhnāmah, written by the poet Firdausī, who died about 1025 A. D. Firdausī used old traditions which were mythology that had been turned into pseudo-historical legends. It is of interest to note that not long after the time when Firdausī treated the fragments of an Aryan mythology as historical traditions and romantic tales, a like work was accomplished at the other side of the Aryan world—in Wales where the fragments of Celtic mythology were made over into the collection of romantic stories that we know as the Mabinogion.

JEWISH: POST-CHRISTIAN PERIOD

The Jewish stories that have come down to us in the Haggadah are more akin to the Persian than they are to any other stories. Their monotheism seems to be nominal, veiling a real dualism. Thus, God creates the Angels on the second day "lest man believe that the Angels assisted God in the creation of the heavens and the earth." This suggestion of rivalry is in many of the stories: God is on one side, the Angels on the other. The Angel Samael who becomes Satan is, in his opposition to the Most High, like Angra Mainyu in relation to Ahura Mazda. The stories that form the Haggadah were developed between the second and the fourteenth century of our era. They are accessible in "The Legends of the Jews" by Louis Ginzberg. [11]

GREEK

The myths given are mainly from Hesiod's Theogony and the Homeric Hymns, works composed between the eighth and the sixth century B.C. Little remains to be said on the subject of Greek mythology. But it is worth while repeating some sentences written by Miss Jane Harrison:

All men, in virtue of their humanity, are image-makers, but in some the image is clear and vivid, in others dull, lifeless, wavering. The Greeks were the

[10] Iranian Mythology, Volume VI of Mythology of All Races.
[11] Four volumes. Philadelphia, Jewish Publication Society.

supreme *ikonists*, the greatest image-makers that the world has ever seen, and, therefore, their mythology lives on today.[12]

LATIN

It is important to separate the Greek and Latin mythologies: Iuppiter, though akin to, is not the same as Zeus; Iuno is not the same as Hera. Minerva is not the same as Athena, Neptune is not the same as Poseidon. "The Romans worshipped not gods, not *dei*," writes Miss Jane Harrison, "but powers, *numina*":

These numina were only dim images of activities. They had no attributes, no life histories; in a word, no mythology. We must always remember that mythology, the making of images, is only one and, perhaps, not the greatest factor in religion. Because the Romans were not *ikonists*, it does not follow that they were a people less religious than the Greeks. The contrary is probably true. A vague something is more awe-inspiring than a known something.[13]

Mars the Death-dealer was the central object of Italian worship, according to Mommsen, in that epoch when the Italian stock dwelt by itself in the Peninsula. He was the champion of the burgesses, hurling the spear, protecting the flock, and overthrowing the foe. Mommsen goes on to say:

To Mars was dedicated the first month not only in the Roman calendar of the months, which in no other instance takes notice of the gods, but also probably in all the other Latin and Sabellian calendars. Among the Roman proper names, which in like manner contain no allusion to any other god, Marcus, Mamercus, and Mamurius appear in prevailing use from very early times; with Mars and his sacred woodpecker was connected the oldest Italian prophecy; the wolf, the animal sacred to Mars, was the badge of the Roman burgesses, and such sacred national legends as the Roman imagination was able to produce referred exclusively to the god Mars and to his duplicate, Quirinus. . . . While abstraction, which lies at the foundation of every religion, elsewhere endeavoured to rise to wider and more enlarged conceptions and to penetrate ever more and more deeply into the essence of things, the forms of Roman faith remained at, or sank to, a singularly low level of conception and insight. . . . In the religion of Rome there was hardly anything secret except the names of the gods of the city, the Penates; the real character, moreover, even of these gods was manifest to everyone. . . . Of all the worships of Rome, that which, perhaps, had the deepest hold was the worship of the

[12] Myths of Greece and Rome. London, Ernest Benn, Ltd.   [13] *Ibid.*

tutelary spirits that presided in and over the household and storechamber: these were, in public worship, Vesta and the Penates, in family worship the gods of the forest and field, the Silvani, and especially the gods of the household in its strict sense, the Lases or Lares, to whom the share of the family meal was regularly assigned. . . . Respecting the world of spirits, little can be said. The departed souls of mortal men, the "good" (*manes*), continued to exist as shades haunting the spot where the body reposed (*dii inferi*), and received meat and drink from the survivors. But they dwelt in the depths beneath, and there was no bridge that led from the lower world either to men ruling on earth or upward to the gods above. The hero-worship of the Greeks was wholly foreign to the Romans. . . . Numa, the oldest and most venerable name in Roman tradition, never received the honours of a god in Rome as Theseus did in Athens.[14]

The stories of Romulus and of Numa are taken from Plutarch's Lives and Livy's History where the personages are treated as historical characters. The story of Pomona and Vertumnus is taken from Ovid.

GRAECO-ROMAN

The story of Cupid and Psyche is a literary production; however, it is given in this collection of stories from the mythologies because it became something of a sacred story—a focus for religious thought. And, besides, the literary production was based on an old Greek folktale that had in it religious elements. It must be remembered that the mother of Cupid is not the Venus of early Roman mythology nor the Venus Genetrix of Lucretius's poem; she has been merged with Aphrodite, the goddess who belonged to the southern and eastern islands of the Greek archipelago. In the form we know it the story belongs to a late period: it was written by Apuleius of Medaura who was born A.D. 124, and it forms an episode in the novel which we call "The Golden Ass." There is an Elizabethan translation by Adlington besides the better-known translation which Walter Pater gives in his "Marius the Epicurean."

CELTIC

Celtic mythology is known to us only in the fragments that have come down to us through Irish (Gaelic) and Welsh (Brythonic) romances. Of the mythology of the Continental Celts we know nothing:

[14] The History of Rome, Book I.

On the Continent the Celtic tribes came in contact with the rich and highly organised Graeco-Roman mythology, and discarded their own mythic romance. In the British Isles Celtic mythic romance escaped the destructive influence of Rome, was spared by Christianity, and served, almost down to the present day, as a backbone and rallying centre to the peasant lore about the fairies, which is substantially the old agricultural faith, preserved in rude and crude form, and partly reshaped by the fierce opposition or the insidious patronage of Christianity. Gaelic peasant lore only differs from that of other parts of Europe, because Gaeldom has preserved, in a romantic form, a portion of the pre-Christian mythology. Thanks to the fact that this mythology enters largely into the Arthurian romance, the literature of modern England has retained access to the fairy realm, and has been enabled to pluck in the old wonder-garden of unending joy fruits of imperishable beauty.[15]

In Ireland a learned class who took pride in preserving the relics of the national past, wrote down histories and romances that contained mythological material. We have these histories and romances in documents of the eleventh and twelfth centuries, the Book of Leinster and the Book of the Dun Cow: the material on which they are based is of a much earlier period. In Wales a material less copious and more distorted, was, between 1080 and 1260, shaped into the romances that we know in the Mabinogion.

The Celts were known in the ancient world for their positive beliefs concerning the survival of the soul. They appear to have had a conception of a Happy Otherworld which was similar to that of the early Greeks:

Although from fifteen hundred to two thousand years separate the earliest recorded Greek and Irish utterances in a form, substantially speaking, yet extant, yet both stand on much the same stage of development, save that Ireland has preserved, with greater fulness and precision, a conception out of which Homeric Greece had already emerged. Examination of the mythologies due to other Aryan races, or rather, to prejudge nothing, to peoples speaking Aryan tongues equally with the Greeks and Irish, reveals the remarkable fact that Greeks and Irish alone have preserved the early stage of the Happy Otherworld conception in any fulness.[16]

The Celtic religion appears to have been the worship of the Powers of Life and Increase:

[15] Alfred Nutt: The Voyage of Bran, Vol. 2, in the Grimm Library.
[16] Ibid.

In Greece the Powers of Life and Increase, worshipped by the primitive agriculturists, are but one element in the completed Hellenic Pantheon, and this has been subjected to so much change, to such enlargement and glorification, as to be well-nigh unrecognizable. In Ireland, to judge by extant native texts, these powers must have constituted the predominant element of the Pantheon, and cannot have departed very widely from their primitive form. . . . In the main that mythology had for its *dramatis personae* the agricultural Powers of Life and Increase, in the main it was made up of stories of which the ultimate essence and significance were agricultural.[17]

The same authority offers the following conclusions on the subject of Celtic mythology as it is revealed in the Irish romances:

The features common to Greek and Irish mythology belong to the earlier known stage of Aryan mythical evolution, and are not the result of influence exercised by the more upon the less advanced race. Survivals in Greece, they represent the high-water mark of Irish pre-Christian development; hence their greater consistency and vividness in Ireland. Fragmentary as they may be in form and distorted as it may be by its transmission through Christian hands, we thus owe to Ireland the preservation of mythical conceptions and visions more archaic in substance if far later in record than the great mythologies of Greece and Vedic India.[18]

The Celtic stories given here deal mainly with adventures in the Happy Otherworld, in the Divine Land. The Voyage of Prince Bran is a typical story. Translated by Kuno Meyer, it is published with a comment by Alfred Nutt which is a study of Celtic mythology. The poems form the oldest part of the story; they date back to the eighth, or possibly to the seventh century. In the Divine Land to which Prince Bran voyages take place the events which lead up to the birth of Etain and afterwards to the death of King Conaire. This Divine Land is also the scene of Pwyll's adventures in the Welsh story. Pwyll, Arawn, and Mathonwy were originally divinities in Celtic Britain: their stories are taken from the Welsh Mabinogion.

FINNISH

The mythology out of which the Finnish stories come belonged to the Finno-Ugric stock which includes the Finns and their near relations the Esthonians, and the more remotely related Lapps and Hun-

[17] Alfred Nutt: The Voyage of Bran, Vol. 2, in the Grimm Library.
[18] *Ibid.*

garians. We know this mythology through the folk-epic of Finland, the Kalevala, and the Magic Songs of the Finns and the Esthonians. As we have them now, the Finno-Ugric traditions reflect a definite locale—the land of forests and lakes of North Europe. Until the last century these traditions existed in peasant memory and speech. Scattered parts of the poem that is now known as the Kalevala were published in 1822 by Zacharias Topelius. Elias Lönnrot collected the remainder and arranged the twenty-two or twenty-three thousand verses into fifty runes. The metrical form in which the Kalevala has come down has been imitated by Longfellow in Hiawatha.

It is startling to realize that a mythology existed on the lips of a European people in our time. There has been, of course, a Christian influence on the traditions out of which the folk-songs that make the Kalevala have come. A large part of this poetry had its rise in the Middle Ages and Catholicism had an influence on a few incidents.

The episode given here is from the Kalevala, W. F. Kirby's translation, Runo XIII and XIV. John Abercromby's "The pre- and protohistoric Finns with the Magic Songs of the West Finns" has also been used.

ICELANDIC

When we realize that in France, Britain, and Ireland, Christianity had been established for six hundred years before it was introduced into Iceland and the Scandinavian countries, we are aware of what a long lifetime the mythology of northern Europe had in comparison, let us say, with the mythology of Celtic Britain and Ireland. The Icelandic mythology is part of the Scandinavian which is again part of the mythology of the Germanic people. It had a separate development in Norway, and a separate development, perhaps, in Iceland where the records that we have of it were made. Iceland, at the time, was the centre of the Scandinavian world. As shaped in the Icelandic poems and stories, this mythology has been influenced by Christianity. Of the great poem that tells of the creation of the world and the gods, the "Voluspo," the latest translator, Mr. Henry Adams Bellows, writes:

That the poem was heathen and not Christian seems almost beyond dispute; there is an intensity and vividness in almost every stanza which no archaizing Christian could possibly have achieved. On the other hand, the evidences of Christian influence are sufficiently striking to outweigh the arguments of Finnur

Jonsson, Müllenhof, and others who maintain that the "Voluspo" is purely a product of heathendom. The roving Norsemen of the tenth century, very few of whom had as yet accepted Christianity, were nevertheless in close contact with Celtic races which had already been converted, and in many ways the Celtic influence was strongly felt.[19]

We owe our knowledge of this mythology to the Poetic and Prose Eddas—the first a collection of poems celebrating the gods and heroes of the olden times, and the second a handbook giving an account of the gods and the old system of divinity, with a number of separate stories about the gods and heroes. Scholars now agree that the poems that make up the Poetic Edda were shaped between 900 and 1050. The Prose Edda was composed by an Icelandic scholar, Snorri Struluson, about the year 1220. The rediscovery of this mythology was hailed by the whole Germanic world, and treated as a racial inheritance: it lives as no other European mythology lives to-day through the expression it has been given in the tragic music of Richard Wagner's "Ring" operas.

INDIAN

India's is the most heavily *mythologized* of civilizations; the mythology revealed in its literature is threefold. There is, first of all, that of Aryan India which has connections with the mythologies of Persia, Greece, and Italy: because we know it through the Vedic Hymns (shaped between 1200 and 800 B.C.), we name it the Vedic mythology. Then comes a mythology which nominally arises out of the Vedas but which is quite different in idea and outlook: this is the Brāhmanical, the living mythology of India, revealed to us in the enormous epics which were shaped about the fourth century B.C., the Rāmāyana and the Mahābhārata. Buddhism, a movement which originally aimed at simplifying the Brāhmanical system, added new entities to the country's mythology: out of it came a mythology connected with beings who incarnate from period to period in order to redeem mankind: the stories of these incarnations and of the efforts of the Buddhas-to-be to attain enlightenment are its subjects; connected with it are cycles of animal-stories which tell of the incarnations of Buddha in animal forms. Unlike Persia, unlike Europe, India never

[19] Introduction to the Poetic Edda. New York, the American-Scandinavian Foundation.

had her mythology displaced by movements such as Zoroastrianism or Christianity.

India, in respect to her mythology, is like a watershed: there systems which take us to look in opposite directions are close to each other. We have Dyaus Pitar, the Sky Father, who is the same as Zeus and Iuppiter; with him we have Indra, the Storm God, Agni, the Fire God, and the Celestial Twin Horsemen, who are similar to the divinities in European mythology; we have also Yama who assembles the dead, the Yima of old Persia mythology who becomes the Jamshīd of mytho-romance: we are destined to meet this divinity in the Far East where he has become the god of the dead, Emma, in Buddhist Japan. This, the Vedic, was the mythology of a simple-minded, agricultural, cattle-raising people. Then comes the Brāhmanical, which arises out of philosophical ideas: time and space are conceived of in dimensions that are frightening to one of European culture; there are unnumbered worlds, unnumbered periods of creation; the gods are immortal, but they are destined to be absorbed in the absorption of the universe at the end of a cosmic cycle. The Brāhmanical mythology as presented in the epics is a very rich one. Four stories in this collection are taken from it: the Churning of the Ocean and the Birth of the Ganges from the Rāmāyana, Savītiī and the God of the Dead and Damayantī's Choice from the Mahābhārata. The story of Gotama's Attainment is out of Buddhist mythology, and is one of the scriptural stories of the Buddha who, historically, was Prince Siddhāratha who lived in the fifth century B.C. In the early Vedas the story-material is meagre: these Indian hymns are voluminous as compared with the Homeric Hymns, but none of them give us, as most of the Homeric Hymns do, a consecutive story. The Heavenly Nymph and her Mortal Husband is told from the only extended statement in the hymns. The story is also told in later literature. But in the later version the atmosphere has been changed. In the Vedas the Apsarases are nymphs who have something austere about them; in later literature they are types of voluptuousness. An attempt has been made to get the atmosphere of the early Aryan world in the retelling of the story, and to reveal the simple forms of the Vedic gods. It is of interest to note that these gods, the devas, become in Persia, after the Zoroastrian movement, the daēvas who are demons. Later, these fallen daēvas become the divs, or demonic beings, of the Arabian story-tellers.

CHINESE

There is not in China, as there is in India and there was in Greece, any dramatization of divine activities—at least, not in literature; there is no Chinese Hesiod, nor Homer, nor Vālmīki. The Chinese people seem to have had no curiosity about their origin which could be thought of as the origin of mankind; the philosophers have concerned themselves with ethics and politics, and the poets with human relations and the influences of nature. According to Confucius's disciples, the subjects on which the master declined to speak were "extraordinary things, feats of strength, disorder and spiritual beings." This attitude, transmitted to the literate classes, did away with interest in mythology. Undoubtedly, Chinese popular traditions contain a variety of stories about personages who might be regarded as mythical. But such stories are so prosaic and fantastic, so literal and ingenious, that we have no way of retelling them with becoming seriousness. To literate Chinese the universe has been created and is sustained by impersonal forces; that which makes a mythology—personification of supernatural powers and their identifications with some of the interests of mankind—is not conceived of by them.

The story of the creation by P'an Ku is a popular one, deriving from Taoism: Chinese scholars maintain that it was introduced from some outside country. The Celestial Weaver Maid and the Herdsman is a stellar myth, and has to do with the stars Aquilia and Vega. The personages in the story are honoured by women who practise the crafts of needlework and embroidery. The story is popular in Japan as well as China.

JAPANESE

In distinction to Taoism, Confucianism, and Buddhism, Shintoism is the primitive body of beliefs of the Japanese people. The two cosmological myths given here are from Shinto sources. The triumph of the Sun Goddess over darkness and disorder is identified with the triumph of the Imperial dynasty over forces that were hostile to it: the Imperial family claim descent from the Sun Goddess.

POLYNESIAN

The widely spread Kanaka or Maori people have a rich and remarkably homogeneous mythology: the same divine beings figure in stories told in most of the islands of the Pacific Ocean. "We find," writes Miss Martha Warren Beckwith, "the same story told in New Zealand and Hawaii, scarcely changed, even in name." [20] In one sense, practically all Polynesian stories are mythological, for, to quote Miss Beckwith again:

Gods and men are, in fact, to the Polynesian mind, one family under different forms, the gods having superior control over certain phenomena . . . the supernatural blends with the natural exactly the same way as to the Polynesian mind gods relate themselves to men, facts about one being regarded as, even though removed to the heavens, quite as objective as those which belong to the other, and being employed to explain social customs and physical appearances in actual experience.

The Polynesians, like the ancient Egyptians, thought of the soul as being double: a part of it could go wandering and be brought back, or be taken away and restored by spells of sorcerers.

The most direct and significant statement of Polynesian myth is "Pele and Hiiaka" by N. B. Emerson. In this narrative we have the mythical history of the Hawaiian Fire Goddess taken down from the lips of people for whom it was still a belief by a man who knew the people and understood their traditions. Only a bare outline of it is given here: as published it extends to over 200 pages; 170 mele, or dramatic poems, are given in the course of the narrative.[21] When we read this myth we realize how separate Polynesian culture is. The Polynesian Creation Myth is from New Zealand, and is given by Sir George Grey in his "Polynesian Mythology." The story of Maui's attempt to win immortality for men is from the same work. The other story about Maui is in part from New Zealand and in part from Hawaii: it is told in my own "At the Gateways of the Day," [22] but is ultimately based on stories given by Mr. W. D. Westervelt in his

[20] The Hawaiian Romance of Laieikawai: Thitry-third Annual Report of the Bureau of American Ethnology.
[21] Pele and Hiiaka, a Myth from Hawaii, by N. B. Emerson: Honolulu, 1915.
[22] Published by the Yale University Press.

"Maui the Demi-god." Maui is a pan-Polynesian hero, and stories about him are told upon nearly all the islands which the Kanaka-Maori people reached.

PERUVIAN

The two great civilizations of America, the Middle American and the South American, appear to have had their rise about the same time, and in each a period of decadence seems to have set in just before the advent of the European conquerors. We have much less information about the civilization we name Inca than the one we name Aztec. Most of what we know about the antiquities of Peru comes from the writings of Garcilasso de la Vega, whose father was Spanish and whose mother was Peruvian, and who regarded himself as a descendant of the Incas and an interpreter of their traditions. Garcilasso has been translated into English by Sir Clements Markham, whose own books upon Peru tell us practically all that is known about the ancient monuments, literature, and traditions of the Incas. In the first story, I have imagined someone like Garcilasso speaking. The second is not mythological; it is probably a folk-tale. But the mythological survivals of the Incas are so scanty that any story that has even a slight connection with their mythology, and that has some portion of their imagination in it, is of interest. "The Llama-herder and the Virgins of the Sun" is retold from a version given by Sir Clements Markham; it was told to Fray Martin de Morua, who was a Quichua scholar, in 1583.

CENTRAL AMERICAN AND MEXICAN

In regarding Central America and Mexico as a single cultural area, I accept the authority of Eduard Seler, who, grouping Guatemala, Yucatan, and the area that includes Mexico City together, writes:

The unity of this entire region of ancient civilization is most clearly expressed by the calendar, which these people considered the basis and alpha and omega of all high and occult knowledge.[23]

According to this view, the Mayan, the Toltec, and the Aztec are varieties of a single culture.

[23] Unity of Mexican and Central American Civilization: Report to Bureau of American Ethnology, Bulletin 28.

The most dramatic rendering of the mythology belonging to this culture is in a book written in Guatemala, in a Mayan language, some time in the seventeenth century. This is the "Popul Vuh." The Spanish version of the native text was translated into French by the Abbé Brasseur de Bourbourg, and our main knowledge of this curious and exciting book is derived from this translation. Two stories in this collection are from the "Popul Vuh"—the story of the Creation, and the story of the adventures of the Twin Heroes. A little material has also been taken from an English version of parts of another native book—the "Annals" of the *Cakchiquel* Indians. The rest of the stories are Aztec; they belong to the people whose capital was where Mexico City now stands. The political and material power that this people had attained to is revealed in the impression that their great city, Tenochtitlan, made on the chronicler of the Spanish Conquest, Bernal Diaz:

> We counted amongst us soldiers who had traversed different parts of the world: Constantinople, Italy, Rome; they said that they had seen nowhere a place so well aligned, so vast, ordered with such art, and covered with so many people.

Of the Aztec stories, the most appealing is the one that tells of Quetzalcoatl, his beneficence and his banishment from Tollan. Scholars maintain that Quetzalcoatl was a Toltec divinity, or that he was the last of the Toltec kings, and bore the name of their principal divinity. His story then symbolizes the fall of the mild and enlightened Toltec civilization before the onslaught of the war-like Aztec tribes. Another interpretation is given by Mr. Lewis Spence:

> From April or May to the beginning of October the trade-wind blows from the east coast over the Plateau of Anahuac, bringing with it abundance of rain, and accelerating vegetable growth, thus actually "sweeping the ways for the rain-gods." Its advance is comparatively slow, the rains beginning three or four weeks earlier in Vera Cruz than in Puebla and Mexico. At the beginning of October, however, it is invariably modified by the local monsoon, which interrupts it over wide areas, or in certain districts invades it in violent cyclonic storms, dissipating its energies and altering its course. Quetzalcoatl represents the gentle trade-wind, which ushers in the growth-making rains. His reign of peace, plenty, and fertility over, he comes into opposition with Tezcatlipoca, who represents the monsoon and who chases his rival "from city to city," ravening at him like a tiger, says Mendieta, and at last hustling

him out of the country. That Tezcatlipoca is also a god of wind is certain, as is proved by one of his names, Yoalli Ehecatl, "Wind of Night," and that he is the monsoon or hurricane is proved beyond all doubt by the circumstance that he is said to have rushed along the highways at night at extraordinary speed, and that Hurakan, his Quiche name, is still employed for the very wind he represented, and has become a generic name for a tempestuous wind in practically all European languages, which have without question adopted it from the American word.[24]

As we look upon the powerful sculptures of the ancient Mexicans and their compact drawings we get the impression of a strangely earthbound civilization: it was as if all of the figures were rooted; in some of the drawings hands are in movement, but it is like the movement of branches of trees, and we can never think of the faces as being lifted to the skies. In their mythology we have the impression of thought which can never become abstract. This literalness leaves theirs the most terrible of the religions connected with any of the great civilizations. Always they wanted rain, and they strove to give example to the rainmaking deities by pouring out human blood. They sacrificed thousands of human victims every year; every Aztec ceremony culminated in human sacrifice. Something, however, can be said for this religion:

Students of religious phenomena not infrequently show distaste for the deeper consideration of the Mexican faith, not only because of the difficulties which beset the fuller study of this interesting phase of human belief in the eternal verities, but also, perhaps, because of the "diabolic" reputation which it has achieved, and the grisly horrors to which it is thought those who examine it must perforce accustom themselves. It is certainly not the most obviously prepossessing of the world's religions. Yet if due allowance be made for the earnestness of its priests and people in the strict observance of a system the hereditary burden of which no one man or generation could hope to remove, and the religion of the Azteca be viewed in a liberal and tolerant spirit, those who are sufficiently painstaking in their scrutiny of it will in time find themselves richly rewarded. Not only does it abound in valuable evidences for the enrichment of the study of religious science and tradition, but by degrees its astonishing beauty of colour and wealth of symbolic variety will appeal to the student with all the enchantment of discovery. The echoes of the sacred drum of serpent-skin reverberating from the lofty pyramid of Uitzilopochtli, and passing above the mysterious city of Tenochtitlan with all the majesty of Olympian thunder, will seem not less eloquent of the soul of a vanished faith

[24] Lewis Spence: The Gods of Mexico.

than do the memories of the choral chants of Hellas. And if the recollection of the picturesque but terrible rites of this gifted, imaginative, and not undistinguished people harrows the feelings, does it not arouse in us that fatal consciousness of man's helplessness before the gods, which primitive religion invariably professes and which reason almost seems to uphold? [25]

ZUÑI

The pueblo-dwelling Indians, of whom the Zuñi are the chief representatives, belong to a stage of culture that the great civilizations of Middle and South America had come directly out of. And as in Middle and South America, the whole form of Zuñi culture, the whole trend of Zuñi religious thought, is conditioned by the cultivation of maize. The story given here is taken from Cushing's "Zuñi Creation Myth," published as a report of the Bureau of American Ethnology in 1896. Cushing's remarks on Zuñi culture which are here quoted come out of observations which he made in the period between 1879 and 1881:

The Zuñi faith . . . is a drop of oil in water, surrounded and touched at every point, yet in no place penetrated or changed inwardly by the flow of alien belief that descended upon it. . . . Yet a casual visitor to Zuñi, seeing, but unable to analyze the signs above noted, would be led to infer quite the contrary by other and more potent signs. He would see horses, cattle, donkeys, sheep, and goats, to say nothing of swine and a few scrawny chickens. He would see peach orchards and wheat fields, carts (and weapons now), and tools of metal; would find, too, in queer out-of-the-way little rooms, native silversmiths plying their primitive bellows and deftly using a few crude tools of iron and stone to turn their scant silver coins into bright buttons, bosses, beads, and bracelets which every well-conditioned Zuñi wears, and he would see worn also, especially by the men, clothing of gaudy calico and other thin products of the looms of civilization. Indeed if one did not see these things and rate them as at first the gifts to this people of those noble old Franciscan friars and their harder-handed, less noble Spanish companions, infinitely more pathetic than it is would be the history of the otherwise vain effort I have above outlined; for it is not to be forgotten that the principal of these gifts have been of incalculable value to the Zuñi. They have helped to preserve him, through an era of new external conditions, from the fate that met thirty other and less favored Pueblo tribes—annihilation by the better-armed, ceaselessly prowling Navajo and Apache, and for this alone, their almost sole accomplishment of lasting good to the Zuñi, not in vain were spent and given the lives of the early mission fathers.

I have called the collection "Orpheus," naming it after the minstrel who, according to the poet of the Argonautica, sang "how the earth, the heaven, and the sea once mingled together in one form, after deadly strife were separated each from the other; and how the stars and the moon and the paths of the sun ever keep their fixed place in the sky; and how the mountains rose, and how the resounding rivers with their nymphs came into being, and all creeping things." [26]

PADRAIC COLUM.

[26] Apollonius Rhodius: The Argonautica, translated by R. C. Seaton, the Loeb Library.

CONTENTS

CONTENTS

EGYPTIAN

EGYPTIAN

OSIRIS AND ISIS: RÊ, HIS GOING-DOWN AND UPRISING

OSIRIS AND ISIS

When Osiris reigned death was not in the land. Arms were not in men's hands; there were not any wars. From end to end of the land music sounded; men and women spoke so sweetly and out of such depth of feeling that all they said was oratory and poetry.

Osiris taught men and women wisdom and he taught them all the arts. He it was who first planted the vine; he it was who showed men how and when to sow grain, how to plant and tend the fruit-trees; he caused them to rejoice in the flowers also. Osiris made laws for men so that they were able to live together in harmony; he gave them knowledge of the Gods, and he showed them how the Gods might be honoured.

And this was what he taught them concerning the Gods: In the beginning was the formless abyss, Nuu. From Nuu came Rê, the Sun. Rê was the first and he was the most divine of all beings. Rê created all forms. From his thought came Shu and Tefênet, the Upper and the Lower Air. From Shu and Tefênet came Qêb and Nut, the Earth and the Sky. The Earth and the Sky had been separated, the one from the other, but once they had been joined together. From the eye of Rê, made out of the essence that is in that eye, came the first man and the first woman.

And from Qêb, the Father, and Nut, the Mother, Osiris was born. When he was born a voice came into the world, crying, "Behold, the Lord of all things is born!"

And with Osiris was born Isis, his sister. Afterwards was born Thout, the Wise One. Then there was born Nephthys. And, last, there was born Sêth. And Sêth tore a hole in his mother's side—Sêth the Violent One. Now Osiris and Isis loved each other as husband and wife, and together they reigned over the land. Thout was with them, and he taught men the arts of writing and of reckoning. Nephthys went with Sêth and was his wife, and Sêth's abode was in the desert.

3

Sêth, in his desert, was angered against Osiris, for everywhere green things that Sêth hated were growing over the land—vine, and grain, and the flowers. Many times Sêth tried to destroy his brother Osiris, but always his plots were baffled by the watchful care of Isis. One day he took the measurement of Osiris's body—he took the measurement from his shadow—and he made a chest that was the exact size of Osiris.

Soon, at the time before the season of drought, Sêth gave a banquet, and to that banquet he invited all the children of Earth and the Sky. To that banquet came Thout, the Wise One, and Nephthys, the wife of Sêth, and Sêth himself, and Isis, and Osiris. And where they sat at banquet they could see the chest that Sêth had made—the chest made of fragrant and diversified woods. All admired that chest. Then Sêth, as though he would have them enter into a game, told all of them that he would give the chest to the one whose body fitted most closely in it. The children of Qêb and Nut went and laid themselves in the chest that Sêth had made: Sêth went and laid himself in it, Nephthys went and laid herself in it, Thout went and laid himself in it, Isis went and laid herself in it. All were short; none, laid in the chest, but left a space above his or her head.

Then Osiris took the crown off his head and laid himself in the chest. His form filled it in its length and its breadth. Isis and Nephthys and Thout stood above where he lay, looking down upon Osiris, so resplendent of face, so perfect of limb, and congratulating him upon coming into possession of the splendid chest that Sêth had made. Sêth was not beside the chest then. He shouted, and his attendants to the number of seventy-two came into the banquetting hall. They placed the heavy cover upon the chest; they hammered nails into it; they soldered it all over with melted lead. Nor could Isis, nor Thout, nor Nephthys break through the circle that Sêth's attendants made around the chest. And they, having nailed the cover down, and having soldered it, took up the sealed chest, and, with Sêth going before them, they ran with it out of the hall.

Isis and Nephthys and Thout ran after those who bore the chest. But the night was dark, and these three children of Qêb and Nut were separated, one from the other, and from Sêth and his crew. And these came to where the river was, and they flung the sealed chest into the river. Isis, and Thout, and Nephthys, following the tracks that Sêth and his crew had made, came to the river-bank when it was daylight, but by that time the current of the river had brought the chest out into the sea.

Isis followed along the bank of the river, lamenting for Osiris. She came to the sea, and she crossed over it, but she did not know where to go to seek for the body of Osiris. She wandered through the world, and where she went bands of children went with her, and they helped her in her search.

The chest that held the body of Osiris had drifted in the sea. A flood had cast it upon the land. It had lain in a thicket of young trees. A tree, growing, had lifted it up. The branches of the tree wrapped themselves around it; the bark of the tree spread itself around it; at last the tree grew there, covering the chest with its bark.

The land in which this happened was Byblos. The king and queen of the city, Melquart and Astarte, heard of the wonderful tree, the branches and bark of which gave forth a fragrance. The king had the tree cut down; its branches were trimmed off, and the tree was set up as a column in the king's house. And then Isis, coming to Byblos, was told of the wonderful tree that grew by the sea. She was told of it by a band of children who came to her. She came to the place: she found that the tree had been cut down and that its trunk was now set up as a column in the king's house.

She knew from what she heard about the wonderful fragrance that was in the trunk and branches of the tree that the chest she was seeking was within it. She stayed beside where the tree had been. Many who came to that place saw the queenly figure that, day and night, stood near where the wonderful tree had been. But none who came near was spoken to by her. Then the queen, having heard about the stranger who stood there, came to her. When she came near, Isis put her hand upon her head, and thereupon a fragrance went from Isis and filled the body of the queen.

The queen would have this majestical stranger go with her to her house. Isis went. She nursed the queen's child in the hall in which stood the column that had closed in it the chest which she sought.

She nourished the queen's child by placing her finger in its mouth. At night she would strip wood from the column that had grown as a tree, and throw the wood upon the fire. And in this fire she would lay the queen's child. The fire did not injure it at all; it burned softly around the child. Then Isis, in the form of a swallow, would fly around the column, lamenting.

One night the queen came into the hall where her child was being nursed. She saw no nurse there; she saw her child lying in the fire. She snatched the child up, crying out. Then Isis spoke to the queen from the column on which, in the form of a swallow, she perched. She told the queen that the child would have gained immortality had it been suffered to lie for a night and another night longer within the fire made from the wood of the column. Now it would be long-lived, but not immortal. And she revealed her own divinity to the queen, and claimed the column that had been made from the wonderful tree.

The king had the column taken down; it was split open, and the chest which Isis had sought for so long and with so many lamentations was within it. Isis wrapped the chest in linen, and it was carried for her out of the king's house. And then a ship was given to her, and on that ship, Isis, never stirring from beside the chest, sailed back to Egypt.

And coming into Egypt she opened the chest, and took the body of her lord and husband out of it. She breathed into his mouth, and, with the motion of her wings (for Isis, being divine, could assume wings), she brought life back to Osiris. And there, away from men and from all the children of Qêb and Nut, Osiris and Isis lived together.

But one night Sêth, as he was hunting gazelles by moonlight, came upon Osiris and Isis sleeping. Fiercely he fell upon his brother; he tore his body into fourteen pieces. Then, taking the pieces that were the body of Osiris, he scattered them over the land.

Death had come into the land from the time Osiris had been closed in the chest through the cunning of Sêth; war was in the land; men always had arms in their hands. No longer did music sound, no longer did men and women talk sweetly and out of the depths of their feelings. Less and less did grain, and fruit-trees, and the vine flourish. The green places everywhere were giving way to the desert. Sêth was triumphant; Thout and Nephthys cowered before him.

And all the beauty and all the abundance that had come from Rê would be destroyed if the pieces that had been the body of Osiris were not brought together once more. So Isis sought for them, and Nephthys, her sister, helped her in her seeking. Isis, in a boat that was made of reeds, floated over the marshes, seeking for the pieces. One, and then another, and then another was found. At last she had all the pieces of his torn body. She laid them together on a floating island, and re-formed them. And as the body of Osiris was formed once more, the wars that men were waging died down; peace came; grain, and the vine, and the fruit-trees grew once more.

And a voice came to Isis and told her that Osiris lived again, but that he lived in the Underworld where he was now the Judge of the Dead, and that through the justice that he meted out, men and women had life immortal. And a child of Osiris was born to Isis: Horus he was named. Nephthys and the wise Thout guarded him on the floating island where he was born. Horus grew up, and he strove against the evil power of Sêth. In battle he overcame him, and in bonds he brought the evil Sêth, the destroyer of his father, before Isis, his mother. Isis would not have Sêth slain: still he lives, but now he is of the lesser Gods, and his power for evil is not so great as it was in the time before Horus grew to be the avenger of his father.

RÊ, HIS GOING-DOWN AND UPRISING

There were two brothers each of whom possessed an overmastering strength: the name of the first brother was Edfu, and the name of the second was Nefer-ka. Edfu was a soldier, and his strength was in his arms, and Nefer-ka was a scribe; he knew of spells that are written down in a book that has come from Thout, the God of Magic and of Writing and Reckoning. Behold! these two brothers had come to the house of their father, and it had become known to them, as it was known to him, that death was coming upon their father.

Now their father had sent to the scribes for the book in which is written the description of the journey and the trials of the soul after death, and he would not be at peace until he had taken that book into his still living hands. Therefore he called upon his sons to keep guard over him so that no evil spirit might come upon him and take the strength out of his hands or the sight out of his eyes until he held and looked into the book that is called the Book of the Dead.

Each of his sons swore before him that he would hold back such evil spirit, the one thinking of the overmastering strength that was in his arms, and the other thinking of the overmastering strength that was in the spells he possessed. Swift messengers had been sent to the scribes, and these messengers would be back with the morning light.

Behold! Edfu went forth and stood at the east side of the house, his strength knit like the panther of the South, and his brother, Nefer-ka, went forth and stood at the west side of the house, intent as the hawk of Horus.

It was the hour when Rê, the Sun God, goes down into the Underworld. And the soldier, watching that going-down, thought upon the vengeance wrought by Rê: what he thought upon kept Edfu fierce and wakeful.

The soldier thought to himself: Now Rê was mocked by men who said to themselves, "Rê has reigned over us for hundreds of years; he has become old; his bones are like silver, his flesh is like gold. Who is Rê now that he should be a master over us?"

And Rê, hearing men talk like this, said, "These men who make mock of me will flee into the deserts and the mountains when I send forth against them my daughter, even Sekhmet." The soldier watching towards the east recalled the appearance of Sekhmet.

She had a lion's head upon a woman's body. At the word of her father she went forth against men and her voice resounded horribly. She made the rivers run with the blood of men. The soldier, watching in the night, had a vision of men fleeing before lion-headed Sekhmet as before the army of Pharaoh. The mountains did not hide them, the deserts did not hold them. Sekhmet slew and slew, and her voice resounded as a lion's. Those whom she did not reach to slay were overcome by terror because of her resounding voice. So Sekhmet strode through the land of Egypt.

The soldier told himself what had happened afterwards: Rê began to have pity upon men, and he sought to deliver men from Sekhmet. But even Rê could not deliver men from the lion-headed Goddess—of herself she must cease to slay. Rê pondered on how this might be

brought about. At last he said to Thout who had all his counsel, "Call to me the messengers who are as swift as the storm-clouds." Thout called upon them, and the messengers appeared before the majesty of Rê.

He said to the messengers, "Run to Elephantine; hasten; go and bring back to me quickly the fruit that causes sleep, even the mandrake. Be swift, for what has to be accomplished must be accomplished ere dawn."

The messengers hastened as the storm-wind. They came to Elephantine; they took up the fruit that causes sleep, even the mandrake. Scarlet was that fruit; the juice of it was the colour of men's blood. The messengers brought the fruit before the throne of Rê.

Then the Gods and Goddesses—even Shu whose place is in the upper air, and Qêb, and Nut and Nuu from whom came Rê himself—even these great Gods crushed the barley and made the beer. Seven thousand measures of beer the Gods made then. They brewed it in haste, for the dawn was about to break; with the beer they mixed the juice of the mandrake. Rê saw that the mixture was like to the blood of men; he said, "With this beer I can save mankind."

The Gods took the seven thousand measures of beer, and ere the night passed they brought the beer to the place where men and women had been slain by Sekhmet, the lion-headed Goddess. They spilled the beer over the fields; its colour was the colour of blood.

Then came Sekhmet ready to slay. As she passed she looked to this side and to that, looking out for her prey. No thing living did she see. The fields were covered with beer that was the colour of blood. Sekhmet laughed; her laughter was like the roaring of a lioness. She thought in her heart that she had shed all this blood. She stooped and she saw her face reflected therein, and she laughed again. She stooped and drank; again and again she drank. Then laughter came from her no more, for the juice of the fruit that causes sleep had mounted to her brain. No longer could she slay. And she went when Rê called to her, "Come, my daughter; come, my sweet one; come and rest." The lion-headed Goddess rested, and so men were saved from her destructiveness.

Edfu the soldier looked towards the east, and, behold! there was a redness there that was like the redness of the beer that had covered the fields when Sekhmet the lion-headed Goddess saw her face reflected therein. And still Edfu, crouched like the panther of the South, watched against the coming of whatever evil spirit that might strive to enter the house with malice against his father.

At the west side of the house Nefer-ka the scribe watched: on his lips, ready to pronounce, were the spells he had learned. He had watched from the time of the going-down of the sun, from the time of the daily death of Rê.

And Rê, being dead, was laid on the boat that is named Semektet, the boat that is seven hundred and seventy cubits in length. Nefer-ka the scribe knew what journey Rê was to make in that boat: he followed Rê on his journey through the Underworld.

The boat Semektet, with the dead Rê laid upon it, makes its way through the Realm of the Dead. The twelve Goddesses of Night take their places in the boat to guard Rê. With them goes Up-uaut, the Opener of the Ways. With them goes Isis, the sister and the wife of Osiris, she to whom is known the greatest spells.

Slowly goes the boat of Rê, slowly it goes, passing through the Realm of the Dead. At the entrance to every region there, there is a great gate. The guardian of each hour speaks the name at which the gate opens; then the boat of Rê goes through. And when the Goddess of the First Hour has given place to the Goddess of the Second Hour, and when the Goddess of the Second Hour has given place to the Goddess of the Third Hour, the boat of Rê, the boat Semektet, comes into the region named Amentet where Osiris reigns.

Then, thinking of what passes during that Third Hour and in that Third Realm, the scribe Nefer-ka looked up into the sky, and, behold! there were the never-vanishing stars which are the souls of those who have been justified by Osiris.

In the realm of Amentet Osiris reigns, Osiris who is God of the Dead. All who die come before his throne for judgment. Their hearts are weighed against the Feather of Truth. The throne of Osiris is beside a running stream; from its waters a single lotus blossom arises. Upon the blossom the four children of Horus, the son of Osiris, stand, their faces towards Osiris. The first has the face of a man, the second has the face of an ape, the third has the face of a jackal, the fourth has the face of a bird of prey. The heart of the dead man is weighed against the Feather of Truth: if the man has not been purified the feather weighs down the scale, and it sinks lower and lower. If the man has been made pure the feather sinks and the heart rises. Then Thout, the God of Writing and of Reckoning, takes the heart and puts it back into the breast of the man; Horus takes the man by the hand. All this the scribe Nefer-ka saw as though it had been before him, for he had been instructed in all that is in that book that is called the Book of the Dead.

The Goddess of the Third Hour gives place to the Goddess of the Fourth Hour, and the boat in which Rê is laid comes before another gate. The name of the guardian of that gate is pronounced; the gate opens; the boat makes its way through another region. All desert is this region. The Fourth Hour passes and the Fifth Hour is at hand. The Goddess of the Fifth Hour pronounces the name, and the boat that is named Semektet enters the Fifth Region.

On either side guarding this region are creatures whose bodies are the bodies of lions and whose faces are the faces of men; they dig into the sand with talons that are the talons of eagles. Sokar the Fierce is guardian of this region. He stands upright there, he who has the head of a hawk on the body of a man.

The Goddess of the Fifth Hour makes way for the Goddess of the Sixth Hour. The gates are flung wide as the name is pronounced. Then the boat enters the realm that is named Abyss of Waters—the Sixth Realm of the Realm of the Dead.

As the scribe thought upon these mysteries he knew that the Sixth Hour was passing. Behold! The Morning Star that now leads the boat of Rê onward appeared in the sky. This, the Sixth Hour, is an hour that is evil for men. For in the realm that is named Abyss of Waters is the monster 'Apop who holds the world together in his coils, but who waits to destroy Rê the Giver of Light and Life, and plunge the world into lifeless dark. Now as the boat of Rê journeys through the Sixth Realm those on the boat behold on the banks of the river the vast shapes of the Gods. The Gods cry aloud to Rê as he passes lifeless in the boat that is named Semektet; their voices that are as the roaring of bulls come across that vast abyss as the murmur of bees. The monster 'Apop hisses and roars and strains at the chains that bind him. But now Isis takes her place beside Rê. Her spells prevail and the monster is made helpless. The boat goes on and past the great sand-banks; 'Apop struggles to make himself free.

In the Seventh Hour the boat passes through a region of darkness and cold. But in this region is Khepri the Renewer. Here there is a great coiled serpent with five heads, and within his coils is Khepri. In the form of a scarab he flies into the boat of Rê; he awaits the time when he can bring back life to Rê. On goes the boat; the Goddess of the Seventh Hour gives place to the Goddess of the Eighth Hour. In the Eighth Hour the boat passes through the region where are the tombs of the Gods. The tombs stand by a river: high mounds of sand are they: at each end of each tomb the head of a man watches the passing by of Rê. Also a monstrous lion looms out of the darkness.

The Eighth Hour passes; the Ninth Hour passes and the Tenth Hour. Now a name is spoken, and the boat of Rê comes to the Eleventh Region.

The scribe Nefer-ka thought upon this region. It is a region feared by those who are rejected by Osiris. Near by are Pits of Fire. Goddesses whose breaths are of flame hold in their hands gleaming swords of fire. The scribe lifting up his head saw in the sky what seemed to be reflections from these Pits of Fire.

The Goddess of the Eleventh Hour now gives place to the Goddess of the Twelfth Hour. The name of power is pronounced once more, and the last great gate is opened. Now Khepri fastens himself upon Rê; Rê is transformed into Khepri and lives again. Out between pillars of turquoise comes the boat of Rê. And where the boat goes there is a great island on which the Gods rest: there stands the Tree of Life, growing between the ocean and the sky, between the upper and lower worlds. Its fruit keeps the Gods and the souls of the dead who have been justified before Osiris in eternal youth; the past as well as the future is written on its leaves. Now as the boat passes with Rê living once more within it the Gods come as dogs to his feet, rejoicing to greet him.

The Sun, renewed, was showing himself once more to men. The scribe Nefer-ka held his hands out to the disk and chanted his salutation to Rê, the Great One:

He commanded, and the Gods were born.

Men came forth from his eyes, and the Gods from his mouth.

He it is who made the grass for the cattle, and the fruit tree for men; he who created that wherein live the fishes in the stream and the birds in the heaven; he who putteth the breath in the egg, and nourisheth the son of the worm, and produceth the substance of insects; he who maketh what is necessary for mice in their holes and nourisheth the birds on every tree.

It is for love of him that the Nile cometh, he, the sweet, the well-beloved: and at his rising men do live.

And this Chief of the Gods hath yet his heart open to him that calleth on him.

He protecteth the fearful against the audacious man.

Therefore is he loved and venerated by all that doth exist, in all the height of heaven, in the vastness of the earth, and the depth of the sea.

The Gods bow down before thy majesty and exalt their Creator.

They rejoice at the approach of Him who did beget them:

Be praised! say the wild beasts. Be praised! saith the Desert.

Thy beauty conquers hearts.

In the light of the risen Sun, Nefer-ka the Scribe saw the messengers coming towards the house of his father, one of them bearing in his hands the book that described the journey and the trials of the Dead, and behold! Edfu, his brother, was standing before him declaring that his father's living hands were stretched out to hold the book, and that his eyes had sight yet in them to read what was in the book.

BABYLONIAN

BABYLONIAN

IN THE BEGINNING: GILGAMISH: THE STORY OF UTA-
NAPISHTIM AND OF THE DELUGE THAT DESTROYED ALL
THAT WAS ON THE EARTH: ISHTAR'S DESCENT INTO THE
WORLD BELOW

IN THE BEGINNING

In the beginning there was Apsu the Primeval, and Tiāmat, who is
Chaos. There were no other beings. The waters were not separated;
they and the earth mingled, and there was no ground for the growth
of anything. Then nothing bore name; no destinies had been ordained.

Then the Gods came into existence: Lakhmu and Lakhamu. Ages
passed. Other Gods came into existence: Anshar and Kishar. Ages
passed. Then Ea, Anu, and Bel came into existence.

The Gods considered how the waters might be separated from each
other, how the earth might be separated from the waters, how names
might be given and destinies ordained. And as the Gods considered
these things, the realm of Tiāmat, the Mother of All, was made small
for her. She conceived a hatred for the Gods; with Apsu she plotted
the destruction of those whom she had borne.

Then, behold! Tiāmat roused up the Ancient Monsters; she spawned
monsters never known before. She made ready to destroy the Gods.
The Gods felt their realm shake, and they were affrighted.

Then Anshar opened his mouth and spoke to Anu, his son. He said
to Anu, "Go forth and appease Tiāmat, so that the Gods may not be
destroyed by her who bore them." Anu went forth. He saw the monsters that Tiāmat had formed; his heart failed him, and he turned back
to the dwelling-place of the Gods. They were filled with fear when
they looked upon the countenance of Anu.

Then Ea was sent forth to appease Tiāmat. He saw the Ancient
Monsters that she had roused up. They were sharp of tooth and cruel
of fang; they bore merciless weapons. Ea was affrighted, and he turned
back to the dwelling-place of the Gods. The Gods looked upon his
countenance and they were affrighted. The lesser Gods wailed bitterly,
crying, "What has changed that she should conceive this hatred for us?
We do not understand the evil will of Tiāmat!"

Then Marduk, his heart prompting him, rose in the assembly of the Gods. He opened his mouth and spoke, saying, "Lo, I, Marduk, will be the champion of the Gods if ye decree in your council that whatever I do shall remain unaltered, and that whatsoever my mouth speaketh shall never be changed nor made of no avail." Then the Gods said, "Thou shalt be the chiefest among the great Gods; established shall be the words of thy mouth; irresistible shall be thy command; none of the Gods shall transgress thine ordinances! O Marduk, thou art our champion!"

They prepared for him a lordly chamber; they bestowed upon him the sceptre, the throne, and the ring. And the Gods girded weapons upon their champion: they gave him his bow and his spear; they put a club in his right hand and he grasped it; they hung a quiver by his side. He himself prepared a great net for the taking of the monsters that Tiāmat had formed and the Ancient Monsters that she had roused up.

Tiāmat raged; she was full of wrath against the Gods. With terror and with splendour she clothed her monsters so that their crested heads were lifted high. She gave them invincible weapons. With poison instead of blood their bodies were filled. The dwelling-places of the Gods were shaken as she gave the battle signal to her hosts, as Tiāmat uttered the spell that aroused them for battle.

Then Marduk went into his chariot; the lightning and the thunderbolt were in his hands. The Gods beheld him and knew that none could inspire such terror as he. He harnessed his four horses; he yoked them to the chariot. Ferocious, high of courage, swift of pace were Marduk's horses; moreover, they had been trained to trample enemies underfoot. They gnashed with their teeth and their bodies were flecked with foam. So Marduk went forward, and the seven winds he had created followed in his course. They were the Storm and the Hurricane; the Whirlwind, the Four-fold Wind and the Seven-fold Wind; the Wind that has no Equal, and the Wind that is called the Evil Wind. The Gods followed Marduk.

Now when Marduk neared where Tiāmat was, the movement of Tiāmat's host ceased; the monsters were affrighted by the appearance of Marduk. But Tiāmat rushed on; she uttered angry cries; with unbent neck she taunted the Gods. All things were shaken.

Marduk let loose the Evil Wind. Tiāmat's mouth was opened; the wind rushed in and filled her belly. She lay down: no more could she give battle-orders to her monsters. Marduk drove his spear through the heart of Tiāmat. He stood upon her prone body. Then, sweeping his net around, he took the monsters in his net. The whole world was filled with their cries.

He trampled on Tiāmat, and she, the Mother of All, was as a reed that is broken. With his club he shattered her skull. He cut channels for the blood to flow out of her, and he bade the winds bear her blood away into the secret places.

As a man splits a flat fish, Marduk split the body of Tiāmat. He set one half of her above as a covering for the heavens; he fixed bolts there so that the floods that are above may not be voided upon the earth, and he stationed a watchman to guard the bolts. Of the other half of Tiāmat's body he made the earth. He divided all that was made between Anu, Bel, and Ea—the Heavens, the Earth, and the Abyss. He fixed the stars in their places; he ordained the year and divided it; he caused the Moon God to shine, and he gave him the night for his portion.

Thereafter Marduk devised a plan. He opened his mouth and he spoke to Anu, Bel, and Ea. "My blood I will take and bone I will fashion; I will make man to inhabit the earth so that the service of the Gods may not fail ever." So Marduk spoke, and man began to live upon the earth.

GILGAMISH

Into the Temple where his mother dwelt Gilgamish went, and when she saw by the look upon his face that he was bent upon going on some strange journey or upon doing some terrifying deed, his mother cried out to Shamash, the Sun God, asking him why he had given her son a heart that could never keep still. And Gilgamish, hearing her cry, said to her, "Peace, O woman! I am Gilgamish, and it must be that I shall see everything, learn everything, understand everything." Then his mother said to him, "These longings are yours, O Gilgamish, because not all of you is mortal. Two-thirds of your flesh is as the flesh of the Gods and only one-third is as the flesh of men. And because of the

God's flesh that is on you, you must be always daring, always rest-less. But yet, O my son, you have not immortal life. You must die because a part of you is man. Yea, Gilgamish, even you must die, and go down into the House of Dust."

And Gilgamish, hearing his mother say this, groaned loudly, ter-ribly; the tears flowed down his cheeks; no word that was said to him might content him. He groaned, he wept, even although in the courts of the Temple he heard the women sing:

> Who is splendid among men,
> Who is glorious among heroes?

And answer back, one to the other:

> Gilgamish is splendid among men,
> Gilgamish is glorious among heroes.

In a while he rose up and he said, "O Ninsunna, O my mother, what is it to die?"

Then Ninsunna, his mother, made answer, and said, "It is to go into the abode out of which none ever returns: it is to go into the dark abyss of the dread Goddess, Irkalla. They who dwell there are without light; the beings that are there eat of the dust and feed on the mud." So his mother said, and Gilgamish, the great king, groaned aloud, and the tears flowed down his face.

Gilgamish dwelt in Erech, and was king over the people there. The works that he did in Erech were mighty, surpassing the works of men. He built walls round the city that were an hundred cubits in thickness and in height over a hundred cubits. He built towers that were higher than any that men had builded before. He built great ships that went upon the great sea. All these things he did because Gilgamish had a restless heart. But the people of Erech groaned because of the labours he laid upon them; they groaned and sent up prayers to the Gods.

The Gods harkened to the prayers of the people of Erech; they said in the Council of the Gods, "Behold, Gilgamish lays upon the people labours that crush them. The life goes out of them, and they no longer can offer sacrifice to the Gods. He lays these labours upon them because he alone is mighty in the world. But if we make one who is mightier than he, Gilgamish will be abashed when he sees that one, and no longer will he think that he is lord of all; then will he not engage in labours that give his people no rest."

The Gods called upon the Goddess Aruru. And Aruru considered in her heart how she would make one who was mightier than Gilgamish. Thereafter she washed her hands and she took clay and mixed her spittle into it. And Aruru made a being, a living male creature that was in the likeness of the God Anu. His body was covered all over with hair so that he appeared to be clothed in leaves. The Gods named him Enkidu, and they gave him the wild places of the earth for his portion.

And Enkidu, mighty in stature, invincible in strength, lived in these wild places. Gilgamish passed through the land he dwelt in, but saw him not. Gilgamish passed through the land to make war upon Khumbaba who dwelt in the country where the forests of cedars are. Those who went with him were struck with awe when they saw the cedars in their height and in their closeness of growth together; they were worn out because of their journey and the fear that possessed them, and they prayed to the Gods to deliver them from under the hand of a king who had a heart that was so restless. They came upon Khumbaba whose voice was like the roar of a storm, whose breath was like a gale of wind. They fought the armies of Khumbaba, these soldiers of Gilgamish, and Gilgamish himself fought Khumbaba and with his own hand slew him. And then Gilgamish and his army passed through the country where Enkidu maintained himself, but they saw not Enkidu. And Enkidu, mighty in stature, invincible in strength, drank the water that the wild cattle drank and ate the herbs that the gazelles lived on; he was a friend to the wild beasts and he knew not the faces of men.

Now when Gilgamish returned to Erech, his city, after having overthrown Khumbaba, he heard the women in his palace sing:

> Who is splendid among men,
> Who is glorious among heroes?

And he heard the women answer back, one to the other:

> Gilgamish is splendid among men,
> Gilgamish is glorious among heroes.

But he remembered what had been told him about the House of Dust and the Abyss of the Goddess Irkala; he groaned, and the tears coursed down his face.

Below the forest of cedars dwelt a hunter, a young man who dug pits and laid nets for the wild beasts that were upon the mountains. One day, expecting to find many wild beasts in his pits and his nets, he went to them, but behold! the pits he had digged were filled up and the nets he had laid were torn; also the prey had been taken out of the nets and the pits. Then the young man, the hunter, went up the mountain, and coming nigh a pit he had made he watched, for he saw something at the pit. He saw the shoulders and the head of a man. And he watched the man come out of the pit, and he had upon his shoulders a gazelle that had fallen into it. And behold! the man went to where a company of gazelles stood waiting, and they were not fearful of the man. He laid down the gazelle he carried, and the gazelle joined the company of gazelles. Then the man went back and filled up the pit with earth, and went with great strides towards the forest. The young man, the hunter, saw that he was all naked and covered with hair; and that the hair on his head was long and like a woman's. The hunter was affrighted, and he went from the place. He came upon others of the pits he had digged, and they were all filled up; there was no creature near any of them, nor was there one under any of the nets he had laid.

Then was the hunter made anxious. He said within himself, "What shall become of me? I till no land, and I know of no way of living save by my nets and my pits! But if the creatures that have been snared are taken out of my pits and from under my nets, what shall I do to find food for myself and my parents?" He wept as he spoke thus to himself, and, carrying no beast, he went back to the hut where his father was.

His father heard what the young man said and considered it. "This is one who is friendly to the beasts and knows not the faces of men," he said. "What he has done he will do again and yet again, and there will be no prey left for us in the pits or under the nets. Therefore, we must have him led away from this place. Often have you brought beasts to the Temple in Erech to be sacrificed there to Anu and Ishtar and the rest of the Gods. Go to that city and into the place of the mighty Gilgamish, and have those in the Temple give you a woman of the Temple to go with you. And when the one who has not seen the faces of men sees the face of the woman of the Temple, and sees her take off her veil, he will be amazed; he will go to the woman of the Temple, and she will speak with him and will draw him from this place."

The young man, the hunter, did as his father instructed him: he went into Erech, the city that Gilgamish ruled over, and he went within the Temple. He spoke to Ninsunna, the mother of Gilgamish. And having heard what he had to tell, the mother of Gilgamish brought to him a woman of the Temple; she put the woman's hand in the hunter's hand, and the young man brought the woman out of that place and into the mountainous region where he had looked upon Enkidu.

It was then that Ishtar the Goddess stood before Gilgamish in her terrible beauty. She said unto him, "Thou, O Gilgamish, shalt be my man; I shall be thy woman. Thou shalt come into my house, and those who sit upon the thrones shall kiss thy feet. Gifts from the mountain and the lowland shall be laid before thee. I shall make to be harnessed for thee a chariot of lapis-lazuli and gold; the wheels of it shall be gold and the horns upon it shall be precious stones. Thou shalt harness to it mighty horses; they shall prance proudly; there shall be no horses like unto the horses that shall be under thy yoke. All these things shall be for thee when, with perfume of cedar upon thee, thou shalt come into my house."

Gilgamish made answer to the Goddess; in wrath he spoke to Ishtar, the Beautiful One, the Terrible One, answering her: "Thy lovers have perished. Thy love is like to a door that letteth in the storm. Thy love is like a fortress that falls upon and crushes the warriors within it. The lover of thy youth, Tammuz, even he, was destroyed; destroyed are all the men whom thou hadst to do with. The creatures who come under thine influence rejoice, but they rejoice for a while only: the wing of the bird is broken through thee; the lion is destroyed; the horse is driven to death. Thou sayst thou lovest me, Ishtar. Loved by thee I should fare as they have fared."

When Ishtar heard the words that Gilgamish spoke she was filled with wrath. She left the place where he was. She meditated evil against him. In a while she made a fire-breathing bull and sent it down into Erech to destroy Gilgamish and Gilgamish's people.

The young man, the hunter, went back into the mountain regions where he had digged pits before and spread his nets. He brought the woman of the Temple with him. He made her to sit nigh the place where the wild beasts came to drink; he bade her draw to her the wild man if he should come to drink with the beasts.

Then the hunter went away. The Temple woman sat by the pool, plaiting the tresses of her hair. One by one the beasts came to drink, but finding there the scent of a human creature they went away.

At last Enkidu, the wild man, came down to the pool. He did not have the power of scent that the beasts had. He went into the drinking-place and he filled his palms with water, and he raised them up to his mouth, and he drank. The Temple woman saw him there in his great stature, with the hair on his head long and flowing as if it were a woman's, and the hair on his skin making him look as if he were dressed in leaves. She called out; she spoke, and Enkidu heard her voice.

He saw her; she held her arms out to him; she took off her veil. Then Enkidu was astonished. He went towards her, and she took his hand, and she led him away. He came under the spell of the Temple woman's beauty; he would not leave her, but stayed where she stayed at the edge of the forest. On the sixth day he rose up and went away from where she stayed. His heart had become hungry to look upon the wild beasts whose friend he had been. He went towards where the companies of gazelles were. The gazelles fled from him. He went to where the wild cattle grazed, and the wild cattle fled as soon as he came near to them. He went to where the panthers were, and the panthers bounded away when he came near to them. Then Enkidu was sore in his heart. He cried out, "Why do my friends, the beasts, forsake me?" He did not know that the beasts had wind of another human creature in the wind that was from him. Wherever he went the beasts fled from him. Then Enkidu was made ashamed; his knees gave way under him; he swooned away from shame.

When he rose up again he went back to where the Temple woman stayed, and the beasts still fled before him. The Temple woman waited for him; she smiled upon him; she held out her arms to him, and spoke flattering words to him. He stayed with her and she spoke to him of Erech, and of the Temple, and of Gilgamish the Mighty. At last she led him with her to Erech, Gilgamish's city.

It was then that Gilgamish had his struggle with the fire-breathing bull that Ishtar, in her anger, had sent against him and his people. Multitudes of the inhabitants of the city had been destroyed by the bull. Gilgamish—even he—was not able to prevail against the Bull of Heaven. He lodged an arrow in the neck of the bull. Still it came on against him, and Gilgamish had to flee from before it.

And the bull came upon the way along which Enkidu was coming with the woman of the Temple. He laid his hands against the front of the bull, and held it. Then Gilgamish came and delivered mighty blows between its horns and its neck, and when the bull would have trampled upon him, Enkidu, with his mighty strength, pulled it backwards. Gilgamish with Enkidu attacked the bull again. Long they fought against the fury of the fire-breathing bull, but at length the two of them slew Ishtar's mighty creature.

The Goddess appeared upon the battlements and cursed them for having destroyed the Bull of Heaven. And Enkidu, fearless before Gods and before men, tore the flesh from the side of the bull and threw it at the feet of Ishtar. The Goddess and all the women of the Temple made lamentations over the portion of the bull that had been flung up to them.

But Gilgamish called together the people of the city. He showed them the creature that had been slain. They looked, and they marvelled at the size of the horns, for they were horns that could hold six measures of oil. Gilgamish took the horns of the Bull of Heaven to the Temple of the God Lugalbanda, and he hung them before the seat of the God. He made friends with Enkidu. And he and Enkidu went down to the river Euphrates, and there they washed, and they came back and they stood in the market-place. All men marvelled at the stature and power of these two, Gilgamish and Enkidu. Gilgamish took Enkidu to his palace; he gave him the raiment of a king to put on; he gave him a chair, and he had him sit on his left side; he gave him food fit for the Gods to eat, and wine fit for a king to drink. These two mighty men became friends, and they loved each other exceedingly.

Together Gilgamish and Enkidu hunted; together they made war; the lion and the panther of the desert fell to their bows and spears. And at last the people of Erech had rest from their labours, for no longer did Gilgamish make them weary raising great buildings, and they had peace, for no longer did he bring them to make war upon the people of far lands.

A time came when Enkidu longed for the life of the forest. Thither he went. And Gilgamish, when he knew that his friend has gone from Erech, put on coarse attire; he arrayed himself in the skin of a lion, and he pursued Enkidu. And Enkidu was glad because of this, for he knew that his friend, the noble Gilgamish, would not forsake him. Together they lived in the forest; they hunted together and they became more and more dear to each other.

Later Enkidu had a dream that terrified him. He dreamt that there were thunderings in the heavens and quakings in the earth. He dreamt that a being came before him and gripped him in talons that were the talons of an eagle, and carried him down into a dread abyss. There Enkidu saw creatures that had been kings when they were upon the earth; he saw shadowy beings offering sacrifices to the Gods. He saw in the House of Dust priests and magicians and prophets dwelling. He saw there Bêlit-sêri who writes down the deeds done upon the earth.

Enkidu was terrified; he knew not the meaning of the dream that had come to him. To Ninsunna he went, and he told her his dream. She wept when she heard him tell it. But she would not tell him the meaning that it had.

Thereafter Enkidu lay down on the well-decked bed that Gilgamish, his friend, had given him. He groaned upon his bed. Gilgamish came to comfort him, but Enkidu, although he had joy of Gilgamish's coming, could not banish from his heart the thing that had been shown him in his dream. For ten days he lay upon his bed with Gilgamish beside him. In two days more his sickness became more grievous. Then Enkidu lay silent, and Ninsunna said to her son, "Now is Enkidu dead."

Long gazed Gilgamish upon Enkidu, his friend in the palace, his companion in the hunt upon the mountains and in the forest, his brave ally in his fight against the Bull of Heaven. Long gazed Gilgamish upon his friend lying there. Then Gilgamish said:

"What kind of sleep is this that is upon thee?

"Thou starest out blankly and hearest me not.

"Shall this sleep be upon Gilgamish also? Shall I lie down and be as Enkidu?

"Sorrow hath entered into my soul.

"Because of the fear of death that hath come upon me my heart is restless; I shall go; I shall wander through the lands."

Then Gilgamish touched the breast of his friend, and he found that the heart in his breast was still. Tenderly, as though leaving it over a bride, Gilgamish laid the covering over Enkidu. He turned away; he roared in his grief as a lion or as a lioness robbed of her young. And when his roarings had ceased, his mother said to him, "What dost thou desire, my son, and what is it that will quiet the grief and the restlessness that are in thine heart?"

Gilgamish said to her, "My desire is to escape death which hath taken hold of Enkidu, my friend."

His mother said, "Only one hath escaped death; the one is Uta-Napishtim the Remote, thine ancestor."

THE STORY OF UTA-NAPISHTIM AND OF THE DELUGE THAT DESTROYED ALL THAT WAS ON THE EARTH

Now in the Temple there were tables on which were inscribed the history of Uta-Napishtim the Remote, of him whom the Gods had made immortal. These tables had the very words of Uta-Napishtim upon them. And these are the words that were written there:

"I lived in Shurippak, the city of the sun, a city that was old, and had the Gods dwelling in it. The Gods decided in their hearts to destroy mankind by wind and by flood, so that none would be left living on the earth. Anu, the Father of the Gods, was there when this thing was thought upon, and Enlil, the Warrior of the Gods, and En-urta, the Messenger of the Gods. But the Gods considered again, and they decided to leave living on the earth one man and his family.

"Ea went to the place where I was. He cried to me where I slept;

he cried to me to come out of my house and to build a ship; he cried to me to abandon all my possessions and to save my life.

"He told me of the dimensions of the ship I was to build; he told me of the measures of grain I was to take on board that ship. And he commanded that I should go before the elders and people of the city and say to them that Enlil bore ill-will towards them and that he was set upon destroying them. Then I said to Ea, 'Whither shall I sail when I have built the ship?', and he said, 'To the Gods. Trust thy ship upon the flood and be not fearful.'

"I spoke to the elders and the people of the city. They but mocked me. I gathered my servants around me and I began the building of the ship. I made it a hundred and twenty cubits in length; I covered it with pitch and bitumen; I provided a strong steering-pole for it. And when the ship was built I loaded it with grain, and took my family on board it. The beasts of the field and of the wilderness, also the birds came on board it; they came in pairs. When all was made ready the God Shamash appeared before me. He signified to me that at even-tide a great flood would be loosed upon the earth.

"A rain-flood came at even-tide. I watched the darkness coming and the storm. Terror possessed me as I watched. I went within where my family were and the beasts and birds were in pairs, and I bolted down the doors; yea, I bolted down the nine parts which I had made inside the ship. I committed the ship and all that was on board of it to the mercy of the Gods.

"Then a black cloud came up, and out of the black cloud and the whirlwind the Gods thundered. The Star Gods of the Southern Sky brandished their torches. Every gleam of light was turned to darkness. Floods descended out of the heavens. The waters attacked mankind as in a battle. Fathers no longer saw their children; brother no longer saw brother. The rains descended until the waters mounted to the tops of the hills. As they mounted up, the Gods themselves were filled with fright; they went out of their own places; they went into the high heaven of Anu. Ishtar, the Lady of the Gods, cried out like a woman in travail. Yea, Ishtar lamented, crying against herself for speaking of this flood in the presence of the Gods. The Gods of the Southern Sky wailed with her, and for six days and six nights rain fell and the wind beat down all that was upon the land.

"But after the seventh day the raging flood ceased; the whirlwind and the rain-storm ceased, and the waters no longer rose. I looked over the waters; I saw that calm had come. Calm had come, but the land had been laid out flat, and mankind had been turned to mud. I bowed myself down; I fell upon my face and tears flowed down my cheeks. I looked to the four quarters of the world and all that I saw was the open sea. Then for twelve days the ship went on. The ship rested on the mountain of Nisir and it moved no more.

"And when, after seven days, the ship still rested, I opened an air-hole and light fell upon my face. I let a dove fly forth. The dove came back to the ship for there was no place for her to light. I let a swallow fly forth. The swallow also returned. I let a raven fly forth. The raven did not return; she saw the land come up through the sinking waters; she ate; she pecked on the ground; she croaked, and did not come back to me.

"Then I brought out all that was on board the ship; I brought all to where the four winds blew. I offered up a sacrifice. I poured out a libation where I stood upon the peak of the mountain. There Ishtar, the Lady of the Gods, appeared before me; she cursed Bel for having brought about the flood.

"The God Bel was wroth seeing that a portion of mankind had been saved from the flood. He raged. He cried out, 'None shall be left alive; no man shall be left living in this destruction.' But the God En-urta pleaded with Bel for mankind, and Bel relented. Then the God Ea went to the ship, and took me by the hand, and brought me forth and brought my wife forth; he turned our faces towards one another and made us kneel together. He blessed us, saying, 'Formerly Uta-Napishtim and his wife were mortals; now let Uta-Napishtim and his wife be like the Gods themselves, having immortal life.'"

The tables having been read to the end, Gilgamish said, "How may I go to where Uta-Napishtim is, and what is the way to his dwelling? I would go to him whom the Gods have made undying and find out from him how a man may save himself from going down into that abyss that is Irkalla's."

His mother said, "All that we know is that the dwelling-place of Uta-Napishtim is beyond Mount Mashu, where the sun rises and sets."

Thereupon Gilgamish set out for Mount Mashu. In the foothills of the mountains he was attacked by lions; he killed many of the lions, but others followed him almost till he had reached the top of the mountain. And when he came nigh to the top of the mountain he saw the dread guardians of the place where the sun rises and sets. They were the Scorpion Men, and they were fearful even to look upon. And Gilgamish said when he saw them, "Would that Enkidu, my friend, were with me now, for only with his help might I overcome the guardians here, the glance of whose eyes makes me tremble." He went on; he came before the dread guardians of the mountain-top, and he, even Gilgamish, bowed himself humbly before them.

The Scorpion Men said, one to the other, "The bodies of those who come this way we devour, but behold! the man who comes towards us has flesh that is two-thirds flesh of the Gods. We may not devour his body." With voices that made shake the rocks of the mountain-top they bade Gilgamish pass by. And they cried out to him that he was entering into a region of darkness, and that no one who had gone that way had ever come out of that darkness.

And, lo! Even as they spoke Gilgamish went into the darkness. The sight of the sky and the mountain was cut off from him. The darkness became thicker and heavier as he went on; no mortal had ever gone through darkness such as this darkness. For a space that was equal to a day and a night, Gilgamish went on, went through a deep and deeper darkness. He thought that the light would never come into his eyes again. And then he came into a place where there was light. He saw bright daylight all round him. He saw before him a garden that was filled with bright flowers and glowing fruits.

This was the place and this was the garden of the Goddess Siduri-Sabitu. In the garden was the Tree of the Gods: Siduri-Sabitu guarded it. Gilgamish saw the Goddess. Siduri-Sabitu sat upon a throne beside the sea. She said to him:

"Who are you who come to this place with wasted cheeks, and with face bowed down?

"Your heart is sad; your form is dejected, and lamentation is in your heart! None such as you come here, to the garden in which is the Tree of the Gods."

She ordered her servants to close the gate of the garden against him. Gilgamish laid hands upon the gate and he shook it so that its foundations rocked. He said to the Goddess, "I go to where Uta-Napishtim the Remote is, to Uta-Napishtim, my ancestor."

She spoke to him from her throne while his hands were still upon the gate, making its foundations rock. And he said to her, "I am Gilgamish, and Enkidu, who was my friend, has become like the dust. The fate of my friend lies heavily upon me, and therefore do I travel this way so that I may speak with my ancestor, Uta-Napishtim, and be rid of my fear of death. O Sabitu, thou who sittest by the sea, and hast charge of the gate, speak to me, and tell me the way to the land where Uta-Napishtim abides. Give to me a description of the way. If it be possible, I will cross the sea to come to his country. If it be impossible to cross the sea, I will cross over the land, even if it be a land that darkness rests upon."

Then the Goddess Siduri-Sabitu, the guardian of the gate, knowing that two-thirds of his flesh was as the flesh of the Gods, made answer to Gilgamish. She said to him, "The sea that I sit beside and that thou dost look upon is the Waters of Death. None have crossed these waters heretofore save Shamash, the Sun God."

"I would cross these waters," Gilgamish said.

Said Siduri-Sabitu, sitting on her throne beside the sea, "There is a Ferryman, Ur-Shanabi, who crosses this water. Find him, and mayhap he will ferry thee across to where Uta-Napishtim is."

He waited by the sea until he saw the Ferryman, Ur-Shanabi. He went into his boat. For fifty days and nights they voyaged across the Waters of Death, and the Ferryman warned Gilgamish not to touch with his hand the waters they passed over. They reached the limits of the Waters of Death; they came to the land where Gilgamish's ancestor, Uta-Napishtim, had his abode.

Uta-Napishtim the Remote walked with his wife by the waters. He saw the boat of Ur-Shanabi coming towards him. He, astonished that another beside Ur-Shanabi was in the boat, waited by the shore.

Gilgamish came out of the boat, and he went to the two figures that stood by themselves. Uta-Napishtim knew his descendant, and he spoke kindly to Gilgamish.

Then Gilgamish told him of what had happened to him in the world of men; he told how his friend Enkidu had been taken from him, becoming as dust, he who had been like the panther of the desert, he who had aided him to destroy the Bull of Heaven. "Shall not I myself also be obliged to lay me down and never rise up to all eternity?" he cried to Uta-Napishtim. And again he cried, "I was horribly afraid. I was afraid of death, and therefore have I fled from my own country." But Uta-Napishtim the Remote made answer to Gilgamish, and he said, "None may find out the day of their death, for Mammitum, the Arranger of Destinies, has settled it, and none knows but Mammitum."

And as Uta-Napishtim spoke Gilgamish ate and refreshed himself. Having refreshed himself he lay in the boat and drowsiness overpowered him; he fell into a slumber. Then Uta-Napishtim said to his wife, "Behold the one who would find immortality; he cannot keep drowsiness away from him." Gilgamish slept. For six days the wife of Uta-Napishtim baked bread and laid it beside him. On the seventh day when she brought him bread, she touched him, and Gilgamish wakened up.

Then all day he questioned Uta-Napishtim about the ways of escaping death. Uta-Napishtim told him that at the bottom of the sea that he had crossed, and in the middle of it, there grew a plant, and that he who ate of it nine days after it had been gathered would escape death. Having told him this, Uta-Napishtim told the Ferryman to make ready to take Gilgamish back across the Waters of Death.

The Ferryman made ready; the wife of Uta-Napishtim gave Gilgamish bread to last him for his journey across. When they came to the middle of the sea, Gilgamish fastened stones to his feet and let himself sink down in the water. He found the plant that grew at the bottom of the sea, and, rejoicing, he gathered it. He went into the boat and they came to a land under the mountain. The land was pleasant, and Gilgamish rested himself there. Not yet had come the time for him to eat the plant he had gathered.

A serpent smelled the plant and came to where Gilgamish was. Now Gilgamish would bathe in the water of a pool, for he needed the refreshment of water. He went into the pool. And while he was in the pool the serpent came upon the plant and ate it—yea, ate all of the plant. Then was Gilgamish left without that which would have given him escape from death. He wept, and the spirit of Enkidu came before him, and told him of the Land of the Dead and of how men fared who entered into it.

ISHTAR'S DESCENT INTO THE WORLD BELOW

A time came when the Lady of the Gods, even Ishtar, thought upon the spouse of her youth, upon Tammuz; her heart inclined her to go down into the realm of Irkalla, into the Place of Darkness where Tammuz had gone. So, in all the magnificence of her apparel, in all her splendour and power, the Lady Ishtar went into the cavern that goes down to the realm of Irkalla. She came to the place that is surrounded by seven walls, that has seven gates opening into it, the place where the Dead sit in unchanging and everlasting gloom. Before the first gate she called upon the Watchman, Nedu: "Ho, Watchman! Open thou the gate that I may enter in!" The Watchman looked at her from over the gate; he did not speak to her; he did not open the gate to her. "If thou openest not the gate, I will smite upon it; I will shatter the bolt, and beat down the doors! Yea, I will bring away the Dead that are under the rule of thy mistress! I will raise up the Dead so that they will devour the Living, so that the Dead shall outnumber those that live!" So spoke the Lady of the Gods standing before the gate in all her power and splendour.

And hearing her commanding voice and looking upon her in all her power and splendour, Nedu, the Watchman of Irkalla's realm, said, "Great Lady, do not throw down the gate that I guard. Let me go and declare thy will to the queen, to Irkalla." He went before the queen. And hearing of the coming of the Lady of the Gods, Irkalla was angered terribly. She bade the Watchman open the gates and take possession of the new-comer according to the ancient usages. He returned to the first gate. He laid hands upon that side of the gate on which the dust lies thick; he drew the bolt on which the dust is scattered. "Enter, O Lady, and let the realm of Irkalla be glad at thy coming; let the palace of the land whence none return rejoice at thee." He said this and he took the great crown off Ishtar's head. "Why hast thou taken the great crown off my head?" "Enter so, O Lady; this is the law of Irkalla."

So Ishtar entered through the first gate and saw the second wall before her. With head bent she went towards it. The Watchman at her coming opened the second gate. "Enter, O Lady, and let the realm of Irkalla be glad at thy coming; let the palace of the land whence none return rejoice at thee." He said this and put forth his hand and took that which was at her neck, the eight-rayed star. "Why, O Watchman, hast thou taken the eight-rayed star?" "Enter so, O Lady; this is the law of Irkalla."

So the Lady Ishtar, her head bent, the radiance gone from her, went through the second gate and saw the third wall before her. The Watchman opened the gate that was there. "Enter, O Lady. Let the realm of Irkalla be glad at thee; let the palace of the land whence none return rejoice before thee." He said this and he took the bracelets from off her arms—the bracelets of gold and lapis-lazuli. "Why, O Watchman, hast thou taken the bracelets from off mine arms?" "Enter so, O Lady; this is the law of Irkalla."

So Ishtar, her head bent, the radiance gone from her, and no longer magnificent in the gold of her ornaments, went through the third gate and saw the fourth wall before her. The Watchman opened the gate that was there. "Enter, O Lady. Let the realm of Irkalla be glad at thee; let the palace of the land whence none return rejoice before thee." He said this and he took the shoes from off her feet. "Why, O Watchman, hast thou taken the shoes from off my feet?" "Enter so, O Lady; this is the law of Irkalla."

So the Lady Ishtar, her head bent, the radiance gone from her, no longer magnificent in the gold of her ornaments, with stumbling and halting steps went through the fourth gate and saw the fifth wall before her. The Watchman opened the gate that was there. "Enter, O Lady. Let the realm of Irkalla be glad at thee; let the palace of the land whence none return rejoice before thee." He said this, and he put forth his hand, and he took her resplendent veil away. "Why hast thou taken the veil from me?" "Enter so, O Lady; this is the law of Irkalla."

So Ishtar, her head bent, the radiance gone from her, no longer magnificent in the gold of her ornaments, no longer resplendent in her apparel, with stumbling and halting steps went through the fifth gate and saw the sixth wall before her. The Watchman opened the gate that was there. "Enter, O Lady. Let the realm of Irkalla be glad at thee; let the palace of the land whence none return rejoice before thee." He said this, and he took off her outer robe. "Why hast thou taken my outer robe?" "Enter so, O Lady; this is the law of Irkalla."

So the Lady Ishtar, her head bent, the radiance gone from her, no longer magnificent in the gold of her ornaments, with apparel no longer full nor resplendent, with stumbling and halting steps went through the sixth gate and saw the seventh wall before her. The Watchman opened the gate that was there. "Enter, O Lady. Let the realm of Irkalla be glad at thee; let the palace of the land whence none return rejoice before thee." He said this, and he took off her garment. "Why hast thou taken off my garment?" "Enter so, O Lady; this is the law of Irkalla."

And naked, with her splendour, and her power, and her beauty all gone from her, the Lady of the Gods came before Irkalla. And Irkalla, the Goddess of the World Below, had the head of a lioness and the body of a woman; in her hands she grasped a serpent. Before her stood Bêlit-sêri, the Lady of the Desert, holding in her hands the tablets on which she wrote the decrees of Irkalla.

Ishtar saw the Dead that were there. They were without light; they ate the dust and they fed upon mud; they were clad in feathers and they had wings like birds; they lived in the darkness of night. And seeing their state, Ishtar became horribly afraid. She begged of Irkalla to give her permission to return from the House of Dust where dwelt high priests, ministrants, magicians, and prophets; where dwelt Tammuz, the spouse of her youth. But Irkalla said to her:

Thou art now in the land whence none return, in the place of darkness;
Thou art in the House of Darkness, the house from which none who enter
   come forth again;
Thou hast taken the road whose course returns not;
Thou art in the house where they who enter are excluded from light,
In the place where dust is their bread and mud their food,
Where they behold not the light, where they dwell in darkness,
And are clothed like birds in garments of feathers.
Over the door and across the bolt the dust is scattered.

Then Irkalla cursed Ishtar; she called upon Namtar, the demon of the plague, to smite the Lady of the Gods. And Namtar went to her and smote her, so that the plague afflicted every member of her body. Ishtar saw the light no more; feathers came upon her; she ate dust and fed upon the mud; she was as one of those whom she had sent down into Irkalla's realm.

She stayed in Irkalla's realm and went no more upon the earth. A season passed. The earth was not as it had been when Ishtar went upon it. No longer did the cow low for the bull; no longer did the bull bellow so that the cows might hear of his might. The ewe did not run to ram; the mare was not drawn to the stallion; the he-goat, chief of a flock, browsed with the flock as though there were no longer male and female; the birds did not call to each other. The hero did not take the maid in his arms; the warrior returning did not embrace his wife; his wife uttered no words of love to the warrior. None sought the women in the temple of Ishtar. The women in the temple did not call to the men who went by. So it was on the earth when Ishtar was in the World Below.

Shamash, the Sun God, beheld all this; he knew of the calamity that had befallen men and birds and beasts and all things upon the earth. The generation of creatures would die; no life would be left after them, and the creation of the Gods would perish. So Shamash said in his heart, and in haste he came before Ea, the great God. And when he had heard what Shamash related—that life was not being renewed upon the earth—and when it had been made known to him that this was because Ishtar was being held in the World Below, Ea, the great God, formed a being, Ud-dushu-nāmir, and bade him go down into the World Below, and into the presence of Irkalla, and conjure her by the power of the great Gods to give him the Water of Life with which to sprinkle Ishtar, the Lady of the Gods.

So the being whom Ea had formed went into the presence of Irkalla, and over Ud-dushu-nāmir Irkalla had no power. He conjured her by the power of the great Gods to grant him the Water of Life with which to sprinkle Ishtar, the Lady of the Gods. Irkalla was enraged when she heard his saying; she opened her lion's mouth; her woman's body shook with rage as she cursed Ishtar and cursed the being that was before her. But the being that Ea had formed stood there, not trembling at all at her curses. The Water of Life she had to bring to him. She put the vessel that held it into his hands; she bade Namar bring forth the Lady of the Gods.

Ishtar came from out the dust and the mud; the Water of Life was sprinkled upon her. She stood before Irkalla's seat living, but pale, powerless, naked, and trembling.

Nadu the Watchman put his hand upon the bolt on which the dust lay; he opened the gate on which the dust was scattered. Ishtar passed through the gate. He gave her her garment; she put the garment upon her and her nakedness was covered. She went upon her way. He opened the second gate. He gave her back her outer robe. He gave her back her veil; he gave her back the shoes for her feet; he gave her back her bracelets of gold and lapis-lazuli; he gave her back the eight-rayed star that had been at her neck. At last he opened the outer gate of the realm of Irkalla. He took the great crown and he set it upon her head. Then Ishtar went from the realm of Irkalla. But she did not go in splendour, she did not go in radiance; she went with her head bowed. She went into the world where light was. No blossoms were there, and no birds called.

But no sooner had she come upon the earth than her splendour and power came back to Ishtar; she walked as a Goddess—yea, as the Lady of the Gods. The creatures of the earth heard her voice. Then the bull bellowed; the cow heard and lowed back to him; the stallion neighed and the mare was drawn to him; the warrior returning embraced his wife; his wife said, "Thou shalt be my man, I shall be thy woman"; the hero took the maid in his arms. All creation rejoiced; all creation praised the works of Ishtar. And the Gods rejoiced, knowing that what they had created would not pass away.

PERSIAN

PERSIAN

JAMSHĪD THE RESPLENDENT

A time there was when the works of Angra Mainyu, the Evil One, no longer disturbed the world, and when pain and death were not known amongst men. That time lasted for a thousand years. It was while Jamshīd the Resplendent sat upon the Golden Throne in the Kingdom of Light, and had around his brow the awful Glory that belonged to the Kings of Iran who had the favour of Ahura Mazda, the Beneficent One.

These were the kings and archimages who ruled over men before the time of Jamshīd. First there was Gaya Maretan: in his time men lived on the mountains and clad themselves in the skins of beasts. Then there was Siyamak: he contended with the demon Angra Mainyu, and his life was lost; gloom overcame Gaya Maretan because of this, and the gloom of their ruler spread itself through the minds of all the people. And then came Hoshang, and Hoshang gave fire to men, and showed them how to find and how to use the metals that were in the earth; also he showed them how to lead the rivers so that they might water the land, and he showed them how to till the earth and reap the grain, and he paired sheep and cattle and horses for them. Moreover, he trained hounds for the chase, and showed men how to make coverings for themselves with the skins of the beasts they got in the chase. And Hoshang gave men justice and showed them how to deal justly with each other; his reign, because of the security and prosperity men had during it, was almost as the reign of Jamshīd. To Hoshang was given the Glory that shone around the kings who had the favour of Ahura Mazda, and Hoshang was the first to show it upon his brow. After Hoshang came Tahmurath: he subdued the demon Angra Mainyu, and he rode upon him as upon a horse. The demon would have remained subdued had it not been for the treason of Tahmurath's wife. He came before the woman and offered marvellous presents to her. "Hath Tahmurath any dread of me ever?" he asked of her. "Discover if he hath and tell me of it, and more than these will I give thee." The woman asked Tahmurath if he ever had any dread of the demon whom

41

he rode upon as a horse. "Upon the mountain Albūrz there is a place where dread overcometh me," he told her. "When I, riding upon the demon, come upon that place I shout aloud and I strike him so that he may take me swiftly past that dangerous place." All this Tahmurath's wife told the demon, Angra Mainyu. And the next time when he rode upon Albūrz, and struck the demon that was in the form of his horse, and shouted, Angra Mainyu turned upon him, and threw him upon the ground, and destroyed him. But before he had been destroyed by the demon, Tahmurath had won from the daevas, the creatures of the demon, a boon for men. Once, when he would have destroyed many of them with his great mace, the daevas said to him, "Destroy us not, and we will show you a most useful art." Tahmurath spared them, and the daevas showed him the art of writing, and he taught men that art.

Now Jamshīd won back the Glory from the power of the demon, and it showed upon his brow, and he ruled over the land of Iran, over the Kingdom of Light. And he was called the Resplendent because of the brilliance that was upon him and that was over all things in his time. Death was not known then: father and son walked the land together, each in the flush of youth. Men, birds, and beasts, and daevas obeyed the lord Jamshīd.

In the first hundreds of the years that he reigned he divided men into classes: he formed a class of priests who make sacrifices upon the mountains; he formed a class of warriors who guard the thrones of the kings, and who hold back the foes of the Aryan people; he formed a class of husbandmen who till and reap, and whom none may oppress or reproach; he formed a class of artificers who live together in one place and who are ever turbulent. Over men formed into these classes, Jamshīd, with the Glory upon his brow, reigned in justice.

In the second hundred of the years he reigned he made mighty works—palaces, and temples, and great walled cities. It was then that he built the city of Persepolis—the city that is called the Throne of Jamshīd. In the third hundred of the years he reigned he drew towards his city those who had dwelt far off, or those who wandered about in tribes, and he provided for them, winning out of the earth through his wisdom abundance of provisions. And those who were sick and ailing amongst them he cured, discovering sovereign medicaments through his wisdom and showing men how they were compounded. And more and more Jamshīd was honoured by the multitudes whom he had brought around him and whom he nourished.

And then a change came over Jamshīd. He forgot that all he had was from Ahura Mazda. He thought that all that gave prosperity to men came from him, and from him alone. The first time that he thought this the Glory went from off his brow, leaving him pale and trembling. It departed from him in the shape of the bird Vareghna. Then it was that Mithra seized hold of it and brought the Glory back to Jamshīd—Mithra whom we hymn:

> Thou who drivest over Albūrz
> Coursers that the winds have rousèd—
> Mithra, foremost o' the Immortals!
>
> Thou who seest the gleaming cohorts
> And upholdst hearts of battlers—
> Mithra, foremost o' the Immortals!
>
> Deeds that thou mayst look on grant us—
> Deeds this day from hearts unshrinking—
> Mithra, foremost o' the Immortals!

The Glory again was upon Jamshīd's brow. But soon he said to himself, "The world is mine, for it was I who gave men all that they use." His Glory again departed from him, and he was left pale and trembling. But again it was restored to him.

And once again forwardness entered into Jamshīd. He made a feast and he brought the people around his throne. He had the people honour him even before they had honoured Heaven. And he spoke to them and he said, "Mine is the world. I have formed it according to my will, and from me alone come all the goods that ye possess—your raiment and food, your pleasure and your rest, your health and your happiness. Your lives ye owe to me. Therefore ye should adore me as the maker and the ruler of the world. All who do not adore me belong to the demon, Angra Mainyu."

But when he said this the Glory departed from the brow of Jamshīd; he was left pale and trembling and unguarded. And the Glory was not restored to him. Disease came into the world; contentions came into the world; the multitudes that had gathered around Jamshīd's city strove with one another. Death came amongst men. The demon Angra Mainyu had power in the world.

Now there lived at that time in the land of Arabia a prince whose name was Dahhak. His father had herds of cattle and flocks of sheep past counting, and Dahhak owned a thousand horses. The demon Angra Mainyu went to Dahhak in the guise of a youth, and sought employment from him, and became one of the grooms who attended his horses. And he was serviceable, and he won the favour of Prince Dahhak. After a while the demon tempted the prince, telling him of the power that would be his if his father, the king, were dead. Dahhak listened to him, and consented to the death of his father. And the king was slain as though by a chance, and Dahhak came to be king in Arabia.

Now after Dahhak had become king, Angra Mainyu, the demon, appeared before him once more; again he was in the guise of a young man, and this time he asked Dahhak to let him serve him as cook.

Dahhak consented, and the demon, Angra Mainyu, prepared the dishes for the king and his court. Now up to this time men had nourished themselves upon herbs only; the flesh of animals was not known to them as food. Angra Mainyu prepared dishes of flesh-meat and served them to the king and his nobles. All delighted in these savoury meats, and strength and courage came to them through their eating them, so that the fighting men of Arabia became as lions in battle. And one night, after an especially savoury meal had been served to the court, the king sent for his cook, and said to him, "Is there a boon you would ask of me? If there be one, ask for it, and I swear it shall be granted to thee." Then the demon, with laughter in his black heart, bowed low before the king and said, "There is only one boon that I would ask from the king. I would ask permission from him to let me lay my hands upon the back of his shoulders, and to kiss him between the shoulders."

The king permitted him to do this. Then the demon in the guise of the young man laid his hands upon the back of Dahhak's shoulders and kissed him between the shoulders. And as he did this, the ground opened, and the young man disappeared in the opening, and all who were present were astonished. And behold! From each of the king's shoulders a hissing serpent sprang.

All were horrified at this happening. His nobles tried to tear the serpents from the back of the king, but they could not do this. They took swords and cut off the hissing things. But no sooner were they cut off than they grew again, hissing more dreadfully, and gnawing at the flesh of Dahhak's shoulders. And none knew what could be done to save the king from the serpents that gnawed him.

Then once more Angra Mainyu appeared before Dahhak and his court. This time he came in the guise of a wise man, and he spoke before the king and said, "This ill cannot be healed; always the serpents will stay upon the king's shoulders. But they may be prevented from gnawing his flesh perpetually. The serpents will have to be fed in other ways. Every day feed to each of them the brains of a young man. If this be done the king will have ease."

The word of Angra Mainyu was taken. Every day two young men were killed, and their brains were fed to the serpents upon Dahhak's shoulders. The king had ease from their gnawing, but the land was in gloom and terror because of the slaying of the young men.

And still Angra Mainyu was not content. He would have the gloom and terror that was around Dahhak brought into Iran, the Kingdom of Light. This was the time that Jamshīd had lost his Glory for the third time, and there were sicknesses and woes in the land. Contentions were there also, for his nobles had revolted from Jamshīd and they struggled to take his power from him. They heard of a king in Arabia who was mighty and powerful and a terror to his enemies, and they sent to him—they sent even to Dahhak the Demon-possessed One, and invited him to become king over them and over Iran.

Then Dahhak with his army came into the land. Jamshīd fled from before him. And for a hundred years he who had once been so glorious and who had around his brow the Glory of the kings of Iran, fled from the fury of the demon-possessed Dahhak. Dahhak sought for him in every place. And at last, by the shore of the farthest sea, Dahhak's servitors came upon Jamshīd. They took him who had been called the Resplendent, and they sawed him in twain, and they sent Dahhak the tidings of what had been done.

Then Dahhak put upon himself the Glory and the power of the world as though it were a ring that he slipped upon his finger. He sat upon the golden throne and he ruled over Iran, the Kingdom of

Light, Dahhak the beloved of Angra Mainyu. And in those days the will of the bad man was accomplished, and those who sought good or who spoke of good did so by stealth. Pure sacrifices were no longer offered, and black magic was practised by men who were instructed by the daevas. And every day two young men were slaughtered that the serpents upon Dahhak's shoulders might be fed.

For a thousand years Dahhak ruled, and for a thousand years evil flourished upon the earth. But at last Ahura Mazda heard the cry of his people. He resolved that there should be an end to the sway that evil had upon earth.

Then Dahhak had a dream; he dreamt that he beheld a youth of royal mien, slender like a cypress-tree, and he knew that this youth was of the race of Jamshīd. And the youth came towards him as if to smite him with a mace that he held. Dahhak awakened. He called for his wise men, and when they appeared before him he demanded of them that they interpret his dream.

The wise men were in fear, and for three days they kept silence before the king. He questioned them all the time. At last they spoke and they said to him, "A young man of the race of Jamshīd will arise and will reverse thy fortune." And when they said this, Dahhak the tyrant swooned, and the wise men fled from before him.

Then Dahhak had the world scoured for a youth of the race of Jamshīd. In the terror that had come upon him what judgment he had vanished, and he made wars endlessly, and he filled whole countries with slaughter. But he did not come upon the youth who was in his dream. Such a youth there was, and he was named Farīdūn. His mother heard of the search that was being made for him who was descended from Jamshīd, and she hid him in a thick forest, where he was nourished on the milk of a wondrous cow, and he was trained by those who were the guardians of the cow. And Farīdūn grew to be tall as the royal cypress-tree.

At last the news of the wondrous cow and of the royal youth nourished by her came to the ears of Dahhak. He came with an army towards the forest where they were. But Farīdūn's mother had been warned by a dream: she fled with the youth her son; she brought him to the mountain Albūrz, and she prayed a hermit who lived on the mountain to guard him and to teach him, knowing him to be the descendant of Jamshīd and the one who would destroy Dahhak, the beloved of Angra Mainyu. The hermit hid the youth in his cave. As for the demon-possessed king, when he found out that the youth had been in the forest and had escaped from him, he became enraged and was like to a mad elephant. He slaughtered the wondrous cow, he slew the guardians the cow had had, and he burned and laid waste the whole of the forest. Then, with fear and bitterness in his heart, he went searching again for Farīdūn.

He made his army greater than it had been; he became more and more fearful of what might be said about him. He called upon the people to come before his throne and sign a scroll declaring that he was, and ever had been, a righteous king. People came before the throne; in fear they bent before him; they signed their names to words that they believed not in—that Dahhak was, and ever had been, a righteous king.

Once when men had been assembled to sign this scroll, there came a tumult before the door of the hall, and when the officers asked what was the meaning of the disturbance, a man came into the hall saying, "A wrong has been done me and I demand justice from the king."

Then Dahhak spoke, and he said, "I charge thee to say the name of the man who hath wronged thee. Tell his name that justice may be done to thee in the hall of the king."

Then the man came before the king, and, looking straight at him, he said, "I am Kawa, a blacksmith and a blameless man. I sue for justice. Against thee, O king, is my suit. Seventeen fair sons I have had, and only one remaineth to me now, for all his brothers have been slaughtered that thy accursed serpents might be fed. I pray thee to grant me the life of this last son of mine."

All in the hall were fearful when they heard what Kawa said to the king. But Dahhak spoke softly to the man, saying that the life of his son would be spared to him. And he brought him to where the others were signing their names to the scroll, and he told him to sign the testament as to Dahhak's being a righteous ruler.

When this was said to him the blacksmith lifted up his hands and declared that he would sign no such falsity. And he took up the scroll and he tore it across and he scattered the fragments around the hall.

Then he strode from the palace, leaving those who were there silent and filled with awe.

Kawa went to the market-place and a crowd gathered around him. He related all that had happened in the palace, and he recalled to the people the evil deeds of Dahhak, and all the wrongs he had caused them to suffer. He roused them so that they became ready to strive to shake off the yoke of the servant of the demon, Angra Mainyu. Kawa took off the leathern apron with which blacksmiths cover their knees when they smite the iron, and he stuck it upon a pike, and he raised it up as a standard. And the people declared that they would follow that banner.

So an army was formed with Kawa at the head of it. The soldiers of Dahhak went against them; they fought, and the army of Kawa retreated to another part of the land. They came to the mountain Albūrz, and they encamped beside it. And down from the mountain came Farīdūn, now grown into perfect manhood. He knew now that he was of Jamshīd's race; he knew of the evil deeds of Dahhak, and he was resolved to destroy him. He said to his mother, "I go to the wars, and it remaineth to thee to pray Ahura Mazda for my safety." The army of Kawa knew him to be the one who was destined to overthrow the demon-possessed king.

Now the army with the banner of Kawa before it set out for the West. At Baghdad which is upon the Tigris the army halted. Farīdūn bade the ferrymen who were at the river convey them across. But the ferrymen refused, saying that King Dahhak had crossed the river a while before, and he had given them orders to convey no one across except those who had a seal from his hand. When Farīdūn heard this said he was angry, and in his anger he had no thought for the rushing river nor for the dangers of the flood. He plunged with his steed into the water, and all his army followed him. Many struggled in the midstream, and it seemed as if the flood would bear them away. But Farīdūn on his brave steed crossed the river, and when his army saw him upon the other side of the Tigris they shouted with lifted hearts, and they made their way across.

They turned their faces towards the city that is now called Jerusalem. There was the glorious house that Dahhak had built for himself, a house that was built in a bird's shape. And when Farīdūn came before the city the folk of the city joined his army, for they hated

Dahhak. And Farīdūn entered into the glorious house that the beloved of Angra Mainyu had built, and he cast down the evil talismans that were graven upon the walls, and he made himself the master of that house and of all that was in it.

Then Farīdūn through all that house pursued Dahhak, and he caught him with a rope made out of a lion's hide, and he bound him in bonds that would have held an elephant. Then would he have slain him who had oppressed the world for a thousand years. But it was not destined that he should be slain. The angel Sraosha appeared before Farīdūn as he raised his mace to strike Dahhak, and said, "Strike him not, for Dahhak's hour has not come."

Farīdūn put mighty fetters upon him and carried him to Mount Damavand, and fettered him in a narrow gorge, and bound him to a crag, and left him to hang there through the ages. And the angel Sraosha set upon Farīdūn's brow the Glory that had been upon Jamshīd's. And Farīdūn ruled the world with justice, and in his time men reposed in the gardens of content, in the bowers of undisturbed security. Prosperity drew the bloom of happiness from the vicinity of his pavilion, and victory borrowed brilliance of hue from the surface of his well-tempered sword.

But the ancient story told that Dahhak, fettered by Farīdūn on Mount Damavand, will be released by Angra Mainyu when the powers of evil once more get the upper hand. He will be freed from his chains, and in his fury he will rush forth and swallow everything in his way—he will swallow a third of mankind, a third of the cattle, a third of the sheep. He will smite and strive to destroy water, fire, and the vegetation of the earth. Then water, fire, and vegetation will lament before Ahura Mazda. And Ahura Mazda will send the angel Sraosha to arouse the hero Keresaspa. He will call three times. At the fourth summons of the angel the hero will awake, and he will go forth and encounter Dahhak, and he will strike Dahhak with his great mace, and so will slay the beloved of Angra Mainyu. And when Dahhak has been slain such an era of happiness will begin for men as was in the time of Jamshīd the Resplendent.

JEWISH
POST-CHRISTIAN
PERIOD

JEWISH POST-CHRISTIAN PERIOD

THE ANGELS AND THE CREATION AND FALL OF MAN

When the Holy One, the Almighty (blessed be His name!) would create the world, the twenty-two that are the letters of the alphabet came from His crown and held themselves before His eyes. Each supplicated to have itself made the beginning letter of the creative word. Many were the beginning letters of the various sacred names. But out of the twenty-two, the Most High chose to create the world through BETH: it is the beginning letter in the word BARACH, which signifies to bless.

On the first day the Most High created the heavens and the earth, the light and the darkness, the duration of the day and the duration of the night. From underneath His throne He took a stone and flung it upon chaos: that stone made the centre of the earth, and all that was made was made around it. On the second day God created the angels. On the third day He created the plants, including the plants that are chief of them all, the cedars of Lebanon. But lest these cedars, tallest of trees, should exalt themselves unduly, He created on the same day the iron that would fell the trees; also He created Paradise where the first man was to have his abode, and where the souls of the just were to dwell throughout eternity. On the fourth day He created the sun, moon, and stars. On the fifth day He created the fishes, including the fish that is chief of all of them; namely, Leviathan, and the birds, including the bird that is chief of all of them; namely, Ziz. On the sixth day He created the animals, including the animal that is chief of all of them; namely, Behemoth.

On the sixth day He created man. But the Most Holy One took

counsel with His angels before He created him. And some of the angels said, "What is man that thou art mindful of him?" He stretched forth His finger, and all the angels who said this were consumed with fire—all except their leaders, Michael and Gabriel. Then the Most Holy One commanded Gabriel to fetch dust from the four corners of the earth that man might be made from it. Gabriel went to do as he was commanded. But the earth refused to let the servant of the Lord gather dust from her surface. "I am destined to be cursed by man," the earth said, "and to have my first fair state made unfair through him. If the Almighty One does not take from me the dust for the making of man, no one shall ever be let do it." When God heard the earth say this He stretched forth His hand and He took dust from the four corners of the earth, and He fashioned man out of the dust.

When He would join the body He had formed out of the dust with the soul He had made on the first day, the angelic host who knew the power that man was about to receive from God murmured against his making. And the chief of those who murmured was that angel who was amongst the highest in the angelic host, whose wings were twelve where the others' wings were six, the angel whose name was Samael. Samael said, "Thou didst create us from the splendour of the Shekinah, and now thou dost plan to set above us the creature whom thou hast fashioned out of the dust of the ground." Man would have perished through the fire which Samael would have put upon him if it had not been for the protecting hand that God held over him. The Almighty cast Samael and his host out of heaven, and from that time that angelic prince is known as Satan, and he is the adversary of man.

God named the man whom he had created Adam, and He placed him in the Paradise which He had created on the third day. Another had been created with Adam out of the dust of the earth. This was the woman Lillith. Lillith lived with Adam in Paradise. But she exalted herself over him, knowing that he and she had been made out of the same dust of the earth. And Lillith was able to pronounce the Ineffable Name, and pronouncing it she caused herself to vanish from the sight of Adam. Thereafter she made herself a demoness.

Then Adam was cast into a deep sleep; a rib was taken from his side, and out of this rib God formed a woman to be Adam's wife, and this woman was Eve. Adam was given the east and the north of Paradise with the guardianship of the male animals, and Eve was given the west and south with the guardianship of the female animals. A tree grew in the centre of Paradise: the man and the woman were forbidden to eat of the fruit of this tree.

Samael, who was now Satan, the fallen angel, came riding upon the back of a serpent. The animals saw Samael and the serpent, and they were affrighted by the sight. And Samael, in Eve's hearing, chanted seraphic songs, and she, thinking they were songs in praise of God, listened to him. The serpent ascended the tree and injected the poison of evil inclination into the fruit. He bent the branch on which it grew down to the ground. And Eve, after Samael had spoken to her, took the fruit and ate of it. She summoned Adam and persuaded him to eat of the fruit also. Thereupon the cuirass which was bound across each of them, and which was made of the letters of the Ineffable Name, fell from them, and they had to cover their lower limbs with leaves which the trees had cast off when Eve ate of the forbidden fruit.

Then the Most Holy One put Adam and Eve from Paradise and appointed the Cherubim who are called the Ever-turning Swords of Flame to guard against their return to it. The earth felt the curse of the fall of man. Thenceforward she had to be watered by rain from above; her fruits were subject to failure; she had to bring forth creatures that were noxious to her; also she had to have herself formed into mountains and valleys, and to know that one day she will wax old like a garment. The angels in heaven grieved over the fall of man; the sun grieved also. Only the moon laughed on account of it, and for that God was wroth, and He obscured her radiance.

THE CONFOUNDING OF THE ANGEL OF DEATH

When it came to pass that Moses was about to die, Samael, the angel who is filled with enmity towards man, came before the throne of the Most Holy One and said, "Give me permission to take his soul from Moses." But God said to that angel who is named Severity of God, "How wouldst thou take his soul? From his face? How couldst thou approach the face that looked upon My face? From his hands?

But those hands received the Torah from Me, and how couldst thou be able to approach them? From his feet? But his feet touched My clouds, and how then couldst thou be able to approach them? Thou canst not go near Moses." But Samael said, "I pray thee permit me to take his soul." Then God said, "Thou hast my warrant."

Samael wrapped himself in the red of his wrath, and with his sword upon his thigh he went to where Moses was. And when he came before him Moses was writing the Ineffable Name. Therefore his face was suffused with radiance and his eyes were filled with light. And when he turned his face towards him and his eyes upon him, Samael's eyes grew dim, and his hand trembled upon his sword's handle. Humbly he said, "Yield to me thy soul, for the time is at hand for thee to depart from the world." But Moses said, "Not to thee, hater of man, will I yield my soul." Then holding his staff and standing upright he said to the angel with the sword, "I am he who led sixty myriads of Israel out of Egypt, who turned the bitter water into sweet, who mounted into Heaven and there spoke face to face with God the Almighty, who hewed out the two tables of stone on which God wrote His law, who waged war on the giants Sihon and Og that were created before the Flood, and were so tall that the Flood did not reach to their ankles: with my staff I slew the two of them. How darest thou then, wicked one, presume to seize such a soul as mine? Thou hast no power to sit where I sit nor stand where I stand. Get thee hence; I will not yield to thee my soul." In terror Samael went from before Moses and appeared once more before Almighty God.

Then the Most Holy One said, "In joy thou didst set out to take the soul of my servant Moses, and now thou comest back without it. Thou wretched one! Go fetch me Moses's soul, for if thou dost not, I will discharge thee from the office of taking men's souls!" Then Samael covered himself with the crimson of his fury, and, holding his sword naked in his hand, he went to where Moses was. Moses rose up when he appeared, and with the staff on which was written the Ineffable Name, he drove Samael away.

But even as he did this, Moses heard a voice that said, "Why dost thou strive in vain? Thy last minute is at hand!" Then God Himself appeared before him, and Moses fell upon his face and said, "Lord of the world! In love didst thou create the world, and in love thou guidest it! Treat me with all of Thy love, and deliver me not into the hands of Samael, hater of man."

With the Most High there came the three angels, Michael, Gabriel, and Zagzagel. Gabriel went forward and arranged the couch for Moses, Michael spread a purple garment upon it, Zagzagel laid down a pillow. The Almighty One stayed at Moses's head, Michael at his right side, Gabriel at his left side, and Zagzagel at his feet. "Cross thy feet." Moses did so. "Fold thy hands." Moses did so. "Lay them on thy breast." Moses did so. Then the Almighty said, "Close thine eyes." Moses did so, and God said to the soul that was within, "O my daughter, for one hundred and twenty years I decreed that thou shouldst dwell with this righteous body, but delay not now to leave it, for the time has come for thee to do so." And when Moses heard these words he said unto his soul, "Return to thy rest, O my soul, for the Lord hath dealt bountifully with thee." Thereupon God took Moses's soul by kissing him on the mouth.

God and His angels laid Moses's body in a secret place in the earth, and God took Moses's soul and laid it beside His throne. Samael did not know the doing of God and His angels, and for the third time he sought out Moses so that he might take his soul from him.

But Moses was not in the place he went to. Samael went into the Promised Land, thinking that Moses had gone there, and he asked the land where Moses was, and the land answered him and said, "Long did Moses pray to be here, but Moses is not here."

Then Samael hastened to the sea, and he said to the sea, "Is Moses here?" And the sea made answer and said, "I have not looked upon Moses since the day when he divided me into twelve parts so that the twelve tribes might pass through my waters." Samael went to the abyss, and he said, "Is Moses in the abyss?" And the abyss made answer and said, "I have not seen him, but I have heard his call." Samael went up into the clouds of Heaven, and he said to the clouds, "Is Moses with you?" And the clouds answered and said, "We have not seen him since the day when, at God's command, he went through us to receive the Torah in Heaven." Samael went to where the Tree of Knowledge grows, and he asked of the tree if it had seen aught of Moses, and the tree made answer through its leaves, and said, "Since the day when he came to me for a sliver of my wood with which to

make a pen for the writing of the Torah I have not seen Moses."
And he went to the mountain, and when he asked of it concerning
Moses, the mountain said, "Since he hewed the two tables out of me
for the writing of the Law, I have not seen Moses." Then he asked
of the angels had they seen Moses, and the angels answered and
said, "We have heard lamentations for him on earth, and we have
heard rejoicings over him in Heaven, but him we have not seen."
Then Samael, Severity of God, went amongst men and asked of them
where Moses was, and men looked at him boldly, and said to him,
"What hast thou to do with him? God has taken his soul to Himself,
and it is now in its place beside the throne of God." And when he
heard this said, and saw the spirit that was in the faces of men,
Samael, the Angel of Death, knew himself confounded.

GREEK

GREEK

IN THE BEGINNING

In the beginning Nyx, who is Night, hovered in the darkness. An egg was laid by Nyx, the black-winged bird. From the upper shell of that egg was formed Ouranos, who is Heaven, and from the lower shell, Gaia, who is Earth. And Eros, who is Love, flew forth from the egg. Drawn together by Eros, Ouranos and Gaia married, and they had for children the Titan Gods and Goddesses, Okeanos, Hyperion, Rhea, and Tethys. And then Ouranos, who was father, and Gaia, who was mother, had for their child Kronos, the most cunning of all. Kronos wedded Rhea, and from Kronos and Rhea were born the Gods who were different from the Titan Gods.

Kronos hated Ouranos, his father. With a sickle given him by his mother, Kronos attacked his father and wounded him terribly. Then were Ouranos and Gaia forever put apart from each other. Kronos and Rhea had for children Hestia, Demeter, Hera, Hades, Poseidon, and Zeus, and all these belonged to the company of the deathless Gods. Kronos was fearful that one of his sons would treat him as he had treated his father. So when another child was born to Rhea, he commanded that the child be given to him that he might swallow him. But Rhea wrapped a great stone in swaddling-clothes and gave the stone to Kronos. Kronos swallowed the stone, thinking to swallow his latest-born child.

That child was Zeus. As a child he was hidden away in a deep cave, and those who minded and nursed him beat upon drums so that his cries might not be heard. His nurse was Adrastia; when he was able to play she gave him a ball to play with. All of gold was that ball, with a dark-blue spiral around it. When the boy Zeus would play with this ball it would make a track across the sky, flaming like a star.

The Titan Gods born of Ouranos and Gaia went up to the Mountain Othrys, and there they had their thrones. When Zeus had grown to be a youth he went up to the Mountain Olympos, and there he and Posei-

don, Hades, Hera, Demeter, and Hestia built their shining palaces
Now Kronos was warned that if Zeus married Hera his own reign
would cease: he tried to slay Hera. But Rhea took Hera into the realm
of Okeanos and Tethys. There she wedded Zeus. The Moirai, who
are the Fates, led the bride to her husband; Eros himself drew the
bridal car; Okeanos fashioned for the pair the beautiful Garden of the
Hesperides.

Then Zeus overthrew Kronos, his father. Many children were born
to Zeus and Hera, and the Olympians became powerful. But now the
Titans upon Mount Othrys began a war upon the Olympians. Neither
side might prevail against the other. At last Zeus thought of how he
might help the Olympians to overthrow the Titans.

He went down to the deep parts of the earth where the Giants born
of Ouranos and Gaia had been hidden by their father. They had
been bound; they were weighed down with chains. Now Zeus loosed
them, and the hundred-armed Giants in their gratitude gave him the
lightning and showed him how to use the thunderbolt.

Zeus would have the Giants fight against the Titans. But although
they had mighty strength the Giants had no fire of courage in their
hearts. Zeus thought of a way to give them courage: he brought the
food and drink of the Gods to them—ambrosia and nectar. When they
had eaten and drunk their spirits grew within the Giants, and they
were ready to make war upon the Titans. "Sons of Heaven and Earth,"
said Zeus to them, "a long time now have the dwellers on Olympos
been striving with the Titans. Do you lend your unconquerable might
to the Olympians and help them to overthrow the elder children of
Kronos."

"Divine One," said Kottos, the eldest of the Giants, "through your
devising we are come back again from the murky gloom of the mid
earth; we have escaped from the hard bonds that Kronos laid upon us.
Our minds are fixed to aid you in the war against the Titans."

Then the Giants, with their fifty heads growing from their shoulders and with their hundred arms, went forth against the Titans. The
boundless sea rang terribly and the earth crashed loudly; high Olympos reeled on its foundations. Holding huge rocks in their hands the
Giants attacked the Titans.

Zeus entered the war. He hurled the lightning; the bolts flew thick and fast from his strong hand; there was thunder with lightning and flame. The earth crashed, the forests crackled, the ocean seethed with fire. The hot flames wrapped the Titans all around. Three hundred rocks, one upon the other, did Kottos, Briareos, and Gyes hurl upon the Titans. When their ranks were broken the Giants seized upon them and held them for Zeus.

Some of the Titans, seeing in the beginning that the strife for them would be in vain, went over to the side of Zeus. These Zeus became friendly with. But the other Titans he bound in chains and hurled down to Tartaros.

As far as Earth is from Heaven so is Tartaros from Earth. A brazen anvil falling from Heaven to Earth nine days and nine nights would reach Earth on the tenth day. And again, a brazen anvil falling from Earth nine nights and nine days would reach Tartaros upon the tenth night. Around Tartaros runs a fence of bronze and Night spreads in a triple line all about it, as a necklace circles the neck. Zeus imprisoned there the Titans who had fought against him; they are hidden in the misty gloom in a dank place at the ends of the Earth. They may not pass the imprisoning fence; Poseidon fixed gates of bronze to their prison. And Kottos, Briareos, and Gyes are there, ever guarding them.

And there, too, is the home of Night. Night and Day meet each other at that place, as they pass a threshold of bronze. They draw near and they greet one another; the same house never holds them both together, for while one is about to go into the house the other is leaving through the door. One holds Light in her hand, the other holds in her arms Sleep.

There the children of the dark Night have their dwellings—Sleep and Death, his brother. The sun never shines upon these two. Sleep may roam over the wide earth, and come upon the sea, and he is kindly to men. But Death is not kindly, and whoever he seizes upon, him he holds fast.

There, too, stands the hall of the Lord of the Underworld, Hades, the brother of Zeus. Zeus gave him the Underworld to be his dominion when he shared amongst the Olympians the world that Kronos had ruled over. A fearful hound keeps guard outside the hall of Hades: Kerberos he is called; he has three heads. On those who go within the hall Kerberos fawns; on those who come out of it he springs and would devour them.

Not all the Titans did Zeus send down to Tartaros. Those of them who joined with him stayed in the Upperworld. Kronos, now made harmless, stayed with these friendly Titans. And Zeus reigned over Olympos, becoming the ruler of Gods and men.

PROMETHEUS

The Gods upon Olympos more than once made a race of men. The first was the Golden Race. Very close to the Gods was the Golden Race; the men of that race lived justly, although there were no laws to compel them. In the time of the Golden Race the Earth knew only one season; that season was everlasting spring. The men and women of the Golden Race lived through a span of life that was far beyond that of the men and women of our day, and when they died it was though sleep had become everlasting with them. They had all good things, and they had them without labour, for the Earth without any forcing bestowed fruits and crops upon them. They had peace all through their lives, and after they had passed away their spirits remained above the Earth, inspiring the men of the race who came after them to do great and gracious things and to act justly and kindly to one another.

After the Golden Race had passed away, the Gods made for the Earth a second race—the Silver Race. Less noble in spirit and in body was the Silver Race, and the seasons that visited them were less gracious. In the time of the Silver Race the Gods made the seasons—summer and spring, autumn and winter. The men of the Silver Race knew parching heat; they knew the bitter winds of winter, and snow, and rain, and hail. It was the men of the Silver Race who first built houses for shelter. They lived through a span of life that was longer than our span, but it was not long enough to give them wisdom. Children were brought up at their mothers' sides for a hundred years, playing at childish things. And when they came to years beyond a hundred they quarrelled with one another, and wronged one another; moreover, they did not know enough to give reverence to the immortal Gods. Then, by the will of Zeus, the Silver Race passed away as the Golden Race had passed away. Their spirits stay in the Underworld, and they are called by men the blessed spirits of the Underworld.

And then there was made the Third Race—the Race of Bronze. They were a race great of stature, terrible and strong. Their armour was of bronze, their swords were of bronze, their implements were of bronze, and of bronze, too, they made their houses. No great span of life was theirs, for with the weapons that they took in their terrible hands they slew one another. And so they passed away; they went down under the Earth and they left no name that men might know them by.

Then the Gods created a fourth race—our own—a Race of Iron. We have not the justice that was amongst the men of the Golden Race; we have not the simpleness that was amongst the men of the Silver Race; we have not the stature nor the great strength that the men of the Bronze Race possessed. We are of iron that we may endure. It is our doom that we must never cease from labour and that we must very quickly grow old.

But miserable as we are to-day, there was a time when the lot of men was more miserable. With poor implements they had to labour on hard ground. There was less justice and kindliness in those days than there is now.

Once it came into the mind of Zeus to destroy this fourth race and to leave the Earth to the nymphs and the satyrs. He would destroy it by a great flood. But Prometheus, the Titan who had given aid to Zeus—Prometheus who was named the Forethinker—would not consent to the race of men being destroyed utterly, and he considered a way of saving some of them. To a man and a woman, Deukalion and Pyrrha, just and gentle people, he brought word of the plan of Zeus, and he showed them how to make a ship that would bear them through what was about to be sent upon the Earth.

Then Zeus shut up in their caves all the winds except the wind that brings rain and clouds. He bade this wind, the South Wind, sweep over the Earth, flooding it with rain. He called upon Poseidon and bade him let the sea pour in on the land. And Poseidon commanded the rivers to put forth all their strength, and sweep dykes away, and over-flow their banks.

The clouds and the sea and the rivers poured upon the Earth. The flood rose higher and higher, and in places where pretty lambs had gambolled the ugly sea-calves now played; men in their boats drew fishes out of the tops of elm-trees, and the water-nymphs were amazed to come on men's cities under the waves.

Soon even the men and women who had boats were overwhelmed by the rise of the water—all perished then except Deukalion and Pyrrha, his wife; them the waves had not overwhelmed—they were in a ship that Prometheus had shown them how to build. The flood went down at last, and Deukalion and Pyrrha climbed up to a high and a dry ground. Zeus saw that two of the race of men had been left alive. But he saw that these two were just and kindly and had a right reverence for the Gods. He spared them, and he saw their children again peopling the Earth.

Prometheus, who had saved them, looked upon the men and women of the Earth with compassion. Their labour was hard, and they wrought much to gain little. They were chilled at night in their houses, and the winds that blew in the daytime made the old men and women bend double like a wheel. Prometheus thought to himself that if men and women had the element that only the Gods knew of—the element of fire—they could make for themselves implements for labour, and they could build houses that would keep out the chilling winds, and they could warm themselves at the blaze.

But the Gods had not willed that men should have fire, and to go against the will of the Gods would be impious. Prometheus went against the will of the Gods. He stole fire from the altar of Zeus, and he hid it in a hollow fennel stalk, and he brought it to men.

Men, possessing fire, were then able to hammer iron into tools; they were able to cut down forests with axes, and sow grain where the forests had been. They were able to make houses that the storms could not overthrow, and they were able to warm themselves at the hearth-fires. They had rest from their labour at times. They built cities; they became beings who no longer had their heads and backs bent, but were able to raise their faces even to the Gods.

Zeus spared the men who had now the sacred element of fire. But Prometheus he did not spare. He knew that Prometheus had stolen the fire even from his own altar. And he thought on how he might punish the great Titan for his impiety.

He brought up from the Underworld, from Tartaros, the Giants

Kottos, Briareos, and Gyes. He commanded them to lay hands on Prometheus and to fasten him with fetters to the highest, blackest crag upon Caucasus. And Kottos, Briareos, and Gyes seized upon the Titan, and carried him to Caucasus, and fettered him with fetters of bronze to the highest, blackest crag—with fetters of bronze that may not be broken. They left the Titan stretched there, fettered, under the sky, with the cold winds blowing upon him and with the sun streaming down upon him. And, that his punishment might exceed all other punishments, Zeus sent a vulture to prey upon him—a vulture that tears at his liver each day.

And yet Prometheus does not cry out that he has repented of what he has done for man; although the winds blow upon him, and the sun streams upon him, and the vulture tears at his liver, Prometheus will not cry out his repentance to Heaven. And Zeus may not utterly destroy him. For Prometheus the Forethinker knows a secret that Zeus would fain have him disclose. He knows that, as Zeus overthrew his father and made himself the ruler in his stead, so, too, another will overthrow Zeus. One day Zeus will have to have the fetters broken from around the limbs of his victim, and will have to bring from the rock and the vulture, and even into the Council of the Olympians, the unyielding Titan, Prometheus.

PANDORA

Prometheus the Forethinker had a brother who was named Epimetheus the Afterthinker. He was slow-witted and scatter-brained. His wise brother once sent him a message bidding him beware of the gifts that Zeus might send him. Epimetheus heard, but he did not heed the warning; thereby he brought upon the race of men troubles and cares.

Zeus was wroth with men now because fire, stolen from him, had been given them; he was wroth with the race of Titans, too, and he pondered in his heart how he might injure men, and how he might use Epimetheus, the mindless Titan, to further his plan.

While he pondered there was a hush on high Olympos, the mountain of the Gods. Then Zeus called upon the artisan of the Gods, lame Hephæstos, and he commanded him to make a being out of clay who would have the likeness of a lovely maiden. With joy and pride Hephæstos worked at the task that had been given him, and he fashioned a being that had the likeness of a lovely maiden, and he brought the thing of his making before the Gods and Goddesses.

All strove to add a grace or a beauty to the work of Hephæstos. Zeus granted that the maiden should see and feel. Athene dressed her in garments that were as lovely as flowers. Aphrodite, the Goddess of Love, put a charm on her lips and in her eyes. The Graces put necklaces around her neck and set a golden crown upon her head. The Hours brought her a girdle of spring flowers. Then the herald of the Gods gave her speech that was sweet and flowing. All the Gods and Goddesses had given gifts to her, and for that reason the maiden of Hephæstos's making was called Pandora, the All-endowed.

She was lovely, the Gods knew; not beautiful as they themselves are, who have a beauty that awakens reverence rather than love, but lovely as flowers and bright waters and earthly maidens are lovely. Zeus smiled to himself when he looked upon her; he called to Hermes who knew all the ways of the earth, and he put her into the charge of Hermes. Also he gave Hermes a great jar to take along; this jar was Pandora's dower.

Epimetheus lived in a deep-sunken valley. Now one day, as he was sitting on a fallen pillar in the ruined palace that was now forsaken by the rest of the Titans, he saw a pair coming towards him. One had wings, and he knew him to be Hermes, the messenger of the Gods. The other was a maiden. Epimetheus marvelled at the crown upon her head and at her lovely garments. There was a glint of gold all around her. He rose from where he sat upon the broken pillar and he stood to watch the pair. Hermes, he saw, was carrying by its handle a great jar. In wonder and delight, Epimetheus looked upon the maiden. He had seen no lovely thing for ages. Wonderful, indeed, was this Golden Maid, and as she came near him the charm that was on her lips and in her eyes came to the Earth-born One, and he smiled with more and more delight.

Hermes came and stood before him. He also smiled, but his smile had something baleful in it. He put the hands of the Golden Maid into the great soft hand of the Titan, and he said, "O Epimetheus, Father

Zeus would be reconciled with thee, and as a token of his good will he sends thee this lovely Goddess to be thy companion."

Oh, very foolish was Epimetheus the Earth-born One! As he looked upon the Golden Maid who was sent by Zeus he lost memory of the wars that Zeus had made upon the Titans and the elder Gods; he lost the memory of his brother chained to the highest, blackest peak of Caucasus; he lost memory of the warning that his brother, the wisest of all beings, had sent him. He took the hands of Pandora, and he thought of nothing in the world but her. Very far away seemed the voice of Hermes, saying, "This jar, too, is from Olympos; it has in it Pandora's dower."

For long it stood forgotten, this jar, and green plants grew over it while Epimetheus walked in the garden with the Golden Maid, or watched her while she gazed on herself in the stream, or searched in the untended places for fruits that the elder Gods would eat when they feasted with the Titans in the old days ere Zeus had come to his power. Lost to Epimetheus was the memory of his brother now suffering upon the rock because of the gift he had given men.

And Pandora, knowing nothing except the brightness of the sunshine and the lovely shapes and colours of things and the sweet taste of the fruits that Epimetheus brought her, could have stayed forever in the garden. But one day Epimetheus took her by the hand, and brought her out of that garden, and out of that deep-lying valley, and towards the homes of men. He did not forget the jar that Hermes had left with her. All things that belonged to the Golden Maid were precious, and Epimetheus took the jar along.

The race of men at that time were simple and content. Their days were passed in toil, but now, since Prometheus had given them fire, they had good fruit of their toil. They had well-shaped tools with which to dig the earth and build houses. Their homes were warmed with fire, and fire burned upon the altars that were upon their ways.

Greatly they reverenced Prometheus who had given them fire, and greatly they reverenced the race of the Titans. So when Epimetheus came amongst them, tall as a man walking upon stilts, they welcomed him, and brought him and the Golden Maid to their hearths. And Epimetheus showed Pandora the wonderful element that his brother had

given men; she rejoiced to see the fire, clapping her hands with de
light. The jar that Epimetheus brought he left in an open space.

In carrying it up the rough ways out of the valley Epimetheus may
have knocked the jar about, for the lid that had been tight upon it now
fitted very loosely. But no one gave heed to the jar as it stood in the
open space where Epimetheus had left it.

At first the men and women looked upon the beauty of Pandora,
upon her lovely dresses, and her golden crown, and her girdle of
flowers, with wonder and delight. Epimetheus would have everyone
admire and praise her. And this they did for a while. The men would
leave off working in the fields, or hammering on iron, or building
houses, and the women would leave off spinning and weaving, and come
at his call, and stand about and admire the Golden Maid. But as time
went by a change came upon the women: one woman would weep, and
another would look angry, and a third would go back sullenly to her
work when Pandora was admired or praised.

Once when the women were gathered together one who was the
wisest amongst them said, "We used not to think about ourselves; we
used to be content with what we are and what we have. But now we
think about ourselves, and we say to ourselves that we are harsh and
ill-favoured, indeed, compared to the Golden Maid that the Titan is so
enchanted with. And we hate to see our own men praise and admire
her, and often, in our hearts, we would destroy her if we could."

"That is true," the women said. And then a young woman cried
out in a most yearnful voice, "O tell us, you who are wise, how can we
make ourselves as beautiful as Pandora?"

Then the woman who was thought to be wise said, "This Golden
Maid is lovely to look upon because she has lovely apparel and all
the means of keeping herself lovely. The Gods have given her the ways,
and so her skin remains fair, and her hair keeps its gold, and her lips
are ever red and her eyes shining. And I think that the means of
keeping lovely are all in that jar that Epimetheus brought with
her."

When the woman who was thought to be wise said this, those around
her were silent for a while. But then one rose and another rose, and
they stood and whispered together, one saying to the other that they
should go to the place where the jar had been left by Epimetheus, and

that they should take out of it the salves, the charms, and the washes that would make them as beautiful as Pandora.

The women went to that place. On their way they stopped at a pool and they bent over to see themselves mirrored in it, and they saw themselves with dusty and unkempt hair, with large and knotted hands, with troubled eyes, and with anxious mouths. They frowned as they looked upon their images, and they said in harsh voices that in a while they would have ways of making themselves as lovely as the Golden Maid.

And as they went on they saw Pandora. She was playing in a flowering field, while Epimetheus, high as a man upon stilts, went gathering the blossoms off the bushes for her. They went on, and they came at last to the place where Epimetheus had left the jar that held Pandora's dower.

A great stone jar it was; there was no bird, nor flower, nor branch painted upon it. It stood high as a woman's shoulder. And as the women looked upon it they thought that there were things enough in it to keep them beautiful for all the days of their lives. But each one thought that she should not be the last to get her hands into it.

The lid, once tightly fixed down, had been shifted a little. As the hands of the women grasped it to take off the lid, the jar was cast down; the things that were inside spilled themselves forth.

They were black and grey and red; they were crawling and flying things. And, as the women looked on, the things spread themselves abroad or fastened themselves upon them.

The jar, like Pandora herself, had been made and filled out of the ill-will of Zeus. And it had been filled, not with salves and charms and washes, as the women thought, but with Cares and Troubles. Before the women had come to it one Trouble had already come forth from the jar—Self-thought that was upon the top of the heap. It was Self-thought that had afflicted the women, making them troubled about their own looks, and envious of the graces of the Golden Maid.

And now the others spread themselves out—Sickness and War and Strife between friends. They spread themselves abroad and entered the houses, while Epimetheus, the mindless Titan, gathered flowers for Pandora, the Golden Maid.

Lest she should weary of her play he called to her. He would take her into the houses of men. As they drew near to the houses they saw a woman seated on the ground, weeping; her husband had suddenly become harsh to her, and had shut the door on her face. They came upon a child crying because of a pain that he could not understand. And then they found two men struggling, their strife being on account of a possession that they had shared peaceably before.

In every house they went into Epimetheus would say, "I am the brother of Prometheus who gave you the gift of fire." But instead of giving them a welcome the men would say, "We know nothing about your relation with Prometheus. We see you as a foolish man upon stilts."

Epimetheus was troubled by the hard looks and the cold words of the men who had once reverenced him. He turned from the houses and went away. In a quiet place he sat down, and for a while he lost sight of Pandora. And then it seemed to him that he heard the voice of his wise and suffering brother saying, "Do not accept any gift that Zeus may send you."

He rose up and he hurried away from that place, leaving Pandora playing by herself. There came into his scattered mind Regret and Fear. As he went on he stumbled. He fell from the edge of a cliff, and the sea washed away the body of the mindless brother of Prometheus.

Not everything had been spilled out of the jar that had been brought with Pandora into the world of men. A beautiful living thing was in the jar also. This was Hope. And this beautiful living thing had got caught under the rim of the jar and had not come forth with the others. Under the rim of Pandora's jar a weeping woman one day found Hope; she brought this living thing into the houses of men. And now because of Hope they could see an end to their troubles. The men and women roused themselves in the midst of their afflictions; they looked towards gladness. Hope, that had been caught under the rim of the jar, stayed behind the thresholds of their houses.

As for Pandora, the Golden Maid, she played on, knowing only the brightness of the sunshine and the lovely shapes of things. Beautiful would she have seemed to any being who saw her. But now she was strayed away from the houses of men and Epimetheus was not there to look upon her. Then Hephæstos, the lame artisan of the Gods, put down his tools and went to seek her. He found Pandora; he took her back to Olympos. And in his brazen house she stays, though sometimes, at the will of Zeus, she goes down into the world of men.

DEMETER

Once when Demeter, daughter of Kronos and Rhea, was going through the world, making men's fields fertile, she heard a cry that came to her from across high mountains and mounted up to her from the sea. Demeter's heart shook when she heard that cry, for she knew that it came to her from her daughter, from the maiden Persephone.

She stayed not in the fields, but she hurried, hurried away to Sicily and to the fields of Enna, where she had left Persephone. All Enna she searched, and all Sicily, but she found no trace of Persephone, nor of the maidens with whom Persephone had been playing. From all whom she met she begged for tidings, but although some had seen the maidens gathering flowers and playing together, no one could tell Demeter why her child had cried out nor where she had since gone.

There were some who could have told her. One was a nymph. But she, before Demeter came to her, had been changed into a spring of water. And now, not being able to speak and tell Demeter where her child had gone and who had carried her away, she showed in the water the girdle of Persephone that she had caught in her hands. And Demeter, finding the girdle of her daughter in the spring, knew that she had been carried off by violence. She lighted a torch at Ætna's burning mountain, and for nine days and nine nights she went searching for her through the darkened places of the earth.

Then, upon a high and a dark hill, the Goddess Demeter came face to face with Hekate, the Moon. Hekate, too, had heard the cry of Persephone; she had sorrow for Demeter's sorrow: she spoke to her as the two stood on that dark, high hill, and told her that she should go to Helios for tidings—to bright Helios, the watcher for the Gods, and beg Helios to tell her who it was who had carried off by violence her child Persephone.

Demeter came to Helios. He was standing before his shining steeds, before the impatient steeds that drew the sun through the course of the heavens. Demeter stood in the way of those impatient steeds; she begged of Helios who sees all things upon the earth to tell her who it was who had carried off by violence Persephone, her child.

And Helios, who may make no concealment, said, "Queenly Demeter, know that the King of the Underworld, dark Hades, has carried off Persephone to make her his Queen in the realm that I never shine upon." He spoke, and as he did, his horses shook their manes and breathed out fire, impatient to be gone. Helios sprang into his chariot and went flashing away.

Demeter, knowing that one of the Gods had carried off Persephone against her will, and knowing that what was done had been by the will of Zeus, would go no more into the assemblies of the Olympians. She quenched the torch that she had held in her hands for nine days and nine nights; she put off her robe of Goddess, and she went wandering over the earth, uncomforted for the loss of her child. No longer did she appear as a Goddess gracious to men; no longer did she bless their fields. None of the things that it pleased her once to do would Demeter do any longer.

Persephone had been playing with the nymphs who are the Daughters of Ocean in the lovely fields of Enna. They went to gather the flowers that grow there in the spring-time—irises and crocuses, lilies, hyacinths, and rose-blooms. As they went gathering flowers in their baskets they had sight of the pool that the white swans come to sing in.

Beside a deep chasm that had been made in the earth a wonder-flower was growing—in colour it was like the crocus, but it sent forth a perfume that was like the perfume of a hundred flowers. And Persephone, as she went towards it, thought that having gathered that flower she would have something more wonderful than her companions had.

She did not know that Hades, the Lord of the Underworld, had caused the flower to grow there so that she might be drawn by it to the chasm that he had made.

As Persephone stooped to pluck the wonder-flower, dark Hades, in his chariot of iron, dashed up through the chasm, and, grasping the maiden by the waist, set her beside him. Only Cyane, the nymph, tried to save Persephone, and it was then that she caught her girdle in her hands.

The maiden cried out, first because her flowers had been spilled, and then because she was being reft away. She cried out to her mother, and her cry went over the high mountains and sounded up from the sea. The Daughters of Ocean, affrighted, fled and sank down into the depths of the sea.

In his great chariot of iron that was drawn by black steeds, Hades rushed down through the chasm that had been made. Into the Underworld he went; he dashed across the River Styx, and brought the chariot up beside his throne. And on his dark throne he seated Persephone, the fainting daughter of Demeter.

No more did the Goddess Demeter make fertile the fields of men: weeds grew where crops should be growing; men feared that in a while they would famish for lack of bread.

She wandered through the world, her thought all upon her child, Persephone, who had been taken from her. Once she sat by a well by a wayside, thinking upon the daughter whom she might not come to and who might not come to her.

She saw four maidens come near; their grace and their youth reminded her of her Persephone. They stepped lightly along, carrying bronze pitchers in their hands, for they were coming to the Well of the Maidens beside which Demeter sat.

The maidens thought when they looked upon her that the Goddess was some ancient woman who had a sorrow in her heart. Seeing that she was so noble and so sorrowful looking, the maidens, as they drew clear water into their pitchers, spoke kindly to her.

"Why do you stay away from the town, mother?" one of the maidens asked. "Why do you not come to the houses? We think that you look as if you were shelterless and alone, and we should like to tell you that there are many houses in our town where you would be welcomed."

Demeter's heart went out to the maidens because they looked so young and fair and simple and spoke out of such kind hearts. She said to them: "Where can I go, dear children? My people are far away, and there are none in all the world who would care to be near me."

Said one of the maidens, "There are princes in the land who would welcome you in their houses if you would consent to nurse one of their young children. But why do I speak of other princes beside Keleos, our father? In his house you would, indeed, have welcome. But lately a babe has been born to Metaneira, our mother, and she would greatly rejoice to have one as wise as you to nurse little Demophon."

All the time that she watched them and listened to their voices Demeter felt that the grace and youth of the maidens made them like her Persephone. She thought that it would ease her heart to be in the house where these maidens were, and she was not loath to have them go and ask of their mother to have her come to nurse the infant child.

Swiftly they ran back to their home, their hair streaming behind them like crocus flowers, kind and lovely girls whose names are well remembered—Kallidike and Kleisidike, Demo and Kallithoe. They went to their mother and they told her of the stranger woman whose name was Doso. She would make a wise and kind nurse for little Demophon, they said. Their mother, Metaneira, rose up from the couch she was sitting on to welcome the stranger. But when she saw her at the door, awe came over her, so majestical the stranger seemed.

Metaneira would have her seat herself on the couch, but the Goddess took the lowliest stool, saying in greeting, "May the Gods give you all good, lady."

"Sorrow has set you wandering from your good home," said Metaneira to the Goddess, "but now that you have come to this place you shall have all that this house can bestow if you will rear the infant Demophon, child of many hopes and prayers."

The child was put into the arms of Demeter; she clasped him to her breast, and little Demophon looked up into her face and smiled. Then Demeter's heart went out to the child and to all who were of that household.

He grew in strength and beauty in her charge. And little Demophon was not nourished as other children are nourished, but even as the Gods in their childhood were nourished. Demeter fed him on ambrosia, breathing on him with her divine breath the while. And at night she laid him on the hearth, amongst the embers, with the fire all around him. This she did that she might make him immortal, and like to the Gods.

But one night Metaneira looked out from the chamber where she lay, and she saw the nurse take little Demophon and lay him in a place on the hearth, with the burning brands all round him. Then Metaneira started up; she sprang to the hearth, and she snatched the child from beside the burning brands. "Demophon, my son," she cried, "what would this stranger woman do to you, bringing bitter grief to me that ever I let her take you in her arms?"

Then said Demeter, "Foolish, indeed, are you mortals, and not able to foresee what is to come to you of good or of evil! Foolish, indeed, are you, Metaneira, for in your heedlessness you have cut off this child from an immortality like to the immortality of the Gods themselves. For he had lain in my bosom, and had become dear to me, and I would have bestowed on him the greatest gift that the Divine Ones can bestow. I would have made him deathless and unaging. All this, now, has gone by. Honour he shall have, indeed, but Demophon will know age and death."

The seeming old age that had been upon her had fallen from Demeter; beauty and stature were hers, and from her robe there came a heavenly fragrance. There came such light from her body that the chamber shone. Metaneira remained there, trembling and speechless, unmindful even to take up the child that had been laid upon the ground.

It was then that his sisters heard Demophon wail. One ran from her chamber and took the child in her arms; another kindled again the fire on the hearth; the others made ready to bathe and care for the infant. All night they cared for him, holding him in their arms and at their breasts, but the child would not be comforted; the nurses who handled him now were less skillful than was the Goddess-nurse.

As for Demeter, she left the house of Keleos and went upon her way, lonely in her heart, and unappeased. And in the world that she wandered through, the plough went in vain through the ground; the furrow was sown without any avail, and the race of men saw themselves near perishing for lack of bread.

Once again Demeter came near the Well of the Maidens. She thought of the daughters of Keleos as they came towards the well that day, the bronze pitchers in their hands, and with kind looks for the stranger—she thought of them as she sat by the well again. And then she thought of little Demophon, the child she had held at her breast.

No stir of living was in the land near their home; only weeds grew in their fields. As she sat there and looked around her there came into Demeter's heart a pity for the people in whose house she had dwelt.

She rose up and she went into the house of Keleos. She found the king beside the house measuring out a little grain. The Goddess went to him; she told him that because of the love she bore his household she would bless his fields so that the seed he had sown in them would come to growth. Keleos rejoiced; he called all the people together; they would raise a temple there to Demeter, they vowed. She went through the fields and blessed them, and the seed they had sown began to grow. And the Goddess for a while dwelt amongst the people. The place was Eleusis.

But still she kept away from the assemblies of the Gods. Zeus sent a messenger to her—Iris with the golden wings—bidding her to Olympos. Demeter would not join the Olympians. Then, one after another, the Gods and Goddesses of Olympos came to her; no one was able to make her cease from grieving for Persephone, or to go again into the company of the immortal Gods.

And so it came about that Zeus was compelled to send a messenger down to the Underworld to bring Persephone back to the mother who had grieved so much for the loss of her. Hermes was the messenger whom Zeus sent. Through the darkened places of the earth Hermes went, and he came to the dark throne where Hades sat, Persephone beside him. Then Hermes spoke to the Lord of the Underworld, saying that Zeus commanded that Persephone should come forth from the Underworld that her mother might look upon her.

Persephone, hearing of the word of Zeus that might not be gainsaid, uttered the only cry that had left her lips since she had sent out that cry that had reached her mother's heart. And Hades, hearing the command of Zeus that might not be denied, bowed his dark, majestic head.

She might go to the Upperworld and rest herself in the arms of her mother, he said. And then he cried out, "Ah, Persephone, strive to feel kindliness in your heart towards me who carried you off by violence and against your will. I can give to you one of the great kingdoms that the Olympians rule over, albeit that it is a dark kingdom. And I, who am brother to Zeus, am a fitting husband for you, Demeter's child."

So Hades, the dark Lord of the Underworld, said, and he made ready the chariot with the deathless horses that Persephone might go up from his kingdom.

Beside the single tree in his domain Hades stayed his chariot. A single fruit grew upon that tree, a bright pomegranate fruit. Persephone stood up in the chariot and plucked the fruit from the tree. Then did Hades prevail upon her to divide the fruit; having divided it, Persephone ate seven of the pomegranate seeds.

It was Hermes who took the whip and shook the reins of the chariot. He drove on, and neither the sea nor the water-courses, nor the glens, nor the mountain-peaks, stayed the deathless horses of Hades; soon the chariot was brought near to where Demeter awaited the coming of her daughter.

And when, from a hilltop, Demeter saw the chariot approaching, like a wild bird she flew to clasp her child. Persephone, when she saw her mother's dear eyes, sprang out of the chariot, and fell upon her neck and embraced her. Long and long Demeter held her dear child in her arms, gazing, gazing upon her. Suddenly her mind misgave her. With a great fear at her heart she cried out, "Dearest, has any food passed your lips in all the time you have been in the Underworld?"

She had not tasted food in all the time she had been there, Persephone said. And then, suddenly, she remembered the pomegranate that Hades had asked her to divide. When she told how she had eaten seven seeds from it, Demeter wept; her tears fell upon Persephone's face.

"Ah, my dearest," she cried, "if you had not eaten the pomegranate seeds you could stay with me, and always we should have been together. But now that you have eaten food in it, the realm of Hades has a claim upon you. You may not stay always with me here. Again you will have to go back and dwell in the dark places under the earth, and sit upon Hades' throne. But not always will you be there. When the flowers bloom upon the earth you shall come up from the realm of darkness, and in great joy we shall go through the world together, Demeter and Persephone."

And so it has been since Persephone came back to her mother after having eaten the pomegranate seeds. For two seasons of the year she stays with Demeter; for one season she stays with her dark lord. While she is with her mother there is spring-time on the earth. Demeter blesses the furrows, her heart being glad because her daughter is with her once more. The furrows become heavy with grain, and soon the whole wide earth has grain and fruits, leaves and flowers. When the furrows are reaped, when the grain has been gathered, when the dark season comes, then Persephone goes from her mother; going down into the dark places, she sits beside her mighty lord, Hades, upon his throne. Not sorrowful is she there; she sits with her head unbowed, for she knows herself to be a mighty queen. She has joy, too, knowing of the seasons when she may walk with Demeter, her mother, on the wide places of the earth, through fields of flowers and fruit and ripening grain.

ORPHEUS

Many were the minstrels who, in the early days of the world, went amongst men, telling them stories of the Gods, of their wars and their births, and of the beginning of things. Of all these minstrels none was so famous as Orpheus; none could tell truer things about the Gods; he himself was half divine, and there were some who said that he was in truth Apollo's son.

But a great grief came to Orpheus, a grief that stopped his singing and his playing upon the lyre. His young wife, Eurydike, was taken from him. One day, walking in the garden, she was bitten on the heel by a serpent; straightway she went down to the World of the Dead.

Then everything in this world was dark and bitter for the minstrel of the Gods; sleep would not come to him, and for him food had no taste. Then Orpheus said, "I will do that which no mortal has ever done before; I will do that which even the Immortals might shrink from doing; I will go down into the World of the Dead, and I will bring back to the living and to the light my bride, Eurydike."

Then Orpheus went on his way to the cavern which goes down, down to the World of the Dead—the Cavern Tainaron. The trees showed him the way. As he went on, Orpheus played upon his lyre and sang; the trees heard his song and were moved by his grief, and with their arms and their heads they showed him the way to the deep, deep cavern named Tainaron.

Down, down, down by a winding path Orpheus went. He came at last to the great gate that opens upon the World of the Dead. And the silent guards who keep watch there for the Rulers of the Dead were astonished when they saw a living being coming towards them, and they would not let Orpheus approach the gate.

The minstrel took the lyre in his hands and played upon it. As he played, the silent watchers gathered around him, leaving the gate unguarded. And as he played the Rulers of the Dead came forth, Hades and Persephone, and listened to the words of the living man.

"The cause of my coming through the dark and fearful ways," sang Orpheus, "is to strive to gain a fairer fate for Eurydike, my bride. All that is above must come down to you at last, O Rulers of the most lasting World. But before her time has Eurydike been brought here. I have desired strength to endure her loss, but I cannot endure it. And I have come before you, Hades and Persephone, brought here by love."

When Orpheus said the name of love, Persephone, the queen of the dead, bowed her young head, and bearded Hades, the king, bowed his head also. Persephone remembered how Demeter, her mother, had sought her all through the world, and she remembered the touch of her mother's tears upon her face. And Hades remembered how his love for Persephone had led him to carry her away from the valley where she had been gathering flowers. He and Persephone stood aside, and Orpheus went through the gate and came amongst the dead.

Still upon his lyre he played. Tantalos—who for his crime had been condemned to stand up to his neck in water and yet never be able to assuage his thirst—Tantalos heard, and for a while did not strive to put his lips towards the water that ever flowed away from him; Sisyphos—who had been condemned to roll up a hill a stone that ever rolled back—Sisyphos heard the music that Orpheus played, and for a while he sat still upon his stone. Ixion, bound to a wheel, stopped its turning for a while; the vultures abandoned their torment of Tityos; the daughters of Danaos ceased to fill their jars; even those dread ones, the Erinyes, who bring to the dead the memories of all their crimes and all their faults, had their cheeks wet with tears.

In the throng of the newly-come dead Orpheus saw Eurydike. She looked upon her husband, but she had not the power to come near him. But slowly she came when Hades, the king, called her. Then with joy Orpheus took her hands.

It would be granted them—no mortal ever gained such privilege before—to leave, both together, the World of the Dead, and to abide for another space in the World of the Living. One condition there would be—that on their way up neither Orpheus nor Eurydike should look back.

They went through the gate and came out amongst the watchers that are around the portals. These showed them the path that went up to the World of the Living. That way they went, Orpheus and Eurydike, he going before her.

Up and through the darkened ways they went, Orpheus knowing that Eurydike was behind him, but never looking back upon her. As he went his heart was filled with things to tell her—how the trees were blossoming in the garden she had left; how the water was sparkling in the fountain; how the doors of the house stood open; how they, sitting together, would watch the sunlight on the laurel bushes. All these things were in his heart to tell her who came behind him, silent and unseen.

And now they were nearing the place where the cavern opened on the world of the living. Orpheus looked up towards the light from the sky. Out of the opening of the cavern he went; he saw a white-winged bird fly by. He turned around and cried, "O Eurydike, look upon the world I have won you back to!"

He turned to say this to her. He saw her with her long dark hair and pale face. He held out his arms to clasp her. But in that instant she slipped back into the gloom of the cavern. And all he heard spoken was a single word, "Farewell!" Long, long had it taken Eurydike to climb so far, but in the moment of his turning around she had fallen back to her place amongst the dead. For Orpheus had looked back.

Back through the cavern Orpheus went again. Again he came before the watchers of the gate. But now he was not looked at nor listened to; hopeless, he had to return to the World of the Living.

The birds were his friends now, and the trees and the stones. The birds flew around him and mourned with him; the trees and stones often followed him, moved by the music of his lyre. But a savage band slew Orpheus and threw his severed head and his lyre into the River Hebrus. It is said by the poets that while they floated in midstream the lyre gave out some mournful notes, and the head of Orpheus answered the notes with song.

And now that he was no longer to be counted with the living, Orpheus went down to the World of the Dead, going down straightway. The silent watchers let him pass; he went amongst the dead, and he saw his Eurydike in the throng. Again they were together, Orpheus and Eurydike, and them the Erinyes could not torment with memories of crimes and faults.

DIONYSOS

A ship lay in a harbour; on a headland that overlooked the harbour a youth appeared. He wore a purple cloak; his hair was rich, dark, and flowing; his face was beautiful. The sailors on the ship thought that he must be a king's son, or a young king's brother. They were Tyrrhenian sea-rovers, and they knew that they could never be called to account for anything that they did in that place. So they made a plan to seize the youth and hold him for ransom, or else sell him into slavery in some far land.

They seized him and they brought him on board the ship in bonds. He did not cry out; he sat upon the deck with a smile on his lips and a gleam in his dark eyes. And when the helmsman looked upon him he cried out to his companions, "Madmen, why have ye done this? I tell you that the one whom you have bound is one of the Olympians! Come! Let us set him free at once! Do not have him turn his rage against us, or the winds and the sea may be stirred up against our ship. I tell you that not even our well-built ship can carry such a one as he!"

But the master of the ship laughed at the words of the helmsman. "Madman yourself," he said, "with your talk of Olympians!" He gave command to have the ship taken out of that harbour. Then to the helmsman he said, "Leave the business of dealing with our prize to us. Mark the wind, you, and help to hoist the sail. As for the youth we have taken, I know what kind of a fellow he is. He will say nothing; he will keep smiling there. But soon he will talk, I warrant you! He will tell us where his friends and his brothers are, and how much we are likely to get by way of ransom for him. Or else he will stand in the market-place until we find out what price he will fetch."

So the master of the sea-rovers spoke, and the mast went up; the sail was hoisted; the wind filled it, and the ship went over the sparkling sea. The sea-rovers sang, well content with all they had accomplished. Then, as they went here and there, making taut the sheets, they saw things that made them marvel. What was this that poured upon the deck, giving such fragrance? Could it be wine? Wine it was, and of a marvellous taste! Could that be fresh ivy that was spreading around the mast—ivy with dark-green leaves and berries? Could that be a vine that was growing along the sail—a vine with bunches of grapes growing from it? And what was this greenery that was garlanding the thole-pins? The sea-rovers marvelled. Then, suddenly, their marvelling was turned to affright. There was a lion on the ship—it was filled with his roarings. The sailors fled to where the helmsman was and they crowded about him. "Turn back—turn back the ship!" they cried. And then the lion sprang upon the master of the ship and seized him; the lion shook him and then flung him into the sea. The sailors waited for no more; they sprang into the sea, every man of them. The helmsman was about to spring into the sea after them. He looked around him; there was no lion there. He saw the youth they had taken aboard; the bonds were no longer upon him; there was a smile on his lips and in his dark eyes, and on his brow was a wreath of ivy rich with berries. The helmsman threw himself on the deck before him. "Take courage, man," said the youth, now known, indeed, for one of the Olympians. "The others have been changed to dolphins in the sea. You have found favour with me. And I am Dionysos whom Semele bore to Zeus."

He was that God who was so marvellously born. Zeus, lord of the thunder, had loved Semele, the daughter of King Kadmos. She had begged her lover to show himself to her in all the splendour of his godhead. Zeus came to her in his radiance; then Semele was smitten and consumed and the life went from her.

Zeus took her unborn child; opening his thigh he laid the unborn thing within and had the flesh sewn over it. The child was born from the thigh of Zeus upon Mount Nysa, in a secret place, remote from the presence of Hera, the spouse of Zeus. The nymphs of the mountain received the child from Zeus; they took him to their bosoms and reared him in the dells of Nysa. He was fed on ambrosia and nectar, the food of the Immortals. He grew up in an ivy-covered cave that was filled with the scent of flowers and of grapes.

He grew into a stripling; then he wandered through the wooded valleys of Mount Nysa, a wreath of ivy always upon his brow. The nymphs followed him, and the woods and valleys were filled with their outcries. A king who heard these outcries, who saw the ivy-crowned stripling and the nymphs following him with wands in their hands, became enraged at the sight. Lykourgos was that king's name. He had his men chase them, striking at the nymphs and at Dionysos with their heavy ox-goads. The nymphs flung their wands upon the ground and flew to the mountain-top. Dionysos went down to the sea-shore. As for Lykourgos, he was smitten with blindness; he did not stay long amongst men afterwards, for he was hated by the immortal Gods.

Now the ship with the faithful helmsman in charge of it brought Dionysos to the island of Naxos. There the daughter of King Minos, Ariadne, became his bride. He went to Egypt and was received with honour by the King of Egypt; he went to India and had his dwelling-place by the River Ganges. And everywhere he went he showed men how to grow the vine and how to make wine that gladdens hearts and liberates minds from their close-pressing cares.

And everywhere he went women followed him; they had a frenzied joy from being near him; they danced; they clashed cymbals; they kept up revels that were hidden from men. With trains of women attending him Dionysos turned back to the land he was born in. He went riding in a car that was drawn by leopards that the King of India had given him, and on his brow was a wreath of ivies and of vine-leaves.

So he came back to Thebes—to Thebes that had been ruled over by Kadmos, the father of Semele. Kadmos was an old man now, and he had given the rule of the country to Pentheus, his daughter's son.

Dionysos came, saying that he was the son of Semele, and Pentheus denounced him as an impostor. Then the women of Thebes, neglecting their households, joined the band that followed Dionysos and had their revels in the mountains—revels which no man was allowed to look upon. Pentheus became more and more angered at what his subjects, under the influence of this rover from India, were being brought to think and do.

He forbade the growing of the vine in Thebes; he would not allow the Thebans to make or to drink wine. And this he did, although his father, a wine-cup in his hand, came before him, and warned him against persecuting the followers of Dionysos.

He shut Dionysos in his prison-house, and he followed the women of Thebes to their secret meeting-place on the top of the mountain. He climbed a pine-tree so that he might overlook their revels. And he was there when the women saw him. In a frenzy they dashed to the tree; they tore the man out of its branches. Pentheus saw the women threatening him; he saw his own mother Agave there—the foremost amongst them. She did not know him, but kept crying, "A boar, a boar has come amongst us; destroy this boar." They tore at him; they tore the body of Pentheus to pieces, his own mother, Agave, in her frenzy, leading the others on. So Pentheus perished, and so Dionysos triumphed in the land where Semele saw her divine lover in his splendour and was crushed by his radiance and his might.

APOLLO

Of Apollo the swan sings as he alights upon the banks of the eddying River Peneios; with clear voice and to the beating of his wings the swan sings of him. And of Apollo, the minstrel, holding the lyre in his hands, sings first and last. He and Artemis, his sister, were the children of Leto and Zeus. Long did Leto wander over the earth, trying to find a place where she could give birth to her children, for Hera, the great spouse of Zeus, was angry and withheld all help from her. At last she came to Delos and begged of that island to grant her a place where she might be delivered of her burthen. And Delos, that little island, said, "Gladly, Lady Leto, would I give a place for the birth of your children. I who am little and ill-spoken of by men on account of my hard and rocky soil would be honoured greatly should their birth take place on any lap of my lands. But I have fear, too—I fear lest your children should become ashamed of their birth-place, and overturn me, and thrust me down into the depths of the sea, and have the strange and ugly creatures of the deep make their lairs on me— sea-lions haunting my vales and not human beings. But all should be well, Goddess, if you would take a great oath that your son shall build a temple upon my land." Leto took an oath by Styx—the oath that the Gods take and may be broken never—that her son should have his temple built upon the island.

So Leto's children were born on Delos, that little island—her twin children, Apollo and Artemis. Although Hera withheld all help many of the Goddesses were present at the birth. They took Apollo and washed him in sweet water; they clothed him in white and they put a golden band about him. And Themis, one of the elder Goddesses, gave him ambrosia and nectar, the food of the immortal Gods.

As soon as he had tasted that divine food the infant sprang from the arms of his nurse. He spoke, and all Delos blossomed and gleamed with golden light. He took into his hands the bow and the lyre. Later he received from Hephaistos a quiver of arrows. With these arrows, shot from his silver bow, he slew Python, the huge dragon that was the offspring of Earth. He slew Typhon, too—Typhon, the monster that had no likeness to anything that the Gods had brought into being.

Leaving there the dead and sprawling monster, he went into the lovely Vale of Tempe. There he saw Daphne; Earth was her mother, her father was Peneios, the River. Her hair was unbound as she ran down the slopes of the Mountain Ossa. She saw him standing upon a peak, his silver bow across his shoulder, with the light striking upon his quiver. She knew him for the most beautiful of the Olympians. But when he called to her she fled from him, for she had vowed that no God nor no man should possess her. She ran as a deer runs. Apollo followed her. Down the slopes of Ossa the chase went, the God in pursuit of the maiden. Daphne knew all the places; she was swift of foot and she thought she could out-distance her pursuer. On she ran. But now her breath came in pants; her heart nearly burst within her body. She heard the words that were called out to her, "Stay, O stay! It is not hate that makes me follow you!" She heard his breathing behind her.

Into a soft place she ran, and her feet sank into the ground. "O Mother Earth, make it that I do not have to yield to him," she prayed. Then she felt his breath upon her neck; she felt his hands upon her shoulders. She swayed; she knew herself changed, and rooted in earth, and safe from pursuit. And Apollo found himself holding the twigs and the leaves of a laurel-tree. "Daphne, O Daphne," he cried, as he felt the blood in the body he held flow down and become sap, as he saw the limbs, and the flesh, and the flowing hair become branches and leaves. He mourned for her where he stood. But as he loved Daphne as a maiden so now he loves her as a tree. He plucked the leaves and put them around his brows. And still Apollo wears and still he gives the laurel.

HERAKLES

I

Herakles, born of Alkmene, a mortal woman, was the son of Zeus. Hera, the spouse of Zeus, bore ill-will towards Alkmene and her hero-son, and when Herakles was still an infant in the cradle she sent two great serpents to destroy him. But the child took the serpents and strangled them with his own hands. Then, while he was still a youth, a madness sent by the Goddess came upon him, and unwittingly he slew the children of Iphikles, his half-brother. Coming to know what he had done, sleep and rest went from him; he went to Delphoi, the shrine of Apollo, to be purified of his crime.

At Delphoi, at the shrine of Apollo, the priestess purified him, saying, "Thou shalt go to Eurystheus, thy cousin, in Tiryns, and serve him in all things. When the labours he shall lay upon thee are accomplished, and when the rest of thy life is lived out, thou shalt become one of the Immortals." Herakles, on hearing these words, set out for Tiryns.

He stood before his cousin who hated him; he, a towering man,

stood before a king who sat there weak and trembling. Herakles said, "I have come to take up the labours that you will lay upon me; speak now, Eurystheus, and tell me what you would have me do."

Eurystheus, that weak king, looking on the young man who stood as tall and as firm as one of the Immortals, had a heart that was filled with hatred. He lifted up his head and said with a scowl:

"There is a lion in Nemea that is stronger and more fierce than any lion known before. Kill that lion; bring the lion's skin to me that I may know that you have truly performed your task." So Eurystheus said, and Herakles, with neither shield nor arms, went forth from the king's palace to seek and combat the dread lion of Nemea.

He went on until he came into a country where the fences were overthrown, and the fields wasted, and the houses empty and fallen. He went on until he came to a waste around that land: there he came on the trail of the lion; it led up the side of a mountain, and Herakles, without shield or arms, followed on the trail.

He heard the roar of the lion. Looking up he saw the beast standing at the mouth of a cavern, huge and dark against the sunset. Three times the lion roared, and then went within the cavern.

Around the mouth were strewn the bones of creatures it had killed and carried there. Herakles looked upon the bones when he came to the cavern. He went within. Far into the cavern he went; he came to where the lion lay gorged with the prey it had taken. The breath from its mouth and nostrils came heavily to him. The beast yawned.

Herakles sprang on it; he put his great, knotted hands upon its throat. No growl came out of the mouth, but the great eyes blazed and the terrible paws tore at Herakles. Against the rock Herakles held the beast; strongly he held it, choking it through the skin that was almost impenetrable. Terribly the lion struggled; the strong hands of the hero held its throat until it struggled no more.

Then Herakles stripped off the impenetrable skin from the lion's body; he put it upon himself for a cloak. As he went through the forest he pulled up a young oak-tree and trimmed it to make a club for himself. With the lion's skin over him—that skin that no spear or arrow could pierce—and carrying the club in his hands he journeyed on until he came to the palace of King Eurystheus.

The king, seeing a towering man all covered with the skin of a monstrous lion coming towards him, ran and hid himself in a great jar. He lifted up the cover to ask the servants what was the meaning of that terrible appearance. His servants told him that this was Herakles come back with the skin of the Nemean lion over him. On hearing this Eurystheus hid himself again. He would not speak with Herakles nor have him come near him, so fearful was he. Herakles was content to be left alone. He sat down in the palace and feasted himself.

The servants came to the king, and when Eurystheus lifted the cover of the jar they told him how Herakles was feasting and devouring all the goods in the palace. The king flew into a rage. Still he was fearful of having the hero stand before him. He issued commands through his heralds ordering Herakles to go forth at once and perform the second of his tasks.

It was the task of slaying the great water-snake that made its lair in the swamps of Lerna. Herakles stayed to feast another day; then, with the lion's skin across his shoulders and the great club in his hands, he started off. But this time he did not go alone; the youth Iolaos, his brother's son, went with him.

Herakles and Iolaos went on until they came to the vast swamp of Lerna. Right in the middle of the swamp was the water-snake, the Hydra. Nine heads it had; it raised them out of the water as the hero and his companion came near. They could not cross the swamp to come to the monster, for a man or a beast would sink in it and be lost.

The Hydra remained in the middle of the swamp belching mud at the hero and his companion. Herakles took up his bow and shot flaming arrows at its head. It became more full of rage; it came through the swamp to attack him. Herakles swung his club. As the Hydra came near he knocked head after head off its body.

But for every head knocked off two grew upon the Hydra. And as he struggled with the monster a huge crab came out of the swamp, and, gripping Herakles by the foot, tried to draw him in. The boy Iolaos came; he killed the crab that had come to the Hydra's aid.

Then Herakles laid hands upon the Hydra; he drew it out of its swamp. He knocked off a head; then he had Iolaos put fire to where the head had been, so that two heads might not grow in that place. The life of the Hydra was in its middle head; that head he had not been able to knock off with his club. Now, with his hands he tore it off, and he placed the head under a great boulder so that it could not rise into life again. The Hydra's life was now destroyed. Herakles dipped his arrows into the gall of the monster, making his arrows deadly; afterwards, no thing that was struck with these arrows could keep its life.

Again he came to Eurystheus's palace, and Eurystheus, seeing him, ran again and hid himself in the jar. Herakles ordered his servants to tell the king that he had returned and that the second labour was accomplished.

Eurystheus, hearing from the servants that Herakles had spoken mildly to them, came out of the jar. Insolently he spoke. "Twelve labours you have to accomplish for me," he said, "and eleven yet remain to be accomplished."

"How?" said Herakles. "Have I not performed two of the labours? Have I not slain the lion of Nemea and the great water-snake of Lerna?"

"In the killing of the water-snake you were helped by Iolaos," said the king, snapping out his words and looking at Herakles with shifting eyes. "That labour cannot be allowed you."

Herakles would have struck him to the ground. But then he remembered that the crime he had committed in his madness would have to be expiated by labours performed at the order of this man. He looked full upon Eurystheus and he said, "Tell me of the other labours, and I will go forth and accomplish them."

Then Eurystheus bade him go and make clean the stables of King Augeias. Herakles came into the king's country. The smell from the stables was felt for miles around. Countless herds of cattle and goats had been in the stables for years, and because of the uncleanness and the smell that came from the stables the crops were withered all around. Herakles told the king that he would clean the stables if he were given one-tenth of the cattle and the goats for a reward.

The king agreed to give him that reward. Then Herakles drove the cattle and the goats out of the stables; he broke a passage through their foundations and he made channels for the two rivers, Alpheios and Peneios. The waters flowed through the stables, and in a day all the uncleanness was washed away. Then Herakles turned the river back into their own courses.

He was not given the reward he had bargained for, however. He went back and told of his labour accomplished. "Ten labours remain for me to do now," he said.

"Eleven," said Eurystheus. "How can I allow the cleaning of King Augeias's stables to you when you did it for a reward?"

Then, while Herakles stood still holding himself back from striking him, Eurystheus ran away and hid himself. Through his heralds he sent word to Herakles, telling him what his other labours would be.

He was to clear the marshes of Stymphalos of the man-eating birds that gathered there; he was to capture and bring to the king the golden horned deer of Keryneia; he was also to capture and bring back alive the boar of Erymanthos.

Herakles came to the marshes of Stymphalos. The growth of jungle was so dense that he could not cut his way through to where the man-eating birds were; they sat upon low bushes within the jungle, gorging themselves upon the flesh they had carried there.

For days Herakles tried to hack his way through to them. He could not get to where the birds were. Then, thinking that he might not be able to accomplish this labour, he sat upon the ground in despair.

It was then that one of the Immortals appeared to him; then, for the first and only time, he was given help by one of the Gods. It was Athena who came to him. She stood apart from Herakles; in her hands she held brazen cymbals. These she clashed together. At the sound of the clashing the Stymphalean birds rose up from the low bushes behind the jungle. Herakles shot at them with his unerring arrows. The man-eating birds fell, one after the other, into the marsh.

Then Herakles went north to where the Keryneian deer had her pasture. So swift of foot was she that no hound nor hunter had ever been able to overtake her. For the whole of a year Herakles kept Golden Horns in chase; at last, on the side of Mount Artemision, he caught her. Then Artemis, the Goddess of the Wild Things, would have punished Herakles for capturing the deer. But the hero pleaded with her. She relented and allowed him to bring the deer to Tiryns and show her to King Eurystheus. And Artemis kept charge of Golden Horns while Herakles went off to capture the Erymanthean boar.

He came to the city of Psophis, the inhabitants of which were in deadly fear because of the ravages of the boar. Herakles made his way up the mountain to hunt it. Now, upon this mountain a band of Centaurs lived, and they, knowing Herakles, welcomed him. One of them, Pholos, took Herakles to the great house where the Centaurs stored their wine. Seldom did the Centaurs drink wine; a draught of it made them wild, and so they stored it away, leaving it in the charge of one of their band. Herakles begged Pholos to give him a draught of wine; after he had begged for it again and again the Centaur opened one of his great jars.

Herakles drank wine and spilled it. Then the Centaurs that were without smelled the wine and came hammering at the door, demanding the draughts that would make them wild. Herakles came forth to drive them away. They attacked him. Then he shot at them with his unerring arrows and he drove them away. Up the mountain and away to the far rivers the Centaurs raced, pursued by Herakles with his bow.

One of the band was slain, Pholos, who had entertained the hero. By accident Herakles dropped a poisoned arrow on his foot. Now he took the body of Pholos up to the top of the mountain and he buried the Centaur there. Afterwards, on the snows of Erymanthos, he set a snare for the boar; he caught him there.

Upon his shoulders he carried the boar to Tiryns, and he led the deer there by her golden horns. When Eurystheus had looked upon the boar and upon the deer, the boar was slain and the deer was loosed; she fled back to the Mountain Artemision.

King Eurystheus thought of more terrible labours that he might make Herakles engage in. Now he would send him oversea, and make him strive with fierce tribes there and more terrible monsters. When he had it all thought out he had Herakles brought before him, and he told him of those other labours.

He was to go to savage Thrace and there destroy the man-eating horses of King Diomedes; afterwards he was to go amongst the dread women, the Amazons, daughters of Ares, the God of War, and take from their queen, Hippolyte, the girdle that Ares had given her; then he was to go to Crete and take from the keeping of King Minos the bull that Poseidon had given him; afterwards he was to go to the Island of Erytheia, and take away from Geryoneus, the monster that had three bodies instead of one, the herd of red cattle that the two-headed hound Orthos kept guard over; then he was to go to the Garden of the Hesperides, and from that garden he was to take the golden apples that Zeus had given Hera for a marriage-gift—where the Garden of the Hesperides was no mortal knew.

So Herakles set out on this long and perilous quest. First he went to Thrace, that savage land that was ruled by Diomedes, son of Ares the God of War. Herakles broke into the stable where the horses were; he caught three of them by their heads, and although they kicked, and bit, and trampled, he forced them out of the stable and down to the sea-shore; his companion Abderos waited for him there. The screams of the fierce horses were heard by the men of Thrace; they, with their king, came after Herakles. He left the horses in charge of Abderos while he fought the Thracians and their savage king. Herakles shot his deadly arrows amongst them. He drove them from the sea-shore, and he came back to where he had left Abderos with the fierce horses.

They had thrown Abderos upon the ground, and they were trampling upon him. Herakles drew his bow and he shot the horses with his unerring arrows—the arrows that had been dipped in the gall of the Hydra. Screaming, the horses of King Diomedes raced toward the sea; one fell and another fell, and then, as it came to the line of the foam, the third of the fierce horses fell. They were all slain with the unerring arrows.

Then Herakles took up the body of his companion; he was dead. Herakles buried the body with proper rites, and he raised a column over it. Afterwards, around that column a city that bore the name of Herakles's friend was built.

Then toward the Euxine Sea he went. There, where the River Themiskyra flows into the sea, he saw the abodes of the Amazons. And upon the rocks and the steep places he saw the warrior women; they were standing there with drawn bows in their hands. Most dangerous did they seem to Herakles. He did not know how to approach them; he might shoot at them with his unerring arrows, but when his arrows were all shot away, the Amazons, from their steep places, might be able to kill him with the arrows from their bows.

While he stood at a distance, wondering what he might do, a horn was sounded, and an Amazon mounted on a white stallion rode

owards him. "Herakles," she cried out, "The Queen Hippolyte permits you to come amongst the Amazons. Enter her tent and declare to
he queen the thing that has brought you amongst the never-conquered
Amazons."

Herakles came to the tent of the queen. There stood tall Hippolyte,
an iron crown upon her head and a beautiful girdle of bronze and
iridescent glass around her waist. Proud as a fierce mountain eagle
looked the queen of the Amazons: Herakles did not know in what
way he might conquer her. Outside the Amazons stood; they struck
their shields with their spears, keeping up a continuous savage din.
"For what has Herakles come to the country of the Amazons?" Queen
Hippolyte asked.

"For the girdle you wear," Herakles said, and he held his hands
ready for the struggle.

"Is it for the girdle given me by Ares, the God of War, that you
have come, braving the Amazons?"

"For that," Herakles said.

"I would not have you enter into strife with the Amazons," said
Queen Hippolyte. And so saying she drew off the girdle of bronze and
iridescent glass, and gave it into his hands.

Herakles took the beautiful girdle into his hands. He was fearful
that some piece of guile was being played upon him. He took the
girdle and put it around his great brows. He thanked the queen, but
even as he did the din outside became more savage. Hera, the Goddess
who was his foe, had appeared amongst the Amazons as an Amazon.
She stirred the warrior-women up against him. They fell upon him
with their spears. Then Herakles drew his bow. Hippolyte came out
of her tent and mounted her stallion to draw her Amazons away from
him. She rode toward the River Themiskyra and they rode with her.
And now the arrows of Herakles flew amongst them, and as they fled
across the river the white flanks of their stallions were stained with
the blood of the Amazons.

He went away from that country with Hippolyte's girdle around
his brows. He sailed over the sea and he came to Crete. There he
found, grazing in a special pasture, the bull that Poseidon had given
King Minos. He laid his hands upon the bull's horns and he overthrew
the bull. Then he drove the bull down to the sea-shore.

His next labour was to take away the herd of red cattle that was owned by the monster, Geryoneus. In the Island of Erytheia, in the middle of the Stream of Ocean, lived the monster; his herd was guarded by the two-headed hound Orthos—the hound that was brother to Kerberos, the three-headed hound that kept guard in the Lower-world. As Herakles came near to that island, making Minos's bull swim with him, the sun beat upon him, and drew all his strength away from him; he was dazed and dazzled by the rays of the sun. He drew his bow and shot his arrows upwards. He shouted out against the sun, and in his anger he wanted to strive against the sun. Far, far out of sight the arrows of Herakles went. And the Sun God, Helios, was filled with admiration for Herakles, the man who attempted what was impossible. Then did Helios fling down to Herakles his great golden cup.

Down, and into the Stream of Ocean fell the great golden cup of Helios. It floated there, wide enough to hold all the men who might be in a ship. Herakles put the bull of Minos into the cup of Helios; the cup bore them away, towards the West, and across the Stream of Ocean.

Herakles came to the Island of Erytheia. All over the island straggled the red cattle of Geryoneus, grazing upon the rich pastures. Herakles, leaving the bull of Minos in the cup, went upon the island; he made a club for himself out of a tree, and he went towards the cattle.

The hound Orthos bayed and ran towards him, the two-headed hound sprang upon Herakles with poisonous foam upon his jaws. Herakles swung his club and struck the two heads off the hound. Where the foam of the hound's jaws dropped a poisonous plant sprang up. Herakles took the body of the hound; he swung it around, and he flung it far out into the Ocean.

Then the monster Geryoneus came upon him. Three bodies he had instead of one; he attacked Herakles by hurling great stones at him. Herakles was hurt by the stones. Then the monster beheld the cup of Herakles; he began to hurl stones at the golden thing, striving to sink it in the sea and so leave Herakles without a way of getting from the island. Herakles drew his bow; he shot arrows into the monster, and left him dead in the deep rich grass of the pastures.

He rounded up the red cattle, the bulls and the cows, and he drove

them down to the shore; he put them into the golden cup of Helios
where the bull of Minos stayed. Then back across the Stream of Ocean
the cup floated. The bull of Crete and the cattle of Erytheia were
brought past Sicily and through the straits called the Hellespont. To
Thrace, that savage land, they were brought. Then Herakles took the
cattle out, and the cup of Helios sank into the sea. Through the wide
lands of Thrace he drove the herd of Geryoneus and the bull of Minos,
and he came to Tiryns once more.

There he did not stay. He started off to find the Garden of the
Hesperides, the Daughters of the Evening Land. Long did he search;
he found no one who could tell him where the garden was. At last
he came to the Mountain Pelion where the Centaur Cheiron was. And
Cheiron told Herakles what journey he would have to make to come
to the Hesperides, the Daughters of the Evening Land.

Far did Herakles journey; weary he was when he came to where
Atlas stood, bearing the sky upon his weary shoulders. As he came
near he felt an undreamed-of perfume being wafted towards him. So
weary was he with his journey and all his toils that he was fain to
sink down and dream in that Evening Land. But he roused himself,
and he journeyed on towards where the perfume came from. Over
that place a star seemed always arising.

He came to where a silver lattice fenced a garden that was full
of the quiet of evening. Golden bees hummed through the air. How
wild and laborious was the world he had come from, Herakles
thought! He felt that it would be hard for him to return to that world!

He saw three maidens. They stood with wreaths upon their heads
and blossoming branches in their hands. When the maidens saw him,
they came towards him, crying out, "O man who has come into the
Garden of the Hesperides, go not near the tree that the sleepless dragon
guards!" Then they went and stood by a tree as if to keep guard over it.
All around were trees that bore flowers and fruit, but this tree had
golden apples amongst its bright green leaves.

He saw the guardian of the tree. Beside the trunk a dragon lay.
As Herakles drew near, the dragon showed its glittering scales and its
deadly claws.

The apples were within reach, but the dragon with its deadly claws
stood in the way. Herakles shot an arrow; then a tremor went through

the sleepless dragon; it screamed, fell down, and lay stark. The maidens cried in their grief; Herakles went to the tree; he plucked the golden apples and he put them into the pouch he carried. Down on the ground sank the Hesperides, the Daughters of the Evening Land; he heard their laments as he went from the enchanted garden that they guarded.

Back from the ends of the earth came Herakles, back from the place where Atlas stood holding the sky upon his weary shoulders. He went back through Asia and Libya and Egypt, and he came again to Tiryns and to the palace of Eurystheus.

He brought to the king the herd of Geryoneus; he brought to the king the bull of Minos; he brought to the king the girdle of Hippolyte; he brought to the king the golden apples of the Hesperides. And King Eurystheus, with his thin, white face, sat upon his royal throne and looked over all the wonderful things that the hero had brought him. Not pleased was Eurystheus; rather was he angry that one he hated could win such wonderful things.

He took into his hands the golden apples of the Hesperides. But this fruit was not for such as he. An eagle snatched the branch from his hand. The eagle flew and flew until he came to where the Daughters of the Evening Land wept in their garden. There the eagle let fall the branch with the golden apples; the maidens set it back on the tree, and, behold! it grew as it had been growing before Herakles plucked it.

The next day the heralds of Eurystheus came to Herakles and they told him of the last labour that he would have to set out to accomplish—this time he would have to go down into the Underworld and bring up from King Hades's realm Kerberos, the three-headed hound.

Herakles put upon him the impenetrable lion's skin and set forth once more. This might be the last of his life's labours: Kerberos was not an earthly monster, and he who would struggle with Kerberos in the Underworld would have the Gods of the Dead against him.

But Herakles went on. He journeyed to the cavern where there is an entrance to the Underworld. Far into that dismal cavern he went; then he went down, down, down, until he came to that dim river that had beyond it only the people of the dead. Kerberos bayed at him from the place where the dead cross the river. Knowing that this was no shade, the hound Kerberos sprang at Herakles. He could neither bite nor tear through the impenetrable lion's skin. Herakles held him by the neck of his middle head so that Kerberos was neither able to bite nor tear, nor was he able to bellow.

Then Persephone to the brink of that river came. She declared to Herakles that the Gods of the Dead would not strive against him if he promised to bring Kerberos back to the Underworld.

This Herakles promised. He turned around and he carried Kerberos; his hands were around the monster's neck; from the monster's jaws foam dropped. He carried him on and upward towards the world of men. Out through a cavern that was in the land of Troizen Herakles came, still carrying Kerberos by the neck of his middle head.

From Troizen to Tiryns the hero went; men fled at the sight of the monster he carried. On he went toward the king's palace. Eurystheus was seated outside his palace that day, looking at the great jar he had so often hidden in, and thinking to himself that Herakles would never appear to affright him again. Then Herakles appeared. He called to Eurystheus; he held the Hound of Hell towards him. The three heads grinned at Eurystheus; he gave a cry and scrambled into the jar. But before his feet touched the bottom of it Eurystheus was dead of fear. The jar rolled over, and Herakles looked upon the body that was all twisted with fright. Then he turned around; carrying the hound he made his way back to the Underworld. On the brink of the river he loosed Kerberos, and the bellow of the three-headed hound was heard once more by the River Acheron.

II

It was then that Herakles was given arms by the Gods—the sword of Hermes, the bow of Apollo, the shield made by Hephæstos; it was then that Herakles, coming to the Caucasus, slew the vulture that preyed upon Prometheus's liver, and, at the will of Zeus, liberated the Titan from his bonds. Thereafter Zeus and Prometheus were reconciled, and Zeus, that neither might forget how much the enmity between them had cost Gods and men, had a ring made for Prometheus to wear; that ring was made out of the fetter that had been upon him, and in it was set a fragment of the rock that the Titan had been bound to.

Now there was a king who had offered his daughter in marriage to a hero who could excel himself and his sons in shooting with arrows. Herakles had seen the maiden, the blue-eyed and child-like Iole, and he longed to win her. The contest began. The king and his sons shot wonderfully well, and so did the heroes who entered the contest with Herakles. Herakles shot his arrows. No matter how far away they moved the mark, Herakles struck it, and struck the very centre of it. The people wondered who the great archer might be. And then a name was guessed at and went round—Herakles!

When the king heard the name of Herakles he would not let him strive in the contest any more. For the maiden Iole would not be given to one who had been mad and whose madness might afflict him again. So the king said, speaking in judgment in the market-place.

Rage came on Herakles when he heard this judgment given. He would not let his rage master him lest the madness that was spoken of should come with this rage. He left the city, declaring to the king and people that he would return.

In Kalydon he saw Deianeira. She was tall, this woman of the mountains; she looked like a priestess, but also like a woman who could cheer camps of men with her counsel, her bravery, and her good companionship; her hair was very dark and she had dark eyes. Straightway she became friends with Herakles; and when they saw each other for a while they loved each other. And Herakles forgot Iole, the child-like maiden whom he had wanted to win. To win Deianeira he strove with Acheloos, the River God. Acheloos in the form of a bull wrestled with him. Herakles broke off one of his horns. Then, that he might be given the horn back, the River God gave up his claim to Deianeira.

Then a dreadful thing happened in Kalydon; by an accident, while using his strength unthinkingly, Herakles killed a lad who was related to Deianeira. He might not marry her now until he had taken punishment for slaying one who was close to her in blood.

As a punishment for the slaying it was judged that Herakles should be sold into slavery for three years. At the end of his three years' slavery he could come back to Kalydon and wed Deianeira.

So Herakles and Deianeira were parted. He was sold as a slave in Lydia; the one who bought him was a woman, a widow named Omphale. To her house Herakles went, carrying his armour and wearing his lion's skin. And Omphale laughed to see this tall man dressed in a lion's skin coming to her house to do a servant's tasks for her.

She and all her household had fun with Herakles. They would set him to do house-work, to carry water, and set vessels on the tables, and clear the vessels away. Omphale set him to spin with a spindle as the women did. And often she would put on Herakles's lion-skin and go about dragging his club, while he, dressed in woman's garb, washed dishes and emptied pots.

But he would lose patience with these servant's tasks, and then Omphale would let him go away and perform some great exploit. Often he went on long journeys and stayed away long times. It was while he was in slavery to Omphale that he made his journey to Troy. At Troy he helped to repair for King Laomedon the great walls that, years before, Apollo and Poseidon had built around the city. As a reward for his labour he was offered the Princess Hesione in marriage. But Herakles permitted Telamon to take Hesione. On the day they married Herakles showed the pair an eagle in the sky. He said it was sent as an omen for their marriage. And in memory of that omen Telamon named his son "Aias," that is, "Eagle."

Omphale, the widow, received him mirthfully when he got back to Lydia; she set him to do tasks in the kitchen while she sat and talked to him about Troy and the affairs of King Laomedon. And afterwards she put on his lion's skin, and went about in the courtyard dragging the heavy club after her. Mirthfully and pleasantly she made the rest of his time in Lydia pass for Herakles; the last day of his slavery soon came; he bade good-bye to Omphale, and he started off to Kalydon to claim his bride, Deianeira.

Beautiful, indeed, Deianeira looked now that she had ceased to mourn; the laughter that had been under her grief now flashed out; her dark eyes shone like stars, and her being had the spirit of one who wanders from camp to camp always greeting friends and leaving friends behind her. Herakles wed Deianeira, and they set out for Tiryns.

They came to the River Evenos. Herakles could have crossed the

river by himself, but at the part he came to he could not cross carrying
Deianeira. He and she went along the river, seeking a ferry that
might take them across. They wandered along the side of the river,
happy with each other, and they came to a place where they had
sight of a Centaur.

Herakles knew this Centaur. He was Nessos, one of the Centaurs
whom he had chased up the mountain on the day when he went to
hunt the Erymanthean boar. The Centaur spoke to Herakles as if
he had friendship for him. He would, he said, carry Herakles's bride
across the river.

Herakles crossed the river. He waited on the other side for Nessos
and Deianeira. Then Herakles heard screams—the screams of his wife.
He saw that the Centaur had attacked her. Herakles leveled his bow.
Arrow after arrow he shot in Nessos's body. The Centaur loosed his
hold on Deianeira. He lay down on the bank of the river, his life-
blood streaming from him.

Nessos, dying, but with his rage against Herakles unabated,
thought of a way by which the hero might be made to suffer for the
death he had brought upon him. He called to Deianeira; she, seeing
he could do her no more hurt, came close to him. He told her that in
repentance for his attack upon her he would bestow on her a great
gift. She was to gather up some of the blood that flowed from him; his
blood, the Centaur said, would be a love-philtre, and if ever her husband's love for her waned it would grow fresh again if she gave to
him something from her hands that would have this blood upon it.

Deianeira, who had heard from Herakles of the wisdom of the
Centaurs, believed what Nessos told her. She took a phial and let the
blood pour into it. Then Nessos plunged into the river and died there
as Herakles came up to where Deianeira stood.

She did not speak to him about the Centaur's words to her, nor
did she tell him that she had hidden the phial that had Nessos's blood
in it. They crossed the river at another point; they came after a time
to Tiryns, to the kingdom that had been left to Herakles.

There Herakles and Deianeira lived, and a son who was named
Hyllos was born to them. And after a time Herakles was led into a
war against Oichalia, the kingdom that Iole's father had ruled over.

Word came to Deianeira that Oichalia was conquered by Herakles and that Iole was taken captive by him. Deianeira knew that Herakles had once tried to win Iole for his wife, and she feared that the sight of the maiden would bring his old longing back to him.

She thought upon the words that Nessos had said to her, and even as she thought upon them messengers came from Herakles to ask her to send him a robe—a beautifully woven robe that she had—that he might wear it while making sacrifice. Deianeira took down the robe; through this robe, she thought, the blood of the Centaur could touch Herakles, and then his love for her would revive. Thinking this, she poured Nessos's blood over the robe.

Herakles was in Oichalia when the messengers returned to him. He took the robe that Deianeira sent, and he went to the mountain that overlooked the sea that he might make sacrifice there. Iole went with him. He put on the robe. When it touched his flesh the robe burst into flame. He tried to tear it off; deeper and deeper into his flesh the flames went. The flames burned and none could quench them.

Then Herakles knew that his end was at hand. He would die by fire; knowing this he had a great pile of wood made, and he climbed up on it. There he stayed with the robe burning upon him, and he begged of those who passed to fire the pile that his end might come more quickly.

None would fire the pile. But at last there came that way a young warrior named Philoktetes, and Herakles begged of him to fire the pile. Philoktetes, knowing that it was the will of the Gods that Herakles should die that way, lighted the pile. For that Herakles bestowed upon him his great bow and his unerring arrows. And it was this bow and these arrows, brought from Philoktetes, that afterwards helped to take Troy, King Priam's city.

The pile that Herakles stood upon was fired. High up, above the sea, the pile burned. All who had been near fled—all except Iole. She stayed and watched the flames mount up and up. They wrapped the sky, and the voice of Herakles was heard calling upon Zeus. Then a great chariot came, and Herakles was borne away to Olympos. Thus, after many labours. Herakles passed away, a mortal passing into an immortal being, in a great burning high above the sea.

ROMAN

ROMAN

THE CHILDREN OF MARS: NUMA THE LAW-GIVER: THE
SIBYL: POMONA AND VERTUMNUS

THE CHILDREN OF MARS

I

In the ancient Latin land there was a city which, because it
stretched out along a ridge, was called Alba Longa. In the old days
Silvius reigned there: he was called by that name because he was
born in a forest. After him there reigned Æneas Silvius and Latinus
Silvius: three kings kept the name that came to their forefathers from
the forest. Then there came a king who was named Proca; he bequeathed the ancient realm of the Silvan family to his son, Numitor.

But Numitor had a brother, a violent and a crafty man named
Amulius. No sooner was Proca dead than this man drove out of
the king's house the one to whom the realm had been bequeathed.
He seized Numitor's young sons and he put them to death. A daughter
only was left in Numitor's house. Amulius, that violent and crafty
man, was afraid of what might happen through this girl; he feared
that she might marry some powerful prince and have children who
would claim the Alban realm. And yet he might not put her to death
as he had put her brothers to death—the people would turn against
him if they knew him for the slayer of a maiden. Not with violence,
therefore, did he deal with her, but with craft: he had the maiden
(Rhea Silvia she was named) placed amongst those who might never
marry, amongst those who tended the sacred fire of Vesta and were
named Vestal Virgins, and this he did under the pretence of honouring
his brother's daughter.

In the forest Rhea Silvia met a man with whom there went a wolf
and a woodpecker. He forced her to espouse him. And he was Mars, the
War God of the Latin people.

The Vestals who made themselves unfit to tend the sacred fire
were condemned to death by the people. Amulius now had an excuse
for destroying what remained of the house of Numitor. He had Rhea

Silvia seized and manacled and cast into prison. She gave birth to twin boys. The king ordered that they be taken out and drowned in the river.

That river was the one that had been called in the old days the Albula: a king of Alba whose name was Tiberinus was drowned in it, and its name then was changed to Tiber. Now at the season of the year when Rhea Silvia's twin boys were born the river spreads its stream beyond its banks, making shallow and stagnant pools. The slaves who had been ordered to drown the children brought them only as far as one of these pools. There they left the basket in which the twins were and went away, thinking that a very little water would drown the babes.

The basket went amongst the sedges and was held there. Then the water receded, leaving the basket upon the mud. A she-wolf came down to that place: she stood over the children and she let them suck from her teats. And a woodpecker came upon the basket and dropped food into their mouths. So the children were nourished by the wolf and the woodpecker that went with Mars, their father.

And in time a shepherd named Faustulus, in chasing a wolf that went very slowly away from him, came to a sedgy place and found a basket there with twin babes in it. He brought them to his hut and gave them to his wife to rear. And so the two grandsons of Numitor were brought up in the hut of this shepherd.

They were brought up as shepherd boys. But, born from the embrace of Mars and having a she-wolf for their foster-mother, they were not lads who were content to be always with their sheep. They ranged the mountains and the forest. They hunted wild beasts. Other boys followed them, taking them for leaders. And after they had grown in hardiness and resoluteness they made attacks upon gangs of robbers and took their spoil from them. Often they did this. And the spoil that was taken the leaders shared with their following.

By this time the twins had names: one was named Romulus and the other Remus. Now at that time the hill that is now called the Palatine was the scene of a festival called the Lupercalia. Youths stripped and ran about naked by way of doing honour to a God. Romulus and Remus and their companions came to the hill and joined in the festival. Remus stripped and ran naked with other youths who were there. And then the companions were set upon by a band of robbers whose spoil they had taken. Remus was not able to defend himself and he was taken by the robbers. Romulus followed them, and saw his brother put into the king's prison.

He went back to the shepherd's hut. When Romulus told his foster-father that Remus was in the prison of King Amulius, Faustulus, the shepherd of Numitor, became all stirred up. He had come to think that the youths whom he had brought up in his hut were the children of the royal house. He knew that Rhea Silvia's twin boys had been cast into the river, and he knew that he had found these twins at a time not long after King Amulius's sentence had been carried out. But always the shepherd had been afraid to disclose his thought to any one.

But when Romulus told him that Remus had been taken and was about to be brought before the king on a charge of making raids upon the land, Faustulus told the youth that he and his brother were, in all likelihood, the grandsons of Numitor—of Numitor to whom Proca had left the Alban realm. Now Romulus had seen Numitor: he had come back to Alba Longa, and, because he was old and feeble and had no children nor friends, his life was left to him, and he was even permitted to live at the king's house.

Romulus sent messages to his grandfather: Numitor was amazed at what was told in them. Then he went to where Remus was imprisoned: he looked upon the features of the youth, he noted his bold bearing, and he thought that he saw in him a likeness to the Silvan kings. Then to Romulus's messengers he declared himself ready to help to deliver Remus.

Romulus came before the king's house; his shepherd friends were with him, and they were armed. Numitor drew off the king's defenders by declaring that the citadel was being attacked by invading enemies. The guards went from the house to the citadel. Then Remus broke out of the prison. The king had few left to defend him, and he was slain by the hand of Romulus.

Numitor brought together the council of the people. He told them of Amulius's crimes, and he reminded them that the Alban realm had been bequeathed to him, Numitor, by King Proca. The people hailed Numitor as king; the youths Romulus and Remus were acknowledged to be of the royal house, and they agreed to serve their grandfather.

After a time they were seized with a desire to found a city in the place where they had been exposed and where they had been brought up. Now in Alba Longa there were already too many folk, especially were there too many young men. The proposal to found a new city under the leadership of the youths Romulus and Remus was pleasing to all the youths of the place.

So the brothers and their followers went to the hills on which they had guarded their sheep and in the glades of which they had hunted game and harried robbers. Romulus took the Palatine Hill for his quarters, and Remus took the Aventine Hill. Unto Remus the first augury was shown. He saw a flight of vultures—six of them. Now the vulture was sacred because it was a bird that did not prey on other birds, but ate only of what was dead. When Remus saw these vultures, those who were with him cried out that he was the one who was to found the city and gave a name to it. But no sooner was the omen reported than another flight of vultures was shown to Romulus—twelve vultures. Thereupon each of the twins was saluted by his own followers as the one who would found the city, give a name to it, and rule over it after it had been built.

A quarrel grew up between the brothers and between the followers of Romulus and the followers of Remus. Romulus, declaring that to him the omen was given because he had been shown twice the number of birds that had been shown Remus, set out to build a wall that would protect the city. Remus mocked at him; in mockery he leaped over the wall. Then Romulus struck his brother down, slaying him. "So perish all who leap over my walls," Romulus said.

So it was Romulus who founded it and named the city—*Rome*—and became king over it. The city at first had only a scanty population, for few people joined themselves to the followers of Romulus and Remus. Then, that he might draw people to the city, Romulus founded a sanctuary between two groves on the way up the hill that is now called the Capitoline Hill; it was a sanctuary for men who had done dangerous things, or who had debts that they could not meet, and for all men who, for one reason or another, were being pursued. Those who came into that sanctuary could have safety. And many dangerous and desperate men came there, and were received

into Romulus's community, adding strength and daring to the popu-
lace of the city upon the hills.

In that city there were few women; many young men who had come
with Romulus and Remus and all the fugitive men who had come to
the sanctuary were without wives. Rome, on account of the lack of children, might not last long as a city. Romulus sent embassies to all
the neighbouring states and cities asking them to make marriage alli-
ances with his people. But this new city was not liked by the neighbouring cities and states: they thought it was a camp rather than a
city—a camp of outcast and dangerous men. The envoys were dis-
missed with scorn. "Unless you open a sanctuary for run-away women
there will be no wives for you," the envoys were told. And those
who said this to them hoped that no families would grow up in Rome
and that the city would become forsaken.

The young men of Rome took what was said as an insult—an
insult that they bitterly resented. Romulus was angered, and he made
up his mind that he would get wives for the men of this city by force
or by guile. At harvest-time the Romans kept the festival of Consus
whose altar was underground: he was the God who helped the people
to garner and store their crops. By a proclamation that Romulus made,
the people of the neighbouring state were invited to a great spectacle
that the Romans promised to show.

The Sabines were the people who lived nearest to the Romans.
They were curious to know what kind of celebration the Romans would
have. Many of them came to the city bringing their wives and children,
their growing boys and girls. They were hospitably received by the
Romans and were given lodging in their houses. They saw the city;
they looked at its wall and its defences, and they marvelled at the
growth that they saw.

And then they were shown the spectacle. It was of young men
upon horses. The Sabines looked on, delighted with the appearance
of the young men and their fine management of their horses. But suddenly the horsemen dashed amongst them. The Sabines were scattered;
fathers and brothers who could defend daughters and sisters were
crowded and held at one end of the field. Then the young Romans
seized the Sabine maidens and carried them off as their brides.

The Sabine fathers and mothers went back to their homes in sorrow and indignation. They cursed the Romans for the crime of violating hospitality.

Romulus sent envoys to the Sabine king. He declared to the king that the maidens would be wedded solemnly to their captors and that they would become sharers in all that Rome possessed. And he declared, too, that each Roman would not only endeavour to be a good husband to his Sabine bride, but that he would strive with all his power to console her for the loss of home and parents.

As Romulus said, so it came about. But first there was war. The Sabine fathers in mourning garments went amongst the people, striving to stir them up to punish the Romans for the violence done to the maidens. And soon Romulus had to defend Rome from the rage of the Sabines.

II

In this war the Sabine people did not have greed for their motive; they warred in what they thought was a just cause and they were able to inflict defeat upon the Romans. They captured the citadel, and in the fight they made they drove the Romans through the ancient gate of the Palatine Hill. Romulus was caught in the rout of his army; he was being dragged out of the city he had built when, lifting up his sword and shield to Heaven, he cried, "O Iuppiter, it was thine omen that directed me when I laid here on the Palatine Hill the first foundations of this, my city. The citadel is already in possession of the invaders; they come from it, sword in hand, to seek us here. But do thou, Father of Gods and men, keep them back from this spot; deliver the Romans from their terror; stay their shameful flight! I here vow to thee, Iuppiter the Stayer, a temple, to be a memorial to our descendants how the city was saved by thy present help." Having uttered this prayer Romulus spoke to the fleeing men as though he knew that the prayer was answered. "Here, Romans, Iuppiter commands us to stand and renew the fight." The Romans stood their ground as though directed by a voice from Heaven. Romulus rushed into the battle again. He met the Sabines as they were driving on, their leader shouting, "We have beaten our faithless hosts, our cowardly enemies! Now they know the difference between carrying off maidens and fighting with men." Even as the Sabine leader spoke, a band of young

Romans assailed his band, and he was forced back into the valley that lay between the two hills.

There the Romans and the Sabines faced each other, ready to renew the battle. And there the Sabine women, their hair loosened, their garments torn as a sign of mourning, came between them, daring the missiles that were flying from both sides. They came between the armies, begging their fathers and brothers not to fight against their husbands. "It will be better for us to perish here," they cried, "than to live lacking either of you. If the fight goes on we shall live either as widows, or as orphans, or as women lacking brothers." All were touched by the plea of the women; the leaders on both sides came forward and made a truce.

And so the war waged because of the carrying off of the Sabine maidens came to an end. The Romans and the Sabines were made into a single people, and a new name was given to those who lived in or near the city: no longer were there Romans and Sabines; both together were given the name Quirites. And a king of the Sabines ruled jointly with Romulus for a while.

So the city drew into itself a new population. Other states and cities, fearful of Rome's growing power, made war upon Romulus. The Etruscans came into Roman territory; Romulus marched against them and defeated them. Afterwards he sat on his chair to review his army in the Campus Martius. Before him, with shouts of salutation, his army came. But even as they did there were loud peals of thunder. A cloud hid Romulus from the sight of his people. When the cloud lifted Romulus was there no longer; he was not in his chair; he was no more upon the earth. The soldiers and the people stood around with bowed heads, awed by the mystery of their loss.

Then one who had been near Romulus said, "Quirites, the father of this city, Romulus, said to me: 'Declare to the people the will of Heaven. My Rome shall be the chief city of the world; let the people cherish the art of war; let them teach their children that no human strength can break the Roman army nor resist the Roman arms. And as for me, my father, Mars, has caused Heaven to take me and give me a place amongst the immortal Gods.'"

Then the soldiers and people became contented, knowing that their king and the father of the Roman city was now made an Immortal.

With prayers they besought his favour. From him they asked protection for their children. And Romulus who was their king upon earth was named Quirinus when they worshipped him—Quirinus which was a name that belonged to the God Mars.

NUMA THE LAW-GIVER

One who was born on the day on which the building of the city was begun was chosen to be king after Romulus. Numa was his name. At the time when the Romans and the Sabines took him to be king over them Numa had no mortal wife—a Goddess was his companion. By a spring of clear water she would meet him and converse with him, instructing him in all affairs that lay between mortals and the immortal Gods. Egeria she was named.

And by a clear spring of water she would meet him and converse with him after he had become king in Rome. Now at that time a plague ravaged all Italy; the Roman people were made despondent by all the deaths they saw around them; their city, so lately built, would not last, they thought, for the folk in it would dwindle away through this plague. Then a sign was given to Numa. A brazen shield fell from Heaven. It was revealed to the king that as long as this shield was amongst them the fortunes of the Roman people would be prosperous. He had eleven other shields made, each in the likeness of the one that had fallen from Heaven: when the twelve shields were left together no one, not Numa himself, could tell one from the other. No single enemy, then, could slip in and take away the shield on which the fortunes of Rome depended. And the Romans, knowing that amongst them was a token of prosperity and that that token was secure, ceased to be despondent. Soon the plague left the land.

"Thou shalt not make libation of wine made from an unpruned vine. Thou shalt not make sacrifice without grain." These were two of the commandments that Numa, instructed by Egeria, gave to the people. And by these commandments he showed the Romans that they were to be cultivators, subduing the earth, and growing grain and pruning their vines. He gave the people arts and crafts; he formed companies of musicians, goldsmiths, metal-workers, carpenters, dyers, shoemakers, and potters; he appointed courts and councils for these companies, and he showed to each of them the particular religious ceremony it was to observe.

Then he built temples. First of all he built a temple for the Goddess of the sacred fire—Vesta she was named. Her temple was circular, and the everlasting fire within it was tended by virgins; as long as they in purity tended Vesta's fire the fortunes of Rome might not sink down. And after he had built the Temple of Vesta he built the Temple of Ianus. As the God Ianus has two faces so this temple has two gates: they stand open in time of war and are closed in time of peace. Very seldom in later times were the gates of the Temple of Ianus shut, but in Numa's time the gates were never seen open—no, not for a single day: for the space of over two score years the gates were unopened. Wars were not waged in those days. And not only were the people of Rome made quiet by Numa's influence, but the people of the neighbouring states and cities were made quiet too; they had peace; their lives were employed in the tilling of the soil, in the rearing of their children, and in the worship of the Gods. Of these days it was said:

> Over the iron shields the spiders hang their webs.

And:

> Rust eats the pointed spear and two-edged sword.
> No more is heard the trumpet's brazen roar;
> Sweet sleep is banished from our eyes no more.

Numa then arranged the months of the year. He put January, which is the month of the God of Peace, Ianus, first; he put March, which is the month of the War God, third; between, he put February, which is the month of purification: in February the Romans make offerings to their dead, and the festival of Lupercalia, a festival of purification, is held in February.

Iuppiter, the great God of the sky and of thunder, was brought down to earth by Numa. "If you would bespell the lighting and thunder so that they will do no harm, you must bespell them with heads," Iuppiter said, repeating an ancient doom. "With heads of onions," Numa answered. "Of men," Iuppiter said. "Hair of men's heads," Numa said. "With living——" "With living pilchards," said Numa.

Iuppiter, without giving him an answer, withdrew from the earth. But to this day the Romans, to charm away the thunder and lightning of Iuppiter, sacrifice, not the heads of men, but onions, and the hair of men's heads, and living pilchards.

And so Numa made even the Gods milder in their dealings with men. Egeria it was who instructed him how to bring Iuppiter, the God of the sky and of thunder and lightning, down to earth so that he might be spoken to. Two very lowly Gods had to be captured by him first. Now there were two demi-gods who loved to play tricks on human beings, but who were very simple themselves and easily tricked: Picus and Faunus they were named; they frequented shady places and came beside clear springs. Into the spring that is on the mountain named Aventine, Numa poured a mixture of honey and wine. Picus and Faunus came to that spring: they bent to drink of the water there and they tasted of the wine and honey that was in the spring. They were delighted with what they tasted, and they lay by the water and drank, and played with each other and drank again. They drank till they became drunken and heavy; they fell into a sleep. Then Numa came upon them and took hold of them. The demi-gods changed themselves into all manner of shapes: Numa thought he had in his grasp a weasel and a bird, a shrub and a bunch of leaves. Still he held to them. He thought he had in his grasp a fish and a wolf-cub, a toad and a lizard. Still he held to them. At last Picus and Faunus came back to their own shapes and changed no more. Then Numa forced them to tell what they, the lowliest of the Gods, knew—how to bring Iuppiter down to the earth. They told him, and he let the odd-looking demi-gods run back into the shades. And thereafter he was able to speak with Iuppiter.

Once Numa invited the elders of the Romans to a feast in his house. They came; they found a house that was bare and a table and benches that were of the plainest kind. They knew that their king lived in this simple way and they honoured him for it. They sat at the table: there were wooden dishes on it, and the food that was set before them was bread and fruit and milk and wine. They ate with the king. Then, as they sat there, they came to know that another had come amongst them. They saw no one, but a great lustre came upon all that was in the room. The wooden dishes became changed into vessels of gold and silver; the simple food that they were eating took on the richest and most appetizing flavours. Those who were with Numa knew that Egeria had come amongst them.

They listened to a wondrous conversation between their king and the Goddess who was wont to instruct him. Not all of what they heard was clear to them. But they knew that Numa was soon to pass from amongst them.

And so it came to be. Numa died soon after that feast had been held. His body, by his own command, was not burned. Two coffins of stone were made ready: in one the King was laid; in the other were put the books he had written and the books he had consulted. The people knew that it was right to put these away; they knew that Numa, through his labours for them, through the training he had given them, had made all that was written in the books a part of their mind and their spirit. Then did they know how wise was the king who had ruled over them since the time that Romulus had departed from amongst them—Romulus who had made their state by means of war. This king had made the Muses known to them. He had taught them to reverence above all the Muse who is named Tacita, the Silent—the Roman Muse. Now he would bring them no more the counsel given him by the Goddess whom he sought beside the clear spring. Under the hill Ianiculum two coffins of stone were laid; one held Numa and the other held his sacred books.

THE SIBYL

An old woman came before where Tarquin the Proud sat, and demanded that she be brought before him, the king. Now Tarquin had had a dream in which an old woman appeared, and when he heard that there was such a one near he let her be brought before him. So she came and she stood before where the king sat in his ivory chair, with his purple robe upon him, and with the men who bore the rods and the axes standing around him. She was very old; she held herself up with a staff; her face was a mass of wrinkles. Nevertheless, the grey hair that fell upon her shoulders was heavy and her eyes were filled with light. She stood before the king, this grey old woman, and she showed him what she held in her hands.

She had nine books. "These books I would sell to you, O king," she said, and her voice was startling to all who were around, either because she spoke like one unused to the utterance of words or because there was a tone in it clearer and stronger than they expected to hear. "These books I would sell to you, king of Rome," she said. "What is in your books?" the king asked her. "A foretelling of events that may befall," she said, "and a way of dealing with them that will help to the safety and the greatness of Rome." "How much do you ask for your nine books?" "Half of all that is in the king's treasury," she said.

"This is a crazy woman," said the king. Those who were around him said, "A crazy crone she is." The old woman asked them to bring near to her the brazier of burning coals that was in the hall where the king sat. They brought it near her. Then the old woman took three of her books and cast them into the fire and watched the flames burn them. When the leaves were in ashes she did not go from the hall. Once more, leaning on her staff, she looked at the king and she said, "I have books for sale; it is for you to buy them, O king." "How much do you ask for the six books that are left?" the king asked. "Half of all that is in the king's treasury," she said. "But this is what you asked before; you had nine books then and now you have six only." "I ask the same price for six as I did for nine." "She must be the craziest woman in Rome," said those who were about the king. "But she does not belong to Rome; she is a stranger; no one here has ever seen her before." "What does the king say?" said the woman. "I cannot pay that price for yours or for anyone else's books," said King Tarquin.

Then the old woman threw into the brazier three of her books and watched them burn to ashes. For a while she remained leaning on her staff and looking down into the brazier; the flames lighted up her face with all its wrinkles, and Tarquin the Proud looking upon her felt in awe of that stranger-woman. She looked at him from across the brazier. "Half of all that is in your treasury, O king," said she, "for the three books that are yet unburned."

Then those who were around the king laughed heartily; but the king did not laugh. He knew that if he did not buy the books she had they would be thrown into the brazier and burned to ashes, and that the old woman would depart and never afterwards be seen in Rome. Long he pondered without answering her. Then he beckoned to her and she came and stood beside his chair. She left the three books with the king, and when she went from the hall she was allowed to go into the king's treasury and take half of all that was there.

The king put the three books that he bought from her in a shrine in the temple of Iuppiter. And there they remained for a thousand years. Fifteen priests guarded them; it was the duty of the fifteen to read them whenever the immortal Gods were to be consulted regarding the welfare of the Roman state. The books were called Sibylline Books, and she who brought them to Rome was known as a Sibyl. Long afterwards it was said that some one had seen the Sibyl: she was in a cage, and she lamented because she could not die.

POMONA AND VERTUMNUS

Once, when the kings of the Silvian House reigned over the Latin people, there lived a nymph whose name was Pomona. She never went near the springs, or lakes, or rivers, nor near the wild woods; she cared only for places where grew trees that were laden with fruits. She was no huntress; the only implement that she ever held in her hands was a pruning-hook or a spade.

She would loosen the earth round the roots of some of her trees; she would cut away growth that was too luxurious; sometimes she would make a cut in a tree and would graft into it a twig from another tree, and she would rejoice to see one tree bearing two kinds of fruit. Sometimes she would train a vine to grow along an elm-tree. But all day she worked where fruits grew, leading water to flow by the roots, or destroying insects that came upon the leaves of her trees.

In the spring-time she would see Flora, her sister-nymph, in the fields, giving color and fragrance to the flowers, giving sweetness to the honey in the combs, giving grace to the boys and girls who came about her. To Pomona Flora would give all that she had to give. But Pomona would never go to her or call Flora to come to her amongst her trees. And sometimes she would see Venus, the great lady who had so many worshippers, but she would not leave her trees to go to where Venus had her shrine.

Pomona grew up supple and robust; she grew sound and hand-some as an apple upon one of her trees. She gave herself no adorn-ments; all she ever wore was a brown dress; all she ever put upon her head was a wreath of leaves to keep the sun from burning her face.

Silvanus and Picus were the first of the demi-gods to see that Pomona was becoming more and more good-looking as the seasons went on. She was shy, they knew; but each thought what a fine sweet-heart she would make, if he could get her to walk or talk with him. And each knew that she had lots to give—a fine garden and fruits of every kind—apples and pears, grapes and cherries. Silvanus was the first to go see her: he went in his hunter's dress, with a spear in his hand, and the game he had just killed in a bag at his side. Pomona would not come near him. Then he chased her so that she had to slip from him behind tree after tree. She wearied him out and he went away. But he came to her at another season: this time he did not come from the hunting; he came from lands that he had cleared and that he had sheep grazing on. He came to her as a shepherd, and he sought to woo her mildly, but she would neither speak to him nor let him come near where she was.

Picus came the very day that Silvanus came as a shepherd—Picus the son of old Saturnus who was god of the grain-sown field. Picus was handsome; Picus wore a scarlet cloak; Picus could talk well to any woman. But when he came near her Pomona dashed water in his face from her stream. Then Picus saw Silvanus and thinking that he was Pomona's favoured suitor, began to abuse him. Silvanus caught hold of him, and beat him, and tore his scarlet cloak from his shoul-ders. Pomona fled from both of them, and after that she would let none of the male divinities come near where she was. She built a wall round where her trees grew; she would not go outside the gate, and she was very careful to let no one who might turn out to be a lover come within it.

Young Vertumnus saw her through the gate; he saw Pomona and he loved her more ardently than either Silvanus or Picus had loved her—Silvanus who was much older than he looked, and Picus who was always in love with some girl. He came to her gate, but she would not let him come in. Back he came in the garb of a reaper, carrying a basket of barley-ears as an offering to her. She bade him go away. Another time he came as a mower, with grass binding his brow. She left him outside the gate, nor would she speak to him at all. And then he came as a ploughman, big and burly, holding in his hand a goad which Pomona might think that he had just used to drive the oxen in the furrows. She left him before the gate, and although he shook it with his hands, he could not force it open. And then, that she might think of him as one who had an interest in trees and fruit and be kind to him on that account, he came bearing a ladder upon his shoulder as if he were ready to mount to where the apples were growing and gather them. But Pomona knew him for one of the male divinities, albeit for one of the youngest of them, and she would not let him come to where she tended her trees.

One day Pomona saw outside her gate a bent and weary-looking old woman. She had on a head-dress that fell across her eyes, and she leaned upon a stick. Pomona, the kindliest of the nymphs, asked her to sit in the shade of one of her trees and rest herself and eat some of her fruit. The old woman came within. "How beautifully your garden is kept!" she said. "I have never been where trees grew so well, or where the fruits looked so bright and so refreshing. Do you live here all alone, my dear?" She ate the fruit that was given her and she looked at Pomona as she stood there in her brown dress and with the leaves about her head. "I have heard of you, my dear," she said. "Everything I heard about you made me think you were beautiful, but you are more beautiful than I thought." And saying this she kissed Pomona.

And as she went from tree to tree the old woman kept calling to her. Pomona came back and stood under an elm-tree near where the old woman sat. The elm-tree supported vines which were covered with bunches of grapes. "Look," said the old woman. "If that elm-tree stood unmated to the vine it would have no value except for its timber. And the vine that grows there! If there was no elm-tree for it to grow upon it would straggle along the ground, flat and unflourishing! So you see what good comes of mating two beings—the vine and the elm-tree. But you, my dear, refuse to be mated, refuse to be wedded, refuse even to know one who might be a sweetheart for you! Listen! Consent to having an old woman like me make a match for you!"

Pomona was so surprised to have someone talk to her in this strain that she sank down on the grass beside the old woman. "Be wise and choose Vertumnus! I know the lad well—I know him as well as I know myself! He is a lad who does not wander idly through the world. He has wide spaces to live in, and he dwells near at hand! He is not like the others who came to woo you—Picus, for instance, who went and fell in love with Canens, and who went on until he had an enchantress fall in love with him, and who, because he would not respond to her, has since been turned into a woodpecker. I'll say nothing about Silvanus! He has been in love with nearly all of the nymphs! Vertumnus is not like either of these divinities. You will be his first love, dear Pomona, and his last. And besides, he is interested in all that you are interested in—he deals in fruits, too! He was made to be yours, and you were made to be his, and I am here to tell you that!"

Even as these words were said the head-dress fell off the head of the one who spoke to Pomona. Bright and ardent were the eyes that she saw then. Pomona stood up and would have run away; but hands held her hands, gently, firmly. "You are Vertumnus," she said. She saw a face before her—a youth's face; the stick that the pretended old woman had leaned on fell away; the cloak fell off the figure. Pomona saw a youth who was tall and fine as one of her own trees. And until the evening star came they stayed amongst the trees, and when they parted Pomona had promised to wed her Vertumnus.

GRÆCO-ROMAN

GRÆCO-ROMAN

CUPID AND PSYCHE

I

In a far country there was a king and queen who had three daughters: each of the maidens was beautiful; the youngest of them, however, had such shape and lineaments that all words said in praise of beauty seemed but poor and empty when used about hers. Men came to where she dwelt as to a shrine; they would kiss the tips of their right hands at the sight of her, thus paying to this maiden (Psyche she was named) the same homage that was paid to Venus, the immortal Goddess.

Indeed, it began to be said that Venus had forsaken the courts of Heaven, and had come down to earth as a mortal maiden, and dwelt amongst men in the person of the youngest daughter of the king and queen of that far country. Then men sailed no longer to where there were the famous shrines of the Goddess Venus. The shrines in Paphos, and Cnidus, and Cythera were forsaken of worshippers, and men paid their devotions to a mortal maiden, to Psyche. When she went forth from her father's house in the morning the folk strewed flowers along the way, and sacrifices that should have been made to no one but to the immortal Goddess were made to her.

The rumours of such happenings soon reached to Venus herself. She said, "Shall I, judged the fairest amongst the immortal Goddesses by the Shepherd of Ida, shall I have mine honours taken away from me by an earthly girl? Not so. Little joy shall this Psyche have of the loveliness that the vain imaginations of the crowd have bestowed upon her." Thereupon Venus called to her son. She brought him with her to that far country, and she showed him the maiden Psyche as she walked the ways of the city. "I pray thee," she said, "to let thy mother have a vengeance that it is fitting she should have. See to it that this girl becomes the slave of an unworthy love." She embraced

him and she left him there, and she sailed for whatever shrine o
hers had still some worshippers.

Her son was Cupid, that winged boy who goes through men's houses
by night, armed with his bow and arrow, troubling their wedded lives
She left him there, gazing on the maiden Psyche. And gazing upor
her, Cupid fell deeply in love with the maiden. He had no mind to
carry out the command of his mother; he did not want to smite her
mind with the madness of an unworthy love; rather he thought upor
how he might win for himself the one who was fairer than any being
upon earth or even in the heaven above.

And Psyche, adored by all for her beauty, had no joy in the
fruit of it. She knew that she was wondered at, but wondered at as the
work of the craftsman is wondered at that has in it some likeness
of divinity. No man sought her in marriage. Her sisters were wedded,
but she came to their age and passed their age and remained unasked
for. She sat at home, and in her heart she cursed the beauty that
pleased all men while it set her apart from the close thought of all.
At last the king, her father, was forced to send and inquire of an
oracle what he should do with this daughter of his. An answer
came that meant a dreadful doom. "Let the maiden be placed on the
top of a certain mountain, adorned as for marriage and for death.
Look not for a son-in-law of mortal birth; he who will take her to
his side is the serpent whom even the Gods are in dread of, and who
makes the bodiless ones on the Styx afraid."

For many days after this doom had been made known there were
lamentations in the king's household. Then, at last, knowing that the
doom told might not be avoided, the queen brought out the adorn-
ments for her daughter's marriage and gathered a company to conduct
the maiden to her dread bridal. All was made ready. But the torch
lighted for the wedding gathered ashes and made a dark smoke; the
joyful sound of the pipe changed into a wail; underneath her yellow
wedding-veil the bride trembled and wept. The ceremonies for the
marriage having been accomplished with hearts bowed down as at a
funeral, Psyche was led from the city and to the place appointed
on the mountain-top.

As she went she said to those who were with her, "This is the fruit
of my much-talked-of loveliness! Ye weep for me now, but when the

olk celebrated me with divine honours—then was the time you should have wept for me as for one already dead! The name and titles given me have been my destruction! Lead me on and set my feet upon the appointed place! I am impatient to behold my bridegroom and give myself up to the serpent whom even the Gods are fearful of."

Then she said to her father and mother, "Do not waste what life you have weeping over me." She bade them good-bye. They left her on the mountain-top and went back mournfully to the city. Then night came down upon them there; they shut themselves in their house and gave themselves up to perpetual night.

As for Psyche, she stood upon the mountain-top in fear and trembling. The breeze came, the gentle Zephyrus. Zephyrus lifted Psyche up; he bore her, her bridal vesture floating on either side, down the side of the mountain, and he set her lightly amidst the flowers of the valley below.

Lightly was it all done. Psyche lay on a dewy bed in the valley, resting from the tumult of the days that had gone by. She awoke. She saw a grove with a fountain of water that was as clear as glass in the midst of it, and, by the fountain, a dwelling-place.

Psyche thought that this dwelling-place must be the abode of one of the immortal Gods. Golden pillars held up the roof. Cedar wood and ivory formed the arches. The walls were latticed with silver. Before the house, creatures of the wood and wild—rabbits, and squirrels, and deer sported, and all the birds that Psyche had ever seen or heard sang in the trees. And the very path that led to the house was set in stones that made pictures and stories.

Upon this path she went. She crossed the threshold of the house and went within. Beautiful things were there, and no locks, no chains, no guardian protected them. As she went through the house, drawn on by more and more delight, she heard a voice that said, "Lady and mistress! All that is here is thine! Rest now and relieve thy weariness. We whose voices thou hearest are servants to thee; when thou wilt, a feast fit for a queen will be made ready for thee."

Psyche went to sleep knowing that some divine being had care for her. She awoke and went to the bath; thereafter she sat down to the food that had been made ready for her—a banquet, indeed! Still she saw no one. She heard voices, but those who served her remained invisible. When the feast was ended one whom she saw not entered and sang for her—sang to the chords of a harp that was played for her by one unseen. The night came and the lamps were lighted by unseen hands. Then they were quenched by unseen hands, and to Psyche, lying in her bed, the bridegroom came. He departed before the dawn, and she was a wife.

The day was before her, and the attendant minstrels sang to her; she heard their voices and she heard the music they made for her. The night came; the lamps were lighted and quenched, and to Psyche her husband came as before. And as before, he departed before the dawn came. And this went on for many nights. Then to his bride one night the bridegroom said, "O Psyche, my life and my spouse! Fortune is becoming ill-favored towards us! Thou art threatened with a danger that may be mortal. Harken! Thy sisters are about to go seeking for traces of thee. They will come to the mountain-top in their search. But if their cries come to thee in this abode, do not answer, nor go forth at all. If thou dost, it may be that thou shalt bring sorrow and destruction upon us both. But that shall be as thou wilt!"

Psyche promised that she would do all he would have her do. The bridegroom departed, going forth ere the darkness had gone. That day Psyche heard the voices of her sisters as they went calling her name. And in that house empty of all save voices, she thought that she was indeed dead and cut off from her sisters and her parents. She thought upon how they had wept for her, and she wept herself to think that she had no power to console them. In the night the bridegroom returned. Kissing her face, he found it wet with tears.

He blamed her; she wept the more. Then, as dawn came, he said, "Be it as thou wilt. Let thy pain cease, and do as thou dost desire. Yet wilt thou, Psyche, remember the warning I have given thee." All this he said when she told him that she would die unless she might see and speak with her sisters who were seeking for her.

"Yet one thing shall I say to thee," he said. "If they come here to thee give them all the gifts thou wilt; but do not yield thyself to their doubts about me. Thou knowest me, thy husband. Do not yield to the counsel of thy sisters and inquire concerning my bodily form. If thou dost, thou and I may never again embrace each other."

Then Psyche wept; she said she would die a hundred times rather than forego his dear embraces. In a while he relented, and he spoke less harshly. Then Psyche said, "For the sake of the love I have given thee bid thy servant Zephyrus bring hither my sisters as he brought me." Her husband promised that this would be done. Then, ere the light appeared, he vanished.

II

Her sisters, coming to the place where Psyche was left, sought for traces of her. Finding none they wept, lifting up their voices. Zephyrus came; he raised them up; he bore them down from that mountain-top. He bore them to the lawn that was before the house where Psyche had her abode.

She heard their cries; she came out of her wondrous house and she brought them within it. "Enter now," she said, "and relieve your sorrow in the company of Psyche, your sister." She displayed to them all the treasures of that wondrous house; they heard the voices and they saw how the unseen ones ministered to Psyche. Her sisters were filled with wonder; but soon their wonder gave place to envy. "Who is he?" they asked, "your husband and the lord of all these wondrous things?" "A young man," said Psyche. "I would have you look upon him, but for the most part of the day he hunts upon the mountain." Then, lest the secret should slip from her tongue, she loaded her sisters with gold and gems, and, summoning Zephyrus with words that she had heard her husband utter, she commanded him to bear them to the mountain-top.

They returned to their homes, each of them filled with envy of Psyche's fortune. "Look now," they said to each other, "what has come about! We the elder sisters have been given in marriage to men we did not know and who were of little account. And she, our youngest sister, is possessed of such great riches that she is able to give us these golden things and these gems as if they were mere keepsakes. What a hoard of wealth is in her house! You saw, sisters, the crowns, and glittering gems, and gold trodden under foot! If her husband is noble and handsome enough to match that house, then no woman in the world is as lucky or as happy as that Psyche whom we left upon the mountain-top!" And, saying this, they became more and more filled with envy, and with the malice that comes from envy unchecked.

Then one said to the other, "This husband of hers may be of divine nature, and through his mere fondness for her, he may make her a Goddess. Yes, as a Goddess she ever bore herself! How intolerable it would be if all that was thought about her were realized, and she became as one of the Immortals."

And so, filled with their envy and malice, they returned to that golden house and they said to Psyche, "Thou livest in folly, and knowst nothing of a danger that threatens thee. Thou hast never seen thy husband—that we know. But others have seen him, and they know him for a deadly serpent. Remember the words of the oracle, which declared thee destined for a devouring beast. There are those who have seen that beast at nightfall, coming back from his feeding and entering this house. And now thou art to be a mother! The beast only waits for the babe to be born so that he may devour both the babe and thee. Nothing can be done for thee, perhaps, because thou mayst delight in this rich and secret place, and even in a loathsome love. But at least we, thy sisters, have done our part in bidding thee beware!" So they spoke, and Psyche was carried away by their words, and lost the memory of her husband's commands and her own promises. She cried out in anguish, "It may be that those who say these things tell the truth! For in very truth I have never seen the face of my husband, nor know I at all what form and likeness he has. He frightens me from the sight of him, telling me that some great evil should befall if I looked upon his face. O ye who were reared with me, help, if you can, your sister, in the great peril that faces her now!"

Her sisters, filled with malice, answered, "The way to safety we have well considered, and we will show it to thee. Take a sharp knife and hide it in that part of the couch where thou art wont to lie. Place a lighted lamp behind a curtain. And when thou hearest him breathe in sleep, slip from the couch, and, holding the lamp, look upon him. Have in thy hand the knife. Then it is for thee to put forth all thy strength and strike his serpent's head off. Then thou wilt be delivered from the doom which the vain talk about thy beauty brought upon thee, and thou mayst return to thy father's house."

Saying this, her sisters departed hastily. And Psyche, left alone, was tossed up and down as on the waves of the sea. The apprehension of a great calamity was upon her: she thought she could avert it by making strong her will for the deed that her sisters had counselled her to carry out. Evening came, and in haste she made ready for the terrible deed. Darkness came; he whom she had known for her bridegroom came to her out of the darkness. In a while she, lying rigidly there, knew by his breath that he was asleep.

She arose, she who before was of no strength at all; she drew forth the knife in the darkness and held it in her right hand. She took up the lighted lamp. And then she saw what lay on the couch. Then indeed she became afraid; her limbs failed under her, and she would have buried the knife in her own bosom. For there lay Love himself, with golden locks, and ruddy cheeks, and white throat. There lay Love with his pinions, yet fresh with dew, spotless upon his shoulders. Smooth he was, and touched with a light that was from Venus, his mother. And at the foot of the couch his bow and arrows were laid.

Then Psyche, with indrawn breath, bent over to kiss his lips. And it chanced that a drop of burning oil from that lamp which she held fell upon his shoulder. At the touch of that burning drop, the God started up. He saw her bending over him; he saw the whole of her faithlessness; putting her hands away he lifted himself from the couch and fled away.

And Psyche, as he rose upon the wing, laid hold on him with her hands, striving to stay his flight. But she could not stay it; he went from her and she sank down upon the ground. As she lay there the dawn came, and she saw through the casement her divine lover where he rested upon a cypress-tree that grew near. She could not cry out to him. He spoke to her in great emotion. "Foolish one," he said, "Venus, my mother, would have devoted thee to a love that was all baseness. Unmindful of her command I would not have that doom befall thee. Mine own flesh I pierced with mine arrow, and I took thee for my love. I brought thee here, I made thee my wife, and all only that I might seem a monster beside thee, and that thou shouldst seek to wound the head wherein lay the eyes that were so full of love for thee. I thought I could put thee on thy guard against those who were ready to make snares for thee. Now all is over. I would but punish thee by my flight hence!"

Prostrate upon the earth Psyche watched, as far as sight might reach, the flight of her spouse. When the breadth of space had parted him wholly from her, she ran without. Far she wandered from that golden house where she had dwelt with Love. She came to where a river ran. In her despair she cast herself into it. But as it happened, Pan, the rustic God, was on the river-bank, playing upon a reed. Hard by, his flock of goats browsed at will. The shaggy God took Psyche out of the stream. "I am but a herdsman," he said to her, "a herdsman and rustic. But I am wise by reason of my length of days and my long experience of the world. I guess by thy sorrowful eyes and thy continual sighing that thy trouble comes from love. Then, pretty maiden, listen to me, and seek not death again in the stream or elsewhere. Put aside thy woe, and make thy prayers to Cupid. He is a God who is won by service; give him, therefore, thy service."

Psyche was not able to answer anything. She left the God with his goats and went on her way. And now she was resolved to go through the world in search of Cupid, her spouse. And he, even then, was in his mother's house: he lay there in pain from the wound that the burning drop from Psyche's lamp had given him. Heart-sick was he, too. The white bird that floats over the waves and is his mother's, seeing him come back, went across the sea, and, approaching Venus as she bathed, made known to her that her son lay afflicted with some grievous hurt. Thereupon she issued from the sea, and, returning to her golden house, found Cupid there, wounded and afflicted in his mind. Soon she found out the cause of his suffering and became filled with anger. "Well done!" she cried. "To trample on thy mother's precepts and to spare her enemy the cross that she had designed for her—the cross of an unworthy love! Nay, to have united yourself with her, giving me a daughter-in-law who hates me! But I will make her and thee repent of the love that has been between you, and the savour of your marriage bitter!" And saying this, Venus hastened in anger from her house.

III

Psyche was wandering hither and thither, seeking her husband, her whole heart set upon soothing his anger by the endearments of a wife, or, if he would not accept her as a wife, by the services of a handmaiden. One day, seeing a temple on the top of a mountain, she went towards it, hoping to find there some traces of her lord. Within the temple there were ears of wheat in heaps or twisted into chaplets; there were ears of barley also; there were sickles and all the instruments of harvest. And Psyche, saying to herself, "I may not neglect the shrines, nor the holy service of any God or Goddess, but must strive to win by my works the favour of them all." And so saying she put the sickles and the instruments of harvest, the chaplets and the heaps of grain, into their proper places.

And Ceres, the Goddess of the harvest, found her bending over the tasks she had set herself. She knew her for Psyche, the wife of Cupid. "Ah, Psyche," said the Goddess, "Venus, in her anger, is tracking thy footsteps through the world; she is seeking thee to make thee pay the greatest penalty that can be exacted from thee. And here I find thee taking care of the things that are in my care!" Then Psyche fell at the feet of Ceres, and sweeping the floor with her hair, and washing the feet of the Goddess with her tears, she besought her to have mercy on her. "Suffer me to hide myself for a few days amongst the heaps of grain, till my strength, outworn in my long travail, be recovered by a little rest," she cried. But Ceres answered, "Truly thy tears move me, and I fain would help thee. But I dare not incur the ill-will of my kinswoman. Depart from this as quickly as may be." Then Psyche, filled with a new hopelessness, went away from that temple. Soon, as she went through the half-lighted woods in the valley below, she came to where there was another temple. She saw rich offerings and garments of price hung upon the door-posts and to the branches of the trees, and on them, in letters of gold, were wrought the name of the Goddess to whom they were dedicated. So Psyche went within that temple, and with knees bent and hands laid about the altar, she prayed, "O Iuno, sister and spouse of Iuppiter, thou art called the Auspicious! Be auspicious to my desperate fortune! Willingly dost thou help those in child-birth! Deliver me, therefore—O deliver me from the peril that is upon me!" And as Psyche prayed thus, Iuno, in all the majesty of the spouse of Iuppiter, appeared before her. And the Goddess, being present, answered, "Would that I might incline to thy prayer; but against the will of Venus whom I have ever loved as a daughter, I may not grant what thou dost ask of me!" Then Psyche went forth from that temple, and filled with more and more dismay, she said to herself, "Whither now shall I take my way? In what solitude can I hide myself from the all-seeing eye of Venus? It is best that I should go before her, and yield myself up to her as to a mistress, and take from her any punishment that even she can inflict upon me." And saying this, Psyche went towards where Venus had her house. And as she went on she said to herself, "Who knows but I may find him whom my soul seeketh after in the abode of his mother?"

When she came near to the doors of the house of Venus, one of the servants ran out to her, crying, "Hast thou learned at last, wicked maid, that thou hast a mistress?" And seizing Psyche by the hair of her head she dragged her into the presence of the Goddess. And when Venus saw her she laughed, saying, "Thou hast deigned at last to make thy salutations to thy mother-in-law. Now will I see to it that thou makest thyself a dutiful and obedient daughter-in-law."

Saying this she took barley and millet and every kind of grain and seed, and mixed them all together, making a great heap of them. Then she said to Psyche, "Methinks that so plain a maid can only win a lover by the tokens of her industry. Get to work, therefore, and show what thou canst do. Sort this heap of grain, separating the one kind from the other, grain by grain, and see to it that thy task is finished before the evening." Then Venus went from her, and Psyche, appalled by her bidding, was silent and could not put a hand upon the heap. Listlessly she sat beside it and the hours passed. But a little ant came before her; he understood the difficulty of her task and he had pity upon her. He ran hither and thither and summoned the army of the ants. "Have pity," he said to them, "upon the wife of Love, and hasten to help her in her task." Then the host of the insect people gathered together; they sorted the whole heap of grain, separating one kind from the other. And having done this they all departed suddenly.

At nightfall Venus returned; she saw that Psyche's task was finished and she cried out in anger. "The work is not thine; he in whose eyes thou hast found favour surely instructed thee as to how to have it done." She went from Psyche then. But early in the morning she called to her and said, "In the grove yonder, across the torrent, there are sheep whose fleeces shine with gold. Fetch me straightway shreds of that precious stuff, having gotten it in whatever way thou mayst."

Then Psyche went forth. She stood beside the torrent thinking that she would seek for rest in the depth of it. But from the river-bed the green reed, lowly mother of music, whispered to her and said, "O Psyche! Do not pollute these waters by self-destruction! I will tell thee of a way to get the gold shreds of the fleece of yonder fierce flock. Lie down under yonder plane-tree and rest yourself until the coming of evening and the quiet of the river's sound has soothed the flock. Then go amongst the trees that they have been under and gather the shreds of the fleeces from the trees—the leaves hold the golden shreds."

Psyche, instructed by the simple reed, did all that she was told to do. In the quiet of the evening she went into the grove, and she put into her bosom the soft golden stuff that was held by the leaves. Then she returned to where Venus was. The Goddess smiled bitterly upon her, and she said, "Well do I know whence came the instruction that thou hast profited by; but I am not finished with thee yet. Seest thou the utmost peak of yonder mountain? The dark stream which flows down from it waters the Stygian fields, and swells the flood of Cocytus. Bring me now, in this little cruse, a draught from its inner-most source." And saying this, Venus put into Psyche's hands a vessel of wrought crystal.

Psyche went up the mountain, but she sought only for a place in which she could bring her life to an end. She came to where there was a rock steep and slippery. From that rock a river poured forth and fell down into an unseen gulf below. And from the rocks on every side serpents came with long necks and unblinking eyes. The very waters found a voice; they said in stifled voices, "What dost thou here?" "Look around thee!" "Destruction is upon thee!" All sense left her, and she stood like one changed into rock.

But the bird of Iuppiter took flight to her. He spread his wings over her and said, "Simple one! Didst thou think that thou couldst steal one drop of that relentless stream, the river that is terrible even to the Gods! But give me the vessel." And the eagle took the cruse, and filled it at the source, and returned to her quickly from amongst the raised heads of the serpents.

Then Psyche, receiving the cruse as the gift of life itself, ran back quickly and brought it to Venus. But the angry Goddess was not yet satisfied. "One task more remains for you to do," she said to Psyche. "Take now this tiny casket, and give it to Proserpine. Tell her that Venus would have of her beauty as much as might suffice for one day's use. Tell her this and take back in the casket what the Queen of Hades will give thee. And be not slow in returning."

Then Psyche perceived that she was now being thrust upon death, and that she would have to go, of her own motion, down to Hades and the Shades. Straightway she climbed to the top of a high tower, thinking to herself, "I will cast myself down hence, and so descend more quickly to the Kingdom of the Dead." But the tower spoke to her and said, "Wretched maiden! If the breath quit thy body, then wilt thou indeed go down to Hades, but by no means return to the upper air again. Listen to me. Not far from this place there is a mountain, and in that mountain there is a hole that is a vent for Hades. Through it is a rough way; following it one comes in a straight course to the castle of Orcus. But thou must not go empty-handed. Take in each hand a morsel of barley-bread, soaked in hydromel, and in thy mouth have two pieces of money. When thou art well forward on the way thou wilt overtake a lame ass laden with wood, and a lame driver; he will beg thee to hand to him certain cords to fasten the burden which is falling from the ass: heed him not; pass by him in silence. Thou wilt come to the River of the Dead. Charon, in that leaky bark he hath, will put thee over upon the farther side. Thou shalt deliver to him, for his ferry-charge, one of these two pieces of money. But thou must deliver it in such a way that his hand shall take it from between thy lips. As thou art crossing the stream an old man, rising on the water, will put up his mouldering hands, and pray thee to draw him into the ferry-boat. But beware that thou yield not to unlawful pity.

"When thou art across the stream and upon the level ground, certain grey-haired women, spinning, will cry to thee to lend thy hand to their work. But again beware! Take no part in that spinning! If thou dost thou wilt cast away one of the cakes thou bearest in thine hands. But remember that the loss of either of these cakes will be to thee the loss of the light of day. For a watchdog lies before the threshold of the lonely house of Proserpine. Close his mouth with one of thy cakes, so he will let thee pass. Then thou shalt enter into the presence of Proserpine herself. Do thou deliver thy message, and taking what the Queen of the Dead shall give thee, return back again, offering to the watchdog the other cake, and to the ferryman the other piece of money that thou hast in thy mouth. After this manner mayst thou return again to the light of day. And I charge thee not to look into, nor open, the casket thou bearest with the treasure of the beauty of the divine features hidden therein."

So the stones of the tower spoke. Psyche gave heed to all that they said. She entered the lonely house of Proserpine. At the feet of the Goddess of the Dead she sat down humbly; she would not rest upon the couch that was there nor take any of the food that was offered her. She delivered her message and she waited. Then Proserpine filled the casket secretly and shut the lid, and handed it to Psyche. She went from the house; she remembered the sop she had to give the watchdog and the fee she had to give the ferryman. She came back into the light of day. Now even as she hasted into the presence of Venus she said to herself, "I have in my hands the divine loveliness. Should I touch myself with a particle of it I should have a beauty indeed that would please him whom I still seek, him whom I still hope to be beside." Saying this, she raised the lid of the casket. Behold! what was within was sleep only, the sleep that was like the sleep of the dead! That sleep overcame Psyche, and she lay upon the ground and moved not.

But now Cupid, being healed of the wound from the burning oil, and longing for Psyche, his beloved, flew from the chamber in his mother's house. He found Psyche lying in slumber. He shook that slumber from her, and awakened her with the point of his arrow. Then he rose upon the air, and he went vehemently upon his way until he came into the highest court of Heaven. There sat Iuppiter, the Father of Gods and men. When Cupid went to him, Iuppiter took his hand in his, and kissed his face and said to him, "At no time, my son, hast thou regarded me with due honour. With those busy arrows of thine thou hast often upset the harmony that it is mine to bring about. But because thou hast grown up between these hands of mine, I will accomplish thy desire." He bade Mercury call the Gods together. And the Gods being assembled, Iuppiter said to them, "Ye Gods, it seems good to me that this boy should be confined in the bonds of marriage. And he has chosen and embraced a mortal maiden. Let him have the fruit of his love, and possess her for ever."

Thereupon the Father of the Gods bade Mercury produce Psyche amongst them. She was brought into the highest court of Heaven. The Father of the Gods held out to her his ambrosial cup. "Drink of it," he said, "and live for ever. Cupid shall never depart from thee." Then the Gods sat down to the marriage-feast. On the first couch was the bridegroom with his Psyche at his bosom. Bacchus served wine to the rest of the company, but his own serving-boy served it to Iuppiter. The Seasons crimsoned all things with their roses. Apollo sang to his lyre. Pan prattled on his reeds. Venus danced very sweetly to the soft music. And thus, with all due rites, did Psyche, born a mortal, become the immortal wife of Love. From Cupid and Psyche was born a daughter whom men call Voluptas.

CELTIC

CELTIC

IRISH

MIDIR AND ETAIN

A comb of silver was held in Etain's hand, and the comb was adorned with gold. Beside her was a basin of silver whereon four birds had been wrought, and there were little gems on the rim of the basin. A mantle of bright purple was about her, and beneath it was another mantle ornamented with silver fringes; the outer mantle was clasped over her bosom with a golden brooch. A tunic she wore with a long hood attached to it; it was stiff and glossy with green silk beneath red embroidery of gold, and it was clasped over her breasts with marvellously wrought clasps of silver and gold, so that men saw the bright gold and the green silk flashing against the sun. Her hair was in two tresses, and each golden tress had been plaited into four strands, and at the end of each strand was a little ball of gold. And the maiden was undoing her hair that she might wash it and her two arms were out through the armholes of her smock. Each of her arms was as white as the snow of a single night, and each of her cheeks was as rosy as the foxglove. Even and small were the teeth in her head, and they shone like pearls. Her eyes were as blue as a hyacinth, her lips delicate and crimson; very high, soft, and white were her shoulders. Tender, polished, and white were her wrists; her fingers long and of great whiteness; her nails were beautiful and pink. White as snow, or the foam of a wave, was her neck; long was it, slender, and as soft as silk. Smooth and white were her thighs; her knees were round and firm and white; her ankles were as straight as the rule of a carpenter. Her feet were slim and as white as the ocean's foam; evenly set were her eyes; her eyebrows were of bluish black, such as you see upon the shell of a beetle. With her fifty

141

maidens she had gone to a woodland pool to wash her hair, and there the King of Ireland saw her, and so she appeared to him and his followers. As they looked upon her they knew that there was never a maid fairer than she, or more worthy of love. And it seemed to some who were with the king that Etain must be one of those who have come from the Fairy Mounds.

Eochaid, the King of Ireland, wooed Etain, the daughter of an Ulster prince, and married her, and brought her as his queen to Tara. Not long were they there when strange events began to befall. One morning early, Eochaid, as he went upon the high ground of Tara, saw a young warrior at his side. The tunic that the warrior wore was purple in colour, his hair was of golden yellow, and of such length that it reached to the edge of his shoulders. His eyes were lustrous and grey; in one hand he held a pointed spear, in the other a shield with a white central boss, and with gems of gold upon it. The stranger went from his sight; the king held his peace about what he had seen, for he knew that he would be told that no such warrior had been in Tara on the night before, and that the gate through which such a one might have entered had not yet been thrown open. Then Eochaid walked alone upon the high place and looked out upon the plain of Breg; beautiful was the colour of that plain, and there was upon it excellent blossom glowing with all the hues that are known.

And after that the king's brother, Ailill, fell into a sickness, and no leech could cure his sickness. The king had to go from Tara to make the circuit of Ireland. He begged his queen to care for his brother. He made her promise that she would do everything to bring about Ailill's cure, and that, if he died, she would give him a burial befitting a prince even to putting a stone inscribed in Ogham letters above his grave. Etain promised to do all this, and when the king left Tara she went to visit Ailill.

She asked the sick youth what might be done for him. He told her that he was pining away for love of her, and that if she did not yield to his desire he would assuredly die. Etain said to him at last, "You shall not die if my granting your desire will keep you in life." Then she promised Ailill that she would keep tryst with him in a house outside Tara the next day.

Etain went to that house. He came to where she was; but he did not take her hand. He stood before her and spoke reproachfully to her. "You are one who has forgotten," he said. Then he went away. The next day, too, Etain waited for him in the trysting-house. He came and he stood before her. "You are one who has forgotten," he said again, and without saying more to her he went away. The third time she waited for him. When he stood before her this time he chanted a lay. "O fair-haired woman, will you come with me?" he chanted.

O fair-haired woman, will you come with me to the marvellous land, full of music, where the hair is primrose-yellow and the body white as snow?

There none speak of "mine" or "thine"—white are the teeth and black the brows; eyes flash with many-coloured lights, and the hue of the foxglove is on every cheek.

Pleasant to the eye are the plains of Eirinn, but they are a desert to the Great Plain.

Heady is the ale of Eirinn, but the ale of the Great Plain is headier.

Smooth and sweet are the streams that flow through it; mead and wine abound of every kind. It is one of the wonders of the land that youth does not change into age.

We see around us on every side, yet no man seeth us. O lady, if thou wilt come to my strong people, the purest of gold shall be on thy head—thy meat shall be swine's flesh unsalted, new milk and mead thou shalt drink with me there, O fair-haired woman.

Then he said, "I am not Ailill. Him I cast into a deep sleep; him I filled with a longing for you—a longing that will pass from him. But you, you know me not, you have forgotten. I am Midir the Proud, a king amongst the Immortals. In the land of the Immortals I loved you and you loved me. Then Fuamnach, my queen, jealous of you, caused her Druid to bespell you, changing you into a fly. She blew a tempest upon you and drove you through the world. At last you were driven into Oengus's palace—Oengus the God of Love, my foster-son. And Oengus made for you a bower of glass and set within it for your sustenance and delight a garden of honey-laden flowers. You were lost to me, for I did not know that Oengus guarded you. But Fuamnach found it out. And when you were outside the bower of glass she blew a tempest again upon you and you were driven through the air. Into the house of Etar, your mortal father, you went:

his wife had a drinking-cup in her hand. You went into the cup, and you were swallowed with the draught that was in the cup. Thereafter you were born as the daughter of Etar. All that was before this mortal birth of yours you have forgotten. I have remembered, and I claim you as the bride who was mine in the land of the Immortals."

Etain said, "I am the wife of the King of Ireland; I know nought of your country, and to me you are a nameless man." "If Eochaid gives you to me, will you come with me?" "If he bids me go to you and let your arms be put around me, I will go with you." When Etain said this to him, he who had the appearance of Ailill went from her. She hastened to where Ailill lay; she found him awakening from a deep sleep, and when she told him of the strange things that had been made known to her, all longing that he had had for her left Ailill.

Eochaid returned. Now one morning early when he ascended the height of Tara to behold the plain of Breg, he saw the warrior whom he had seen there before. And the king knew that he had not been within Tara on the night before, and that the gate through which he might have entered had not yet been thrown open. The stranger spoke to the king and said that he had come to play a game of chess with him. That evening they played a difficult game. Eochaid won and claimed much treasure from the stranger. The treasure was brought to him. He played again, and won and demanded that a great work be accomplished for him. That work was accomplished. They played again; the stranger won, and when the king asked him what he desired in payment, the stranger said, "That I may hold Etain in my arms and obtain a kiss from her." Eochaid was silent for a while upon hearing this demand. He might not deny it, for he had taken from the stranger the forfeits that had become due to him. "In a month," he said, "come into this place and the forfeit shall be granted you." And when the king said this the stranger went from Tara.

Then Eochaid caused Tara to be surrounded by a great host of armed men. None who were not known to the king's household might enter the palace. When a month had gone by Eochaid and his nobles sat at a feast in the hall. Etain was there and she handed around the wine-cup. Suddenly the one whom all now knew for Midir the Proud appeared amongst them, and glorious was his appearance and his raiment. "I claim the forfeit from you, King of Ireland," he said. Then Eochaid bowed his head, and bade Etain go to him and permit that he put his arms around her. She went to him; he put his right arm around her, and as he did this she remembered all that love that had been between them in the Land of the Immortals. They rose in the air; they went through the roof-window of the palace, and when Eochaid and the company who were with him hurried out of the hall they saw two swans flying towards Slievenamon, where was Midir the Proud's fairy palace.

THE DEATH OF CONAIRE MÓR, THE KING OF IRELAND

I

When Eterscel, the king, died, a bull was slain; then one who was a diviner drank of the broth and ate of the flesh of the bull and went into a slumber, and truth-compelling spells were chanted over him. All this was done so that it might be shown to the people what man was destined to be king over them. In his slumber the diviner cried out that he saw the one who was destined to be the King of Ireland: he saw him as a naked man carrying a sling, and with a stone in the sling, coming by night along the road to Tara. Messengers were forthwith sent to meet this naked man, and to bring him into the king's house and proclaim him king.

Now at that time a youth who had been brought up in Eterscel's house and recognized as Eterscel's son was playing with his foster-brothers along the plain of the Liffey. This youth was Prince Conaire. And while he was with his foster-brothers he saw a flock of birds that were wonderful for their size and their colour, and he drove towards them. The birds flew, and lighted on the ground, and flew again as Conaire followed them; always they kept a spear-cast ahead of his chariot. He became separated from his foster-brothers. At last the birds lighted on the shore of the sea; then Conaire dismounted from his chariot, and went towards them, a sling in his hand.

Thereupon the flock of birds turned themselves into men; they came towards him with spears and swords. One of them protected Conaire. "Know," he said to him, "that I am Nemglan, king of thy father's birds, and there is no one here but who is kin to thee."

"Until now," said Conaire, "I knew not this."

It was then that the youth learned of his parentage and of his descent. His mother was Mess Buachalla. She was called by that name which means "The Cowherds' Fosterling" because, from her infancy, she was brought up by two cowherds. She was reared in a hut of wattles, but her fosterers taught her many accomplishments, and no king's daughter was fairer than she was. One of King Eterscel's folk looked into the wattled hut one day; he saw there the fairest maiden in all Ireland, and be brought back to the king's household word of what he had seen. Now it had been told King Eterscel that he would marry a maiden of a strange race: when he heard of the Cowherds' Fosterling, he said, "This is the woman who is to be mine according to the prophecy."

Now that day, while Mess Buachalla sat within her wattled hut with the last of the daylight coming through the wattles, a bird flew down through the opening of the roof. The bird changed into a man, a radiant being, and Mess Buachalla knew that he was one of the Danaan lords and from the Land of the Ever-living. They became lovers, he and she, and Conaire was the child of their love. Eterscel sent for Mess Buachalla, and she became his queen, and it was thought that Conaire was the son of King Eterscel.

Now those who were of the Danaan folk both loved and hated the race from which Mess Buachalla had come. She was sprung from Etain who, in the Land of the Ever-living, was loved by Midir the Proud. Etain became a mortal and married Eochaid, the King of Ireland. And when Midir had drawn Etain back to the Land of the Ever-living, Eochaid had laid waste the places where the Danaan folk dwelt. From Eochaid who had laid waste these places, through Mess Buachalla, daughter of his daughter, Conaire was descended.

Thus Conaire learned from Nemglan of his parentage and of his descent. "Thou shalt be made King of Ireland," Nemglan told him, "and these are things that thou must never do." Then Nemglan gave Conaire a list of *geise*, of things that were prohibited to him to do.

"If thou dost break any of these prohibitions," he said, "nothing will stand in the way of the Danaan vengeance upon thy house." Thereafter he said, "A man stark naked who shall go at the end of the night along the road to Tara, having a sling and a stone in the sling—'tis he shall be made king." Then Conaire stripped off his raiment and went naked through the night to Tara. Messengers were watching the roads for him. When they met the naked man they clothed him in royal garments and brought him into the king's house. All rejoiced to find that it was Prince Conaire who was given to them for king. His foster-brothers were there—Ferrogain, Fergobar, and Lomna Dru—and greatly did they rejoice at his being made King of Ireland.

II

Conaire Mór was the most splendid, noble, and beautiful king that ever was in Ireland, and of the kings of the world he was the mildest and gentlest. There was no defect in him whether in form, shape, or vesture; in vision, skill, or eloquence; in knowledge, valour, or kindred. In Ireland during his reign not a cloud veiled the sun from the middle of spring to the middle of autumn; not a dew-drop fell from the grass till it was past mid-day. In his reign from year's end to year's end peace was kept with the wolves even. No man slew another; to everyone in Ireland his fellow's voice was as sweet as the strings of harps. Ireland had the three crowns upon her then—the crown of corn-ears, the crown of flowers, and the crown of oak-mast.

These were the prohibitions that were laid upon Conaire Mór:

He was not to permit rapine in the land;

He was not to go out on a ninth night from Tara;

He was not to go right-handwise round Tara, nor left-handwise round Bregia;

He was not to hunt the evil beasts of Cerna;

He was not to let three Reds go before him to the house of a Red;

He was not to let a solitary woman come into a house where he was after sunset.

The peace of his reign was broken by Conaire's foster-brothers. Pride and wilfulness possessed them, and they went reiving through Ireland. Year after year, for three years, they went reiving. And when all complained against them, the king said, "Let every father slay his own son, but let my foster-brothers be spared." He permitted rapine to be wrought, and so one of the prohibitions laid upon him was broken. At last he withdrew his protection from his foster-brothers. They took ships and went upon the seas. And on the seas they met Ingcel the One-eyed, the son of the King of Britain, who was a banished man also. With him they joined forces. They raided Britain; they destroyed a fortress there; Ingcel's father and his seven brothers were in it and they were slain unwittingly by the raiders.

Ingcel demanded destruction for destruction, and he had Conaire's foster-brothers join him in a raid on Ireland. They beached their ships and they landed, a force of fierce marauders, upon the plain of the Liffey, south of Tara. "What mansion is it I have seen," said Ingcel to Ferrogain, "where the light of a fire comes from the main door and shines through the spokes of the chariot-wheels outside?" "Surely it is the guest-house that stands on the road to Tara—the guest-house of Da Derga," said Ferrogain. "But a guest-house is sanctuary in every land—'tis wrong to sack a guest-house," said Lomna Dru. "Lomna, when we made our oaths, we made no reservations as to a guest-house," said Ingcel. "Unless the earth break under us," said Fergobar, "the destruction of this guest-house shall be wrought. Neither old men nor historians shall declare that I quitted the destruction until I had accomplished it." "Rouse up, then, ye champions," cried Ingcel, the one-eyed outlaw of Britain, "we will plunder that guest-house and destroy it, and destroy all who are in it. A rich plunder will be ours to carry to our ships." Ferrogain and Lomna Dru stayed back, but Fergobar joined himself with Ingcel, and the fierce marauders marched towards the guest-house that was called Da Derga's Hostel.

III

King Conaire had broken another of his prohibitions: he went beyond Tara on a ninth night; he went to settle a dispute between two of his thralls. Now as he returned with his household he saw the smoke of a burning country between him and his royal house. With his cavalcade he went another way; in going that way he went right-handwise round Tara and left-handwise round Bregia. Strange beasts rose up in front of him, and he pursued them. These were the evil beasts of Cerna, but Conaire did not know this until the chase was over.

The king knew that he would have to lie that night outside his royal house. He rode towards the guest-house that stood with its seven doors open on the road to Tara. Now the name "Derga" means "Red," and Conaire knew that he must not let three Reds ride before him to the hostel. But even as he thought upon this he saw three clad in red and riding upon red steeds before him on the road. He bade one from his cavalcade ride after them and bid them turn back. But Conaire's horseman could not come upon the red riders. He shouted to them, bidding them turn back at the king's command. One of the riders, looking over his shoulder, shouted back: "A gathering at a hostel; great the destruction; great the tidings." Again Conaire's horseman cried to them to turn back for the sake of the great reward that would be given them. Then the riders chanted: "Weary are the steeds we ride, the steeds from the Land of the Ever-living. Though we are living, we are dead. Great are the signs; destruction of life; sating of ravens; feeding of crows; strife of slaughter; wetting of sword-edges; shields with broken bosses after sundown. Lo, my son!" Still they rode on. Conaire's horseman saw them alight before Da Derga's Hostel, and fasten their red steeds to the portal, and seat themselves within. The horseman rode back and told the king that the red riders had entered before him. "More of my *geise* have now been broken," said Conaire.

So he and his cavalcade rode on, and they entered Da Derga's Hostel. Then were the chariots left outside the hostel, seventeen chariots with steeds small-headed and broad-chested, each steed with a bridle of red enamel. There were grey spears over the chariots, and those on guard there had ivory-hilted swords by their sides and silver shields above their elbows. At one side of the great door as guard stood the King of Ulster's son, Cormac. He was a man of noble countenance, with clear and sparkling eyes. His face was broad above and narrow below. He had golden hair and a proper fillet around it; there was a brooch of silver in his mantle, and in his hand he held a gold-hilted sword. His shield had five golden circles upon it. At the other side of the door stood Conall Cearnach, Conall the Victorious, most famous of Ireland's warriors. Blue as gentians were his eyes; dark as a stag-beetle were his brows. The spear that he held in his hand was as thick as a chariot's outer yoke. He had a blood-red shield on which were rivets of white bronze between plates of gold. Between them stood the king's champion, MacCecht. He was a man of strong and fear-inspiring countenance. The shaft of his lance was the weight of a plough-yoke. He had a wooden shield covered with plates of iron, and upright in his hand he held a spear from the iron point of which blood dripped.

Conaire sat upon the couch. The mantle that was about him was even as the mist of a May day: diverse were the hues and semblances each moment shown upon it. A hand's breadth of his sword was outside its scabbard, and a man in front of the hostel might see by the light of the blade. The colour of the king's hair was like the sheen of smelted gold. Beside him was his little son—a small, freckled lad in a purple cloak; he had the manners of a maiden, and he was loved by all.

The king's juggler played before them. White as mountain cotton were the hairs on his head. He had three shields, three swords, and three apples of gold, and he kept them rising above and falling past each other like bees on a day of beauty. But even as the king and his son looked on, lo! a cry came from the things in the air, and they fell down upon the floor. Then was the head of a man cast into the hostel. Conaire saw that it was the head of Ferrogain, his foster-brother. He took it up, and wept over it, and even then the reivers made their attack upon the hostel.

A woman came and stood by the door-posts of the house. Her cloak was soiled and smelt of damp earth. Great loathing came upon the company at the sight of that woman. The king bade her begone. "It is known," he said, "that it is a prohibition with me not to let a solitary woman be after sunset where I am." The woman said, "If in sooth it has befallen the king not to have in his house room and a meal for a solitary woman, they will be gotten apart from him." "We will have you stay," said Conaire, "albeit another of my *geise* is broken." The woman cast her cloak upon the floor. "To-night," she said, "the king will sleep with me."

Then another shape was shown to Conaire. He saw a man who had

only one eye, one foot, and one hand. He knew him for the Swineherd of Bove Derg, and he knew that ruin was wrought at every
feast at which he was present. And shapes more dreadful than this
shape were shown him. He saw the Daughters of Bav—even those
three that are slaughtered at every destruction. Naked and bleeding,
they hung by ropes from the roof.

There issued from the hostel a band terrible to the reivers, a
band of men whose dress was of rough hair, who had girdles of ox-
hide, and who were armed with flails; each flail they wielded had
chains of iron triple-twisted. These were the giants that had been
taken by Cuchulain at the beleaguerment of Faldal. They went through
the reivers, their savage eyes shining through their thick hair. But
Ingcel called out to them, and made terms with them, and drew
them to his own side. Then was the river that flowed through the
hostel turned aside. Brands were flung upon it; the hostel burned, and
there was no water to quench the burning.

Conall Cearnach went forth with his nine companions. He made
a circuit of the hostel, going through the reivers as a hawk goes
through a flock of small birds. A piper in red was there. He played
before Conall, and led Conall away with his bewildering music. Cormac, the son of the King of Ulster, strove against the reivers. As a
ship goes through the waves so Cormac went through the ranks of
those who attacked the hostel. A piper in red went before him, and,
playing an enchanting strain, led him from the fight.

A thirst came upon the king. There was no water to assuage it.
MacCecht took up the king's golden cup and cut his way through the
ranks of the reivers to bring water to Conaire. The king armed his
household and went forth, and he and his harpers and cup-bearers
and jugglers made their fight. But a piper in red played, and a harper
cried out that the Danaan folk were against the king, because King
Eochaid had lain waste the Danaan places in his search for the queen
who had been taken from the world. The giants who had gone over
to Ingcel turned against the king's company with their iron flails.

MacCecht, the king's champion, failed to find water to assuage
Conaire's thirst. The wells, the rivers, and the lakes of Ireland, at the
bidding of the Danaan folk, hid themselves from him. The Shannon,
the Slaney, the Bann, and the Barrow—all the great rivers—hid them-

selves. The great lakes of Ireland hid themselves from him that night. MacCecht came upon a lone lake far from the hostel—he came upon Loch Gara. Before it could hide itself from him he had dipped the king's golden cup into its water. Then, carrying the water, he returned to the hostel. He found that all its defenders were dead or had been led away by the music of the pipers from the Land of the Ever-living. He came up as one of the reivers was striking off the head of King Conaire. MacCecht slew the man. Taking up his master's head, he poured a drink into his mouth. And Conaire's head spoke to Mac-Cecht, and praised him for his valour and his devotion.

MacCecht found Conaire's son unhurt, and he bore him away from that place of destruction. As he stood by the burning hostel he heard the red pipers chanting to each other: "Great the tidings. Through ancient enchantments a company has perished. Until this was accomplished we might not return. Now we ride the horses of Donn Tetscorach, the horses of Midir's son. Now we ride back to the Land of the Ever-living."

THE VOYAGE OF BRAN TO THE LAND OF THE IMMORTALS

Prince Bran sat in his royal house. The ramparts were closed around and no more could anyone enter it. There was a gathering of the nobles and notables of the countryside, and Prince Bran feasted them in his hall.

A woman came and stood in the doorway of the hall. None knew how she had come there. She was fairer than any woman that Bran or any of the nobles or notables present had ever seen. Her garb was strange; no woman of that part of the country had ever worn a garb such as this woman had on. In her hand she held a branch; white blossoms were on it, and a fragrance came from them. She held the branch towards where Bran sat on his high seat, and as she did the woman chanted this lay to him:

> Crystal and silver
> The branch that to you I show:
> 'Tis from a wondrous isle—
> Distant seas close it;

Glistening around it
The sea-horses hie them:
Emne of many shapes,
Of many shades, that island.

They who that island near
Mark a stone standing:
From it a music comes,
Unheard-of, enchanting.
They who that music hear
In clear tones answer—
Hosts sing in choruses
To its arising.

A folk that through ages long
Know no decaying,
No death nor sickness, nor
A voice raised in wailing.
Such games they play there—
Coracle on wave-ways
With chariot on land contends—
How swift the race is!

Only in Emne is
There such a marvel—
Treason and wounding gone
And sorrow of parting!
Who to that island comes,
And hears in the dawning
The birds, shall know all delight,
All through the ages!

To him, down from a height,
Will come bright-clad women,
Laughing and full of mirth—
Lovely their coming!
Freshness of blossom fills
All the isle's mazes;
Crystals and dragon-stones
Are dropped in its ranges!

But all my song is not
For all who have heard me;

Only for one it is:
Bran, now bestir you!
Heeding the message brought,
In this, my word,
Seeing the branch I show,
Leave you a crowd.

She finished her lay; she held up the branch that was in her hand so that Bran saw the blossoms upon it and felt the fragrance that came from the blossoms. Then she was seen no more. Nor Bran nor any of the company that were in the hall knew how she had gone from where she had been.

When Prince Bran went abroad the next day he heard music whether he stood still or whether he walked on. A wide space was before him, and in it he saw neither man nor woman. He went upon a mound; he stood there and looked towards the sea. Still he could see no one, neither man nor woman. And yet the music was around him; it quieted all stir within him; he sat down upon the mound, and there he slept.

And in his sleep he saw the woman who had appeared with the branch in her hand. "Arouse thee," she said to him in his dream. "Be no longer unheeding, no longer unready. Launch thy ship upon the sea and sail on until thou dost come to the island I sang to thee about."

So Bran made ready his ship. Thrice nine companions he took with him, and over each of the nine he set one of his foster-brothers. They launched the ship from an inlet in their own territory, and they sailed their ship into the outer sea. For two days and two nights they saw only the waves and the monsters of the deep around them. On the third day they saw a sight that was stranger than the sight of any of the monsters of the deep: they saw a chariot coming across the surface of the sea.

The chariot was driven by a man of resplendent appearance; the horses yoked to it came on as if they were galloping over the surface of a plain. When the chariot came near the ship the man who was in it reined his horses and spoke to those who were sailing across the sea.

And this is what that resplendent charioteer said to Bran and his companions, "Manannan MacLer, the Lord of the Sea, am I who speak to thee. I go into your land to seek a queen who will bear a son to me; his teacher I will be, and he shall be beloved by the mortal and the immortal folk. He shall have wisdom and be able to disclose the mysteries without fear. He shall be a dragon before the hosts of battle, a wolf in the forest, an antlered stag upon the plain; he shall be a salmon of changing hues in the river, a seal in the sea, a white swan upon the shore; Mongan he shall be named." Then Manannan chanted a lay to Bran, bidding him sail on, and telling him that he would soon come to the islands where the immortal folk were.

Manannan went over the waves in his chariot, and Bran and his companions sailed on. They came to an island from which a marvellous fragrance was blowing. They saw blossoming trees that grew to the edge of the water. They saw women upon the island, and they saw one who was a queen amongst them. Bran knew the queen, for she was the one who had appeared to him in his royal house, she was the one who had borne the branch with the blossoms. The queen cried to him from the island, "Come, Prince Bran, and land, for thou art welcome!"

But Bran and his companions were fearful of making a landing; they would have sailed off. Then the queen threw a ball of thread towards the ship. Bran caught it, and the thread held to the palm of his hand. The queen kept the other end of the thread, and she began to wind it. As she wound it she drew Bran and his ship to the island. Then Bran and his companions landed.

They went into the high house that was upon the island. There were couches there—couches enough for Bran and his companions. They were entertained there by the queen and her women. The mariners took the queen's women for their companions, and the queen was with Bran.

On the island were all the marvels of which the queen had chanted to Bran when she stood in the doorway of his hall. And this island was one of fifty islands, each one of them larger than Ireland. Silver-cloud Plain. Plain of Sports, Bountiful Land, Gentle Land, were some of the names that these islands bore. All who were on them lived without fear of death, without treachery, without pain of parting.

Again the queen chanted a lay of the marvels of that land. She chanted it to Bran as she stood beside him outside of her own high house:

> Age-old, and yet
> It bears the white blossom,
> This tree wherein
> Birds' songs are loud.
> Hear! with the hours
> The birds change their singing—
> But always 'tis gladness—
> Welcome their strain!
>
> Look where the yellow-maned
> Horses are speeding!
> Look where the chariots
> Are turning and wheeling!
> Silver the chariots
> On the plain yonder;
> On the plain nigh us,
> Chariots of bronze!
>
> And from our grounds,
> Cultivated, familiar,
> No sound arises
> But is tuned for our ear.
> Splendour of colour
> Is where spread the hazes;
> Drops hair of crystal
> From the waves' manes!
>
> And of the many-coloured
> Land, Ildatach,
> We dream when slumber
> Takes us away.
> 'Tis like the cloud
> That glistens above us,
> A crown of splendour
> On beauty's brow!

So it was on the island that was named Emne. But a day came when the first of his foster-brothers said to Bran, "In Ireland the blossoms go off the trees, and even the leaves are blown away. The ravens come with the storms. But I am fain to see again the land to which such changes come. Thou, Bran, didst bring us here. And if one of us only should desire it, it is right that thou shouldst bring us back to look upon our land again."

Bran knew that it was right that he should do this—that he should let those who desired it look upon their own land again. He spoke to the queen; he told her that he would have to bring the mariners to within sight of the land of Ireland. Bitterly grieved was the queen when he told her this. But she gave him permission to go. "Let no one," she said, "neither you nor any of your companions set foot upon the ground of your own country. And when you have looked upon that changing land, return; come to me here in the Land of the Everliving." Bran told her that he would sail only to within sight of the land, and that when he and his companions had looked upon it, they would turn their ship back.

The ship that had brought them to the island was still within a creek there. Nothing had changed on the ship; not a tear was in a sail, not a splinter was off an oar. The mariners went into the ship, and they sailed off. When they had sailed a little way an island appeared before them. They drew near to it, and they saw upon it a multitude of folk. All were playing games, all were merry, all were laughing. Bran sent one of his foster-brothers upon the island. They waited for him to return with tidings from the people.

But they waited for him in vain. For no sooner had this foster-brother of Bran's gone upon the shore than he joined in the sports of the multitude; when he turned his face towards his fellows on the ship they saw that he was laughing happily. Not for all the signals they made would he return to them. Then Bran ordered his companions to sail on, leaving this foster-brother of his on the Island of Merriment.

They sailed on; they sailed to where the seas became misty. They sailed on and they saw the mist around Ireland. Then they sailed to that part of the north where Prince Bran's territory was.

And when they were able to look upon that territory, they saw a throng of people near the shore. There was an assembly there of the people of the countryside. The mariners shouted to the people from the ship. "Bran, the prince of this territory, his foster-brothers, and the men who sailed with him are here," they cried.

"We know no one of that name," the spokesman of the people said, "but in our old stories Prince Bran is spoken of as one who made a voyage overseas."

When Bran heard that said he bade the mariners turn the ship away from the shore. But the foster-brother who had desired so greatly to see the land of Ireland sprang from the ship and dashed through the water to the shore. The people went to where he landed and drew him amongst them. But even as they touched him he fell upon the shingle.

The people drew away from that man. Those who were upon the ship saw him lying there; as they looked upon him it seemed to them that he was like one who had been dead and buried for an age.

Then Bran spoke from the ship to the people upon the shore. He told them all that had befallen him and his companions since they had sailed from that place—a wondrous story it was to those who heard him tell it. And the learned who were amongst them wrote down in Ogham the chants that Bran had heard from the queen of the island. Then he bade the people farewell. He sailed back over the sea with his companions, and from that day to this there has been neither tale nor tidings of Prince Bran.

WELSH

PWYLL, PRINCE OF DYFED AND HIS VISIT TO ANNWFN, THE REALM OF FAËRIE

It is told of Pwyll, Prince of Dyfed, that once he went hunting in Glyn Cuch, and that having loosed his hounds in the wood and sounded his horn, he found that his companions were no longer with him, and that as he went on he heard the cry of other hounds, a cry different from that of his own, and coming in the opposite direction.

It is told of Pwyll that he found himself in a glade in the wood forming a level plain, and that as his hounds came to the edge of the glade, he saw a stag before the hounds that were not his. And lo! as it reached the middle of the glade, these hounds overtook it and brought the stag down. And Pwyll stayed to look on the colour of the hounds rather than to look upon the stag: of all the hounds he had

ever seen in the world, he had never seen any that were like unto these. For their hair was of a brilliant shining white, and their ears were red; and as the whiteness of their bodies shone, so did the redness of their ears glisten. But after he had looked upon them for a while, he drove them off, and he set his own hounds upon the stag.

As he was setting on his hounds he saw a horseman coming towards him; he had a hunting horn round his neck, he was in a hunting garb of grey woollen, and he was mounted upon a large light-grey steed. As the horseman came near he spoke to Pwyll, saying, "Chieftain, I know who thou art, but I salute thee not." "Peradventure," said Pwyll, "art thou of such state that thou shouldst not salute me?" "Verily," answered the other, "it is not my state, great as it is, that prevents my saluting thee." "What is it, then, O chieftain?" asked Pwyll. "Thine own discourtesy and rude behaviour," answered the stranger.

Then said Pwyll, "What discourtesy and rude behaviour hast thou seen in me, O chieftain?" "Greater discourtesy I never saw in any man," said the other, "than to drive away the hounds that were killing the stag and to set on it thine own hounds." "O chieftain," said Pwyll, "all that can be done I will do to redeem thy friendship, for I perceive that thou art of noble kind." "A crowned king am I in the land that I come from," said the stranger. "Lord," said Pwyll, "show me how I may redeem thy friendship."

Said the stranger, "I am Arawn, a king of Annwfn. Thou canst win my friendship by championing my cause. Know that Annwfn has another king, a king who makes war upon me. And if thou shouldst go into my realm and fight that king thou shouldst overthrow him, and the whole of the realm would be mine." "Lord," said Pwyll, "instruct me; tell me what thou wouldst have me do, and I will do it to redeem thy friendship."

Then said Arawn, King of Annwfn, "I will make a firm friendship with thee, and this I will do. I will send thee to Annwfn in my stead, and I will give thee the fairest lady thou didst ever behold to be thy companion; I will put my form and semblance upon thee, so that not a page of the chamber, nor an officer, nor any other man that has always followed me shall know that it is not I. And this shall be for the space of a year from to-morrow, and then we shall meet in this place."

"Yea, Lord," said Pwyll, "but when I have been there for the space of a year, by what means shall I discover him of whom thou speakest?" "One year from this night," said the King of Annwfn, "is the time fixed for combat between him and me. Be thou at the ford in my likeness. With one stroke that thou givest him he will lose his life. And if he should ask thee to give another stroke, do not give it, no, not if he entreat thee even. If thou shouldst give him another stroke he will be able to fight thee the next day as well as ever." "If I go into thy realm," said Pwyll, "and stay there in thy semblance for a year and a day, what shall I do concerning my own dominion?" "I will cause that no one in all thy dominion, neither man nor woman, shall know that I am not thou, and I will go there in thy stead." "Gladly then," said Pwyll, "will I set forward." "Clear be thy path, and nothing shall detain thee, until thou come into my dominion, and I myself will be thy guide." And saying this, the King of Annwfn, who had come into the wood with his hounds for no other purpose than to bring Pwyll into his realm on that day, conducted him until he came in sight of the palace and its dwellings.

"Behold," he said, "the court and the kingdom; all is in thy power. Enter the court; there is no one there who will know thee, and when thou seest what service is done there, thou wilt know the customs of the court." And when he had said this the man who had been with Pwyll went from his sight.

So Pwyll, Prince of Dyfed, went forward to the court, and when he came there, he beheld sleeping-rooms, and halls, and chambers, and the most beautiful buildings ever seen. And he went into the hall to disarray, and there came youths and pages and disarrayed him, and all as they entered saluted him. And two knights came and drew his hunting-dress from about him, and clothed him in a vesture of silk and gold. And the hall was prepared, and he saw the household enter in. And with them came in likewise the queen, and she was the fairest woman he had ever yet beheld. She had on a yellow robe of shining satin. He spoke with her, and her speech was the wisest and the most cheerful he had ever listened to. She was his queen for the year he was there, and of all the courts of kings on the earth this court of Annwfn was, to the mind of Pwyll, the best supplied with food and drink, with vessels of gold and with royal jewels.

A year went by. Every day for Pwyll there was hunting and minstrelsy, there was feasting and discourse with wise and fair companions. And then there came the day on which the combat of the kings was to take place, and even in the farthest part of the realm the people were mindful of that day.

Pwyll went to the ford where the combat was to be, and the nobles of Arawn's court went with him. And when they came to the ford they saw that Havgan, the king against whom the battle was to be, was coming from the other side. Then a knight rose and spake, saying, "Lords, this is a combat between two kings, and between them only. Each claimeth of the other his land and territory. This combat will decide it. And do all of you stand aside and leave the fight to be between the kings."

Thereupon Pwyll in the semblance of Arawn approached Havgan. They were in the middle of the ford when they encountered. Pwyll struck Havgan on the centre of the boss of his shield, so that his shield was broken in two, and his armour was broken, and Havgan himself was flung on the ground over the crupper of his horse, and he received a deadly blow. "O chieftain," he cried, "what right didst thou have to cause my death? I was not injuring thee in any thing; I know not wherefore thou shouldst slay me. But since thou hast begun to slay me, complete thy work." "Ah, chieftain," said Pwyll, "I may yet repent of what I have done to thee. But I will not strike thee another blow." "My lords," said Havgan then, "bear me hence, for my death has come, and I shall be no more able to uphold you." "My nobles," said he who was in the likeness of Arawn, "take counsel, and let all who would be my subjects now come to my side. It is right that he who would come humbly should be received graciously, but he that doth not come with obedience shall be compelled by force of swords." "Lord," said the nobles, "there is no king over the whole of Annwfn but thee." And thereupon they gave him homage. And Pwyll, in the likeness of Arawn, went through all the realm of Annwfn, and he received submission from those who had been Havgan's subjects, so that the two halves of the kingdom were in his power.

Thereupon he went to keep his tryst with Arawn. When he came into the glade in the wood the King of Annwfn was there to meet him, and each rejoiced to see the other. "Verily," said Arawn, "may Heaven reward thee for what thou hast done for me. When thou comest thyself to thine own dominions," said he, "thou wilt see what I have done for thee."

Then Arawn, King of Annwfn, gave Pwyll back his own proper semblance, and he himself took on his own. Arawn went back to the realm of Annwfn, and Pwyll, Prince of Dyfed, went back to his own country and his own dominion, and was lord once more of the seven Cantrevs of Dyfed.

And after he had been a while in his own country and dominion, Pwyll inquired of his nobles how his rule had been in the year that was past, compared with what it had been before. "Lord," said his nobles all, "thy wisdom was never so great before, and thou wast never so kind nor so free in bestowing gifts, and thy justice was never more worthily shown than in this year." "By Heaven," said Pwyll, "for all the good you have enjoyed, you should thank him who hath been with you, for this is the way matters have been." And thereupon Pwyll related to his nobles all that had happened. "Verily, Lord," they said, "render thanks unto Heaven that thou hast made so good a friendship."

After that the friendship between Pwyll and Arawn was made even stronger. Each sent unto the other horses, and greyhounds, and hawks, and such jewels as they thought would be pleasing to each other. And by reason of his having dwelt a year in Annwfn he lost the name of Prince of Dyfed, and he was called Pwyll, Head of Annwfn, from that time forward.

MATH, THE SON OF MATHONWY

I. THE TREACHERY OF GWYDION AND GILVAETHWY

To Pryderi, the son of Pwyll, the King of Annwfn sent as gift a drove of swine. Pryderi then had rule in the South, and Math, the son of Mathonwy, had rule in the North. To Math, the son of Mathonwy, went Gwydion. "Lord," said Gwydion, "I have heard that there have come into the South some animals such as were never known in this island before." "What are they called?" "Pigs, Lord." "And what kind of animals are they?" "They are small animals, and their flesh is better than the flesh of oxen." "Who owneth them?" "Pryderi, the son of Pwyll; they were sent him from Annwfn by Arawn, the King of Annwfn." "And by what means may they be obtained from him?" "I know a way by which they may be obtained. I will go as one of twelve, each of us in the guise of a bard, and we will obtain the swine from Pryderi." "Go forward, then," said Math, the son of Mathonwy, to Gwydion, his sister's son.

But it was not so much to obtain the swine from Pwyll's son as to do a wrong to Math, the son of Mathonwy, that Gwydion offered to go to where Pryderi had his court. For Gwydion's brother had fallen deeply in love with a maiden who was close to Math, and the only way he might obtain her was by bringing Math, the son of Mathonwy, into war.

For it was this way with Math, the son of Mathonwy: he could not exist unless his feet were in the lap of a maiden. Only when he was engaged in war could he separate himself from the maiden foot-holder. Now Goewin was the maiden who was with him at this time, and she was the fairest maiden who was known in Arvon. Gilvaethwy, the son of Math's sister and the brother of Gwydion, set his affections upon Goewin, and loved her so that he knew not what he should do because of her, and therefore, behold! his hue, and his aspect, and his spirits changed for love of her, so that it was not easy to know him.

One day his brother Gwydion gazed steadfastly upon him. "Youth," he said, "what aileth thee?" "Why," replied Gilvaethwy, "what seest thou in me?" "I see," said his brother, "that thou hast lost thine aspect and thy hue; what, therefore, aileth thee?" "My lord brother," answered Gilvaethwy, "that which aileth me, it will not profit me that I should show to any." "What may it be, my soul?" "Thou knowst that Math, the son of Mathonwy, hath this property, that if men whisper together in a tone how low soever, if the wind meet it, it becomes known to him." "Yes," said Gwydion. "Now hold thy peace. I know thine intent."

Then Gilvaethwy, when he found that his brother knew his intent, gave the heaviest sigh in the world. "Be silent, and sigh not," said Gwydion to him. "It is not thereby that thou wilt succeed. I will cause a war," he said, "that will separate Math, the son of Mathonwy, from his maiden foot-holder." It was then that Gwydion went before

Math and obtained permission from him to go seek the swine owned by Pryderi.

Now he and Gilvaethwy departed with ten men with them, and they were all in the guise of bards. They came to the court, and they were received joyfully by Pryderi, the son of Pwyll, and Gwydion was placed beside Pryderi that night.

Said Prince Pryderi, "Gladly would I hear a tale from one of your men yonder." "Lord," said Gwydion, "we have a custom that the first night we come to the court of a prince, the chief of song recites a tale. And gladly will I recite one for you." So Gwydion recited, and diverted all the court that night with tales and pleasant discourse, and he charmed everyone, and it pleased Pryderi to talk with him. And after a while Gwydion said to Pryderi, "Lo, now! My errand! It is to crave from thee the animals that were sent thee from Annwfn." "Verily," said Pryderi, "that were the easiest thing in the world to grant thee, were it not that there is a covenant between me and my land concerning these animals. And the covenant is that they shall not go from me till they have produced double their number in this land." "Lord," said Gwydion then, "give me not the swine to-night, but neither refuse them to me." And so Pryderi, if he did not give them, did not refuse the swine to Gwydion that night.

So Gwydion betook him to the magic arts that he knew, and he began to work a charm. And he caused twelve steeds to appear, and twelve black greyhounds, each of them white-breasted, and having upon them twelve collars and twelve leashes, such as no one who saw them could believe to be other than gold. And upon the steeds were twelve saddles, and every part which should have been of metal was entirely of gold, and the bridles were of the same workmanship. Then, with the steeds and the hounds, Gwydion appeared before Pryderi.

"Lord," said he, "behold! here is a release for thee from the word thou spakest last night concerning the swine—that thou couldst neither give them nor sell them. Thou mayst exchange them for that which is better. And I will give thee these twelve horses, all caparisoned as they are, with their saddles and their bridles, and these twelve greyhounds, with their collars and their leashes as thou seest." Then Pryderi and his council agreed to take the steeds and hounds, and let

Gwydion take the swine. This was done. And all that Gwydion had given was formed out of fungus.

Gwydion and Gilvaethwy and their men took their leave and went forward swiftly with the swine. "It is needful we journey with speed," said Gwydion. "The illusion will not last but from a certain hour to the same hour to-morrow." They hurried on, and they came within Math's dominion, and they made a sty for the swine; they proceeded, and they came before Math, the son of Mathonwy. And as soon as they came before him lo! the trumpets sounded, and the host of Pryderi was advancing into Gwynedd, Math's dominion.

And, lo! there was the tumult of war in Gwynedd. Then Math, the son of Mathonwy, went forth to meet Pryderi; Gwydion and Gilvaethwy went with him. But at night Gilvaethwy and Gwydion returned; Gilvaethwy took the couch of Math, the son of Mathonwy. And while he turned out the other damsels from the room discourteously, he made Goewin unwillingly remain.

When these two brothers saw the day they went back to where Math, the son of Mathonwy, was with his host. Then the battle began, and Pryderi's host was forced to flee. Then Pryderi and Gwydion fought in single combat. And by force of strength and fierceness, and by the magic and charms of Gwydion, Pryderi, the son of Pwyll, was slain. Then Math, the son of Mathonwy, went back to his court, while Gwydion and Gilvaethwy went the circuit of his lands.

Math went within his chamber, and caused a place to be prepared for him whereon to recline, so that he might put his feet in the maiden's lap. "Lord," said Goewin, "seek now another to hold thy feet, for I am not now a maiden. An attack was made unawares upon me, and by thy nephews, Lord, the sons of thy sister, Gwydion and Gilvaethwy: unto me they did wrong, and unto thee dishonour." "Verily," said Math, the son of Mathonwy, "I will do the utmost in my power concerning this matter. First I will cause thee to have compensation, and then I will have amends made to myself. As for thee, I will take thee to be my wife, and the possessions of my dominions will I give into thy hands."

And Gwydion and Gilvaethwy came not near the court, but stayed at the confines of the land until it was forbidden to give them meat and drink. Then, at last, they came before Math. "Lord," they said, "we are at thy will." "By my will I would not have lost my warriors. You cannot compensate me my shame, setting aside the death of Pryderi. But since ye came hither at my will, I shall begin your punishment forthwith." So said Math, the son of Mathonwy.

II. THE TRANSFORMATIONS OF GWYDION AND GILVAETHWY

He took his magic wand, and he struck Gilvaethwy, so that he became a deer, and he seized upon Gwydion hastily lest he should escape from him. He struck him with the same magic wand, and he became a deer also. "Since now ye are in bonds, I will that ye go forth together and be companions, and possess the nature of the animals whose form ye bear. And this day twelvemonth come hither to me."

At the end of a year from that day, lo! there was a loud noise under the wall, and the barking of the dogs of the palace together with the noise. "Look," said Math the son of Mathonwy, "what is without." "Lord," said one, "I have looked; there are there two deer and a fawn with them." Then Math arose and went out. And when he came he beheld the three animals. He lifted up his wand. "As ye were deer last year, be ye wild hogs each and either of you, for the year that is to come." And thereupon he struck them with his magic wand. "The young one I will take and cause to be baptized," he said. "Be ye of the nature of wild swine," he said. "And this time twelvemonth be ye here under the wall."

At the end of the year the barking of dogs was heard under the wall of the chamber. And Math arose and went forth, and when he came forth he beheld three beasts: he saw two wild hogs of the woods and a young one with them. "Truly," said Math, "this one I will take and cause to be baptized. Now as for you, as ye were wild hogs last year, be ye wolves each and either of you for the year that is to come." Thereupon he struck them with his magic wand, and they became wolves. "And be ye of like nature with the animals whose semblance ye bear, and return here this day twelvemonth beneath this wall."

And at the same day at the end of the year, he heard a clamour and a barking of dogs under the wall of the chamber. And Math arose and went forth. And when he came, behold! he saw two wolves, and a cub with them. "This one I will take," said Math, "and I will cause him to be baptized." So the three that were the fawn, the young hog, and the wolf-cub were baptized, and the names given them were Hydwn, Hychdwn, and Bleiddwn, and they were the sons of Gilvaethwy.

Then Gwydion and Gilvaethwy he struck with his magic wand, and they resumed their own nature. "Oh, men," said he, "for the wrong that ye did unto me sufficient has been your punishment and your dishonour." And he said to those who were around him, "Prepare now precious ointment for these men, and wash their heads, and equip them." This was done, and the brothers, the sons of Math's sister, were men that he could speak with once more.

III. GWYDION AND ARIANRHOD

A day came when Math, the son of Mathonwy, said to Gwydion, his councillor, "What maiden shall I seek that my feet may be in her lap?" "Lord," said Gwydion, "it is easy to give thee counsel in this matter; seek Arianrhod, the daughter of Don, thy niece, thy sister's daughter."

Then Gwydion brought Arianrhod before him. "Ha, damsel," said Math, "art thou a maiden?" "I know not, Lord, other than I am." He took up his magic wand, and bent it. "Step over this," said he, "and I shall know if thou art a maiden." She stepped over the magic wand. There were born then two children. Math took one and had him baptized. Gwydion took the other and hid him in a chest.

The boy that was baptized, as soon as they baptized him he plunged into the sea. And immediately when he was in the sea, he took its nature, and swam as well as the best fish that was therein. And for that reason was he called Dylan, the Son of Wave. Beneath him no wave ever broke.

As Gwydion lay one morning on his bed awake, he heard a cry in the chest at the foot of his bed; it was not loud, but it was such that he could hear it. He rose in haste, and opened the chest, and when he opened it, he beheld an infant boy stretching out his arms to him. He took up the boy in his arms, and he carried him to a place where he knew there was a woman that could nurse him. That

year he was nursed by her, and the second year he was a big child
and able to go to the court by himself. Gwydion took charge of him,
and the boy became familiar with him, and loved him better than
anyone else. The boy was reared at the court until he was four years
old, when he was as big as though he had been eight.

Now Gwydion with the boy following him came to the castle of
Arianrhod. Arianrhod rose up to meet Gwydion, and greeted him, and
bade him welcome. "Who is the boy that followeth thee?" she asked.
"He is thy son." "Why shouldst thou shame me thus?" said Arianrhod. "What afflicts thee is that thou canst no longer be called a
maiden," said Gwydion to her, "but unless thou suffer dishonour
greater than that of bringing up a boy like this, small will be thy
disgrace." "What name has he?" "As yet he has no name." "Verily,"
said Arianrhod, "I lay this destiny upon him, that he shall be nameless
until he receives a name from me."

The next day Gwydion arose and took the boy with him, and went
to walk on the sea-shore. And there he saw sedges and sea-weed, and
by his magic and the charms that he made, he turned them into a
boat. And out of dry sticks and sedges he made leather, and he coloured the leather in such a way that no one ever saw leather more
beautiful than it. He put a sail on the boat, and he had the boy sail
with him in it to the port of the castle of Arianrhod. He began forming
shoes and stitching them till he was observed from the castle. "What
men are those in yonder boat?" said Arianrhod to those who were
about her. "They are cordwainers," she was told. "Go, then," said
she, "and see what kind of leather they have, and what kind of work
they can do."

The messengers came back and told her that the leather that
they in the boat had was beautiful, and that no one ever did better
work than they did. "Well," said Arianrhod, "take the measure of
my foot, and desire the cordwainer to make shoes for me." Gwydion
made the shoes for her, yet not according to the measure, but larger.
"These are too large," said she, "but he shall receive their value.
Let him also make some that are smaller than these." He made others
that were much smaller than her foot and sent them to her. "Tell him
that these will not go upon my feet," said she. They went and told
Gwydion this. "Verily," said he, "I will not make her shoes unless

I see her foot." And this was told to Arianrhod. "Truly," said she, "I will go unto him."

So she went down to the boat, and when she came there Gwydion was shaping shoes and the boy was stitching them. And behold! a wren stood upon the deck of the boat, and the boy shot at it, and hit the wren on the leg between the sinew and the bone. Then Arianrhod smiled. "Verily," said she, "with what a sure hand he shoots the bird." Lleu Llaw Gyffes were the words she uttered. "Lion of the Sure Hand is a good name," said Gwydion, "and you, Arianrhod, have given that name to your son."

Then the work disappeared in sea-weed and sedges. "Well," said Arianrhod, "I will lay this destiny upon the boy, that he shall never have armour nor arms until I invest him with them." "By Heaven," said Gwydion, "let thy malice be what it will, Lleu shall have arms."

He taught the boy until he could manage any horse; Lleu was perfect in features, and strength, and stature. But he languished through the want of arms. "Ah, youth," said Gwydion on a certain day, "we will go to-morrow on an errand together. Be therefore more cheerful than thou hast been." "That I will," said the youth.

Next morning, at the dawn of day, they arose. They went towards the castle of Arianrhod. "Porter," said Gwydion to him who was at the gate, "go thou in and say that there are here bards from Glamorgan." And the porter went in. "The welcome of Heaven be unto them, let them come in," said Arianrhod.

So they entered, and their shapes were not their own, so that Arianrhod did not know them. And in the early twilight Gwydion arose, and he called unto him his magic and his power. And by the time that the day dawned, there resounded through the land uproar, and trumpets, and shouts. When it was now day Gwydion and Lleu heard a knocking at the door of their chamber, and therewith Arianrhod asking that it might be opened. Up rose the youth and opened the door to her, and she entered. "Ah, good men," said she, "in evil plight are we in this castle." "Yes, truly," said Gwydion, "we have heard the trumpets and the shouts." "What can we do," said she, "against those who come against us?" "Lady," said Gwydion, "there is no other counsel than to close the castle upon us, and to defend it as best we may." "May Heaven reward you," said Arianrhod, "and do you defend the castle. Here you have plenty of arms."

And thereupon she went forth for the arms, and she returned with suits of armour for two men with her. "Lady," said Gwydion, "do you arm the youth, and I will arm myself with the help of your maidens. Lo! I hear the tumult of the men approaching." "I will arm the youth gladly." Thereupon she armed Lleu fully, and that right cheerfully. "Hast thou finished arming the youth?" said Gwydion. "I have finished," she answered. "I likewise have finished," said Gwydion. "Let us now take off our arms, we have no need of them." "Wherefore?" she asked. "There is no army." "Whence, then, was the tumult?" "The tumult was but to break the prophecy and to obtain arms for this youth, thy son. And now he has got arms without any thanks to thee." "By Heaven," said Arianrhod, "thou, Gwydion, art a wicked man. Many a one might have lost his life through the uproar thou hast caused in this territory to-day. Still I will lay a destiny upon this youth. He shall never a wife of a race that now inhabits this earth." "Verily," said Gwydion, "thou wert ever a malicious woman. But as I have succeeded before, so I shall succeed again, and Lleu, thy son, shall have a wife."

IV. The Maiden Made of Flowers

So Gwydion, taking the youth with him, went to Math, the son of Mathonwy, and complained to him most bitterly of Arianrhod. "Well," said Math to Gwydion, "we will seek, I and thou, to form a wife for him out of flowers. He has now come to man's stature, and he is the comeliest youth that was ever beheld." So they took the blossoms of the oak, and the blossoms of the broom, and the blossoms of the meadow-sweet, and produced from them a maiden, the fairest and most graceful that man ever saw. And they baptized her, and gave her the name of Blodeuwedd.

And after they had feasted and Blodeuwedd had become the bride of Lleu, Gwydion said to Math, "It is not easy for a man to maintain himself without possessions." "Of a truth," said Math, "it is not, and I will give this young man possessions." And Math gave Lleu a Cantrev

to rule over, and the youth built a palace, and there he and Blodeuwedd dwelt, and Lleu and his rule were beloved by all.

Now a day came when he went to visit Math. And on the day he
set out for Math's court, Blodeuwedd walked in the grounds of the
palace. And she heard the sound of a horn. And after the sound of
the horn, behold! a tired stag went by, with hounds and huntsmen
following it. After the hounds and the huntsmen there came a crowd
of men on foot. "Send a page," said she, "to ask who the chief of
these men may be." "Gronw, the Lord of Penllyn, is chieftain here,"
the page was told. And he came back and told this to Blodeuwedd.

Gronw pursued the stag, and by the river he overtook the stag
and killed it. And what with flaying the stag and baiting his dogs, he
was there until the night began to close in on him. As the day departed
and the night drew near, he came to the gate of the court. "Verily,"
said Blodeuwedd, "the chieftain will speak ill of us if we let him
at this hour depart to another land without inviting him in." "Yes,
truly, lady," said those who were with her, "it will be most fitting to
invite him in."

Then went the messengers to meet him and bid him in. And he
accepted the bidding gladly, and came to the court, and Blodeuwedd
went to meet him, and greeted him, and bade him welcome. "Lady,"
said he, "Heaven repay thee thy kindness."

Then Blodeuwedd looked upon him, and from the moment that she
looked upon him she became filled with love for Gronw. And he
gazed on her, and the same thought came unto him as unto her, so
that he could not conceal it from her that he loved her, but he declared
unto her that he did so. Thereupon she was very joyful. And all their
discourse that night was concerning the affection and love which they
felt one for the other, and which in no longer space than one evening
had arisen. And that evening passed they in each other's company.

The next day Gronw sought to depart. But Blodeuwedd said, "I
pray thee go not from me to-day." And that night he tarried also.
They consulted by what means they might always be together. "There
is none other counsel," said he, "but that thou strive to learn from
Lleu in what manner he will meet his death. And this thou must do
under the semblance of solicitude concerning him."

The new day Gronw sought to depart. "Verily," said she, "I will counsel thee not to go from me to-day." "At thy instance will I not go," said he, "albeit, I must say, there is danger that the chieftain who owns this palace may return home." "To-morrow," answered she, "will I indeed permit thee to go forth." The next day he sought to go, and she hindered him not. "Be mindful," said Gronw, "of what I have said unto thee, and converse with him fully, and that under the guise of the dalliance of love, and find out by what means he may come to his death."

That night Lleu returned to his palace. And at night when they went to rest, he spoke to Blodeuwedd once, and he spoke to her a second time. But, for all he said, he could not get from her one word. "What aileth thee?" he said, "art thou well?" "I was thinking," she said, "of that which thou didst never think of concerning me; for I was sorrowful as to thy death, lest thou shouldst go sooner than I." "Heaven reward thy care for me," said he, "but until Heaven take me I shall not easily be slain." "For the sake of Heaven, and for mine, show me how thou mightest be slain. My memory in guarding is better than thine." "I will tell thee gladly," said he.

Then said Lleu, "Not easily can I be slain, except by a wound. And the spear wherewith I am struck must be a year in the forming. Nothing must be done towards it except during the sacrifice on Sundays. And I cannot be slain within a house, nor without. I cannot be slain on horseback nor on foot. Only by making a bath for me by the side of a river, and by putting a roof over the cauldron, and thatching it well and tightly, and bringing a deer, and putting it beside the cauldron. Then if I place one foot on the deer's back, and the other on the edge of the cauldron, whosoever strikes me thus will cause my death." "Well," said Blodeuwedd, "I thank Heaven that it will be easy to avoid this."

But the next day she sent word to Gronw as to how Lleu could be slain. Gronw toiled at making the spear, and that day twelvemonth it was ready. And the very day the spear was ready he caused Blodeuwedd to be informed thereof. "Lord," said she then to Lleu, "I have been thinking how it is possible that what thou didst tell me formerly can be true; wilt thou show me in what manner thou couldst stand at once upon the edge of a cauldron and upon the back of a deer, if I prepare the bath for thee?" "I will show thee," said he.

The next day she spoke thus, "Lord," said she, "I have caused the roof and the bath to be prepared, and lo! they are ready." "Well," said Lleu, "we will go gladly to look at them." They came and looked at the bath. "Wilt thou go into the bath, Lord?" said she. "Willingly will I go in," he answered. So into the bath he went, and he anointed himself. "Lord," said she, "behold! there are deer here." "Well," said he, "cause one of them to be caught and brought here." And the deer was brought. Then Lleu rose out of the bath, and he placed one foot on the edge of the bath and the other on the deer's back.

Gronw was in ambush on a hill. He rose up from his ambush, and he rested on one knee, and flung the poisoned dart and struck Lleu on the side, so that the shaft started out. Thereupon there was a fearful scream, and behold! Lleu flew up in the form of an eagle.

And Gronw and Blodeuwedd went into the palace that night. And the next day Gronw arose and took possession of Lleu's dominion. He ruled over it so that his dominion and Lleu's were under one sway. Then these tidings reached Math, the son of Mathonwy, and heaviness and grief came upon him, and even more of heaviness and grief came upon Gwydion. "Lord," said Gwydion, "I shall never rest until I have tidings of Lleu."

So Gwydion went forth, and in many places, and for a long time he kept up the search for Lleu. One night he alighted at a house, and stayed there that night. The man of the house and his household came in, and last of all there came the swineherd. Said the man of the house to the swineherd, "Well, youth, has thy sow come in to-night?" "She has," said the swineherd. "Where does this sow go?" said Gwydion. "Every day, when the sty is opened, she goes forth and none can catch sight of her, neither is it known whither she goes more than if she sank into the earth." When Gwydion heard this he said, "Wilt thou grant unto me not to open the sty until I am by the sty with thee?" "This I will do right gladly," he answered.

That night they went to rest; and as soon as the swineherd saw the light of day, he awoke Gwydion. And Gwydion arose and dressed himself, and went with the swineherd, and stood beside the sty. Then the swineherd opened the sty. And as soon as he opened it, behold! the sow went forth, and set off with great speed. Gwydion followed her, and she went against the course of a river, and made for a brook, and there she halted and began feeding. Gwydion came under a tree, and looked what it might be the sow was feeding on. And he saw that she was eating putrid flesh. Then he looked up to the top of the tree, and as he looked up he beheld an eagle on the top of the tree, and when the eagle shook itself, there fell vermin and putrid flesh from off it, and these the sow devoured. Then Gwydion sang:

> Oak that grows between the two banks;
> Darkened is the sky and hill!
> Shall I not tell him by his wounds,
> That this is Lleu?

Upon this the eagle came down until he reached the centre of the tree. Then Gwydion sang:

> Oak that grows in upland ground,
> Is it not wetted by the rain? Has it not been drenched
> By nine score tempests?
> It bears in its branches Lleu Llaw Gyffes!

Then the eagle came down till he was on the lowest branch of the tree, and thereupon Gwydion sang:

> Oak that grows beneath the steep;
> Stately and majestic is its aspect!
> Shall I not speak it?
> That Lleu will come to my lap!

Then the eagle came down upon Gwydion's knee. And Gwydion struck him with his magic wand, so that he returned to his own form. No one ever saw a more piteous sight, for Lleu was nothing but skin and bone.

In a year he was healed. Then said Lleu to Math, the son of Mathonwy, "It is full time now that I have retribution of him by whom I have suffered all this woe." "Truly," said Math. Then they called together the whole of Math's dominion. Gwydion went on before Lleu's muster. And when Blodeuwedd heard that he was coming, she took her maidens with her, and fled to the mountain. As for the maidens, as they passed through the river, and went towards a court that was there upon the mountain, through fear they could not proceed except with their faces looking backwards, so that unawares they fell into the lake. Then Gwydion overtook Blodeuwedd. He said unto her, "I will not slay thee, but I will do unto thee worse than that. For I will turn thee into a bird; and because of the shame thou hast done unto Lleu, thou shalt never show thy face in the light of day henceforth. And it shall be the nature of the other birds to attack thee, and to chase thee from wheresoever they may find thee. And thou shalt not lose thy name, but shalt be always called Blodeuwedd." Then he changed her into the owl that is hateful unto all birds, and even now the owl is called Blodeuwedd.

FINNISH

FINNISH

LEMMINKAINEN, HIS DESTRUCTION AND HIS RESTORATION TO LIFE

Into the forest went Lemminkainen. As he went he chanted his Magic Song, "O Tapio, Lord of the Forest, aid me: lead me where I may take my quarry! Nyyrikki, O thou son of the Forest's Lord, red-capped one, mighty hero, make a path for me through your father's domain; clear the ground for me and keep me on the proper roadway!" Lemminkainen, the handsome, the light-stepping one, chanted Magic Songs to win the forest divinities as he went seeking the Elk of Hiisi.

Another Magic Song he chanted: "O Mielikki, Mistress of the Forest, fair-faced, bountiful lady, send the game towards me; turn it into the pathway of the hunter; open the thickets; unlock Tapio's storehouse; make wide the door of his castle in the forest! Do this during this hunting-trip of mine!" Other Magic Songs Lemminkainen chanted as he went through the forest seeking the Elk of Hiisi. "If thou wilt not trouble thyself about me, Mistress of the Forest, charge thy little serving-girls to help me! And thou, Tapio's girl, little maiden of the forest, put the flute to your mouth of honey, whistle through thy pipe so that the Lady of the Forest may rouse herself and harken to my Magic Songs!"

So he went through the forest; but the quarry he sought was not turned towards him. Through the trackless forest he went, across the marshes, over the heaths. At last he went up a mountain; he climbed a knoll; he turned his eyes to the north-west; he turned his eyes to the north; there, across the marshes, he saw Tapio's mansions with their doors and windows all golden.

Then once more the quick-moving, light-stepping Lemminkainen went onward. He dashed through all that lay across his path. Under the very windows of the mansions of the Lord of the Forest he came. Through the windows he saw those whose business it was to dispense the game to the hunters. They were resting; they were lolling; their worst wear they had on them. Under the windows Lemminkainen chanted his Magic Songs:

"Mistress of the Forest, wherefore do you sit here and do you let the others sit here in such shabbiness? You are loathsome to behold! Yet when I went through the forest I saw three castles—one a wooden one, one a bone one, one a stone one; they had six windows, all bright, all golden; they who were within had rustling, golden garments on! Re-array as before thyself and thy household! Put away now your birch-bark shoes, your old garments, your disgusting shabbiness! Mistress of the Forest, put on thy garments of good fortune! Put thy golden bracelets on thy wrists, thy golden rings on thy fingers, a head-dress of gold put on! Put gold coins in thy hair, gold rings in thine ears, gold beads around thy neck! Long and wearily have I wandered hereabouts; I wander for nothing; the quarry I seek is not to be seen by me!

"Greybeard with the pine-leaf hat," he chanted, "with the cloak of moss! Re-array the woods; give the aspens their greyness, give the alders a robe of beauty, clothe the pine-trees in silver, adorn the fir-trees with gold, and the birch-trees with golden blossoms. Make it as in the former years when days were better, when the waste-places flowed with honey. O daughter of Tapio, Tuulikki, gracious virgin, drive the game this way! Take a switch; strike the game on their haunches; drive the game towards the one who seeks for it and waits for it! Master of Tapio's mansions, mistress of Tapio's mansions, make wide the doors, send forth the game that has been shut in!"

So Lemminkainen chanted; for a week he ranged through the forest. His Magic Songs appeased the Lord of the Forest, delighted the Mistress of the Forest, and made glad the hearts of all the Forest Maidens. To where the Elk of Hiisi had his lair they went; they drove forth the Elk; they turned it in the direction of the one who waited for it.

Over the Elk Lemminkainen threw his lasso. And when he held the Elk he chanted his Magic Song once more, "Lord of the Forest, Tapio; Mistress of the Forest, Mielikki, come now and take your reward for the good you have done me! Come now and take the gold and silver I scatter on the ground of the forest!" So he chanted; then to the north, to Pohjola, he journeyed with the Elk he had captured. "I have caught the Elk of Hiisi! Come forth now, ancient one of Pohjola; give me your daughter; give me the bride I have come for!"

Louhi, the Mistress of Pohjola, came out of her dwelling, and she looked upon Lemminkainen and the Elk he had captured. "I will give you my daughter, I will give you the bride you have come for, when you capture the Steed of Hiisi, and bring it to me here."

Then Lemminkainen took a golden bridle and a halter of silver; he went through the green and open meadows; he went out upon the plains. No sign he saw of the Steed of Hiisi. He called upon Ukko, the God of the Sky, and he chanted a Magic Song:

"Open the clefts of the Heavens; cast the hail upon the back of Hiisi's Steed; fling ice-blocks upon him that he may race from where he is, that he may come to where I am!" Ukko rent the air; he scattered ice-blocks; they were smaller than a horse's head, but they were bigger than a man's head. They struck the back of Hiisi's Steed. It raced forward. Then Lemminkainen chanted, "Steed of Hiisi, stretch forth thy silver head; push it into this golden bridle! I will never drive thee harshly; with a rope's end I will never smite thee. No, with silver cords I will lead thee, and with a piece of cloth I will drive thee!" So he chanted, and the Steed of Hiisi put forward his head; the golden bridle with the bit of silver went across his head and into his mouth.

Then to the north went Lemminkainen bringing the chestnut steed with the foam-flecked mane. He called to the Mistress of Pohjola, "I have captured the Steed of Hiisi and the Elk of Hiisi. Now give thy daughter to me, give me the bride that I have come for."

But Louhi, the Mistress of Pohjola, answered him, "I will give thee my daughter, I will give thee the bride thou hast come for when thou hast shot with an arrow, and using one arrow only, the white Swan on Tuonela's dark water." Then Lemminkainen took his bow. He went down into Manala's abysses. He went to where Tuoni's murky river flowed. He went to where the waters made a dread whirlpool.

There the cowherd Märkähattu lurked; there the blind man waited for Lemminkainen. When Lemminkainen had come first to Pohjola he had chanted his Magic Songs; he had chanted them against the swordsmen and the young heroes who were there, and he had driven them all away, banning them with his Magic Songs. One old man he had not banned—Märkähattu the cowherd who sat there, his eyes closed in blindness. Lemminkainen had scorned him. "I have not banned thee," he cried, "because thou art so wretched a creature. The worst of cowherds, thou hast destroyed thy mother's children, thou hast disgraced thy sister, thou hast crippled all the horses, thou hast wearied to death the foals." Märkähattu, greatly angered, left the place where Lemminkainen had scorned him; ever since he had waited by the whirlpool for the coming of Lemminkainen.

The white Swan was on the dark river of Tuonela. Lemminkainen drew his bow. As he did, Märkähattu grasped a water-snake; he hurled it; he pierced Lemminkainen with the serpent. Lemminkainen knew no Magic Songs to relieve himself from the wounds made by water-snakes. He sank into the murky river; he was tossed about in the worst of whirlpools; he was dashed down the cataract; the stream brought him into Tuonela.

There Tuoni's bloodstained son, drawing his sword, hewed him into pieces. He hewed him into eight pieces and he flung the pieces into the dark river. "Be tossed about for ever with thy bow and thy arrows, thou who camest to shoot the sacred Swan upon our sacred River!"

Only through his mother could help come to Lemminkainen. She had bided at home, troubled by his long delay in returning. One day she looked up the comb and the hair-brush he had left behind: she saw blood trickling from the comb, blood dripping from the hair-brush. She knew that blood was coming from the body of her son. She gathered up her skirt and she went off to find him.

Valleys were lifted up as Lemminkainen's mother went on; hills were levelled; the high ground sank before her and the low ground was lifted up. She hastened to Pohjola. She came to the door and she questioned the Mistress of Pohjola.

"Whither hast thou sent my son, Lemminkainen?" "I know no tidings of your son. I yoked a steed for him; I fixed a sledge for him, and he started off from my dwelling; perhaps in driving over a frozen lake he sank into it." "Shameless are the lies thou tellst me. Tell me whither thou hast sent him or I will break down the doors of Pohjola." "I fed him; I gave him meat and drink, and I placed him in his boat; he went to shoot the rapids, but what has befallen him I do not know." "Shameless are the lies thou tellst. Tell me whither thou hast sent him or this instant death will come to thee." "Now I will tell thee, now

I will tell thee truly. Lemminkainen went to shoot the secred bird, the Swan on Tuonela's River."

Then his mother went in quest of him; she questioned the trees, she questioned the pathway, she questioned the golden moon in the sky. But the trees, the pathway, the golden moon in the sky, all had their own troubles, and they would take no trouble for any woman's son. She questioned the sun in the heavens, and the sun told her that her son was in Tuonela's River.

Then to the smith Ilmarinen went Lemminkainen's mother. For her Ilmarinen fashioned a rake, a rake with a copper handle and with teeth of steel—a hundred fathoms was the length of the teeth, five hundred fathoms was the length of the handle. To Tuonela's River she went: there she chanted a Magic Song.

She prayed the sun to shine with such strength that the watchers in Manala would sleep and that the powers of Tuonela would be worn out. And the sun stooped upon a crooked birch-tree and shone in his strength so that the watchers of Manala were worn out—the young men slept upon their sword-hilts; the old men slept resting upon their staffs; the middle-aged men, the spearmen, slept resting upon the hafts of their spears. Then Lemminkainen's mother took her rake; she raked the river against the current; once she raked it, and she raked it again. The third time she raked the river she brought up the hat and stockings of her son Lemminkainen. She went into the river, and she waded in its deepest water. She drew up the body with her rake of iron.

Many fragments were wanting to make up the body of Lemminkainen—half of his head, a hand, many little fragments. Life was wanting in the body. But still his mother would not cast it back into the river. Once again she raked Tuonela's deep river, first along it and then across it; his hand she found, half of his head she found, fragments of his backbone she found, and pieces of his ribs.

She pieced all together; the bones fitted, the joints went together. She chanted a Magic Song, praying that Suonetar would weave the veins together, and stitch with her finest needle and her most silken thread the flesh and the sinews that were broken. She sang a Magic Song, praying that Jumala would fix together the bones. Then the veins were knit together, the bones were fastened together, but still the man remained lifeless and speechless.

Then Lemminkainen's mother sang a Magic Song. She bade the bee go forth and find the honey-salve that would give final healing. The bee flew across the moon in the heavens; he flew past the borders of Orion; he flew across the Great Bear's shoulders, and into the dwelling of Jumala the Creator. In pots of silver, in golden kettles was the salve that would give final healing. The bee gathered it and brought it back to Lemminkainen's mother.

With the salve she rubbed him. She called upon her son to rise out of his slumbers, to awaken out of his dreams of evil. Up he rose; out of his dreams he wakened, and speech came back to him. Even then he would have slain the Swan so that he might win a bride in Pohjola. But his mother persuaded him, and his mother drew him back with her to his home. There the bride awaited him whom he had won in another place and on another day, Kyllikki, the Flower of Saari.

ICELANDIC

ICELANDIC

IN THE BEGINNING

In the beginning was Yawning Gap: to one side of it was the Place
of Fog and Mist; to the other side was the Place of Fire. Ginnunga
Gap, Niflheim, Muspellsheim—these were in the beginning. Yawning
Gap filled up with chill streams flowing from the Place of Fog and
Mist; the heat from the Place of Fire turned the chill streams into
mist; out of the mist was formed two beings—Ymir the ancient Giant,
and the cow Audhumla.

Ymir stayed by Audhumla and drank her milk. Giants and Giantesses came from his feet; the race of Giants multiplied. Then another
race appeared. One day Ymir saw Audhumla breathe upon a cliff of
ice and lick with her tongue the place she breathed on. As her tongue
went over and over the place the Giant saw that a figure was being
formed. It was not like a Giant's form; it was more shapely. A head
appeared in the cliff and golden hair fell over the ice. As Ymir looked
upon the being that was being formed he hated him for his beauty.

Audhumla, the giant cow, went on licking the place where she had
breathed. At last a man completely formed stepped from the cliff.
Ymir, the ancient Giant, hated him so much that he would have slain
him then and there. But he knew that if he did this Audhumla would
feed him no more on her milk.

Buri was the name of the one who was formed in the ice-cliff. Buri,
married to one of the Giantesses, had a son. His son, Bur, married to
Bestla, daughter of the Giant Bolthorn, had three sons: they were the
first of the Aesir, the first of the Gods.

Their names were Oithin, Hönir, and Lothur. For a time they
lived in peace with Ymir and his children. Then as the children of
Bur multiplied and the children of Ymir multiplied there was war
between them. The ancient Giant was slain. So huge was Ymir that his
blood when he was slain poured out in such mighty flood that his sons

were all drowned in it, all except the Giant Bergelmir. He was in a boat with his wife when the flood came; they floated away on the flood to the place that came to be called Jotunheim; from them the race of Giants came, and in that place the race of Giants lived.

Now Oithin and his brothers and his sons took the body of Ymir —the vastest body that ever was—and they flung it into Yawning Gap, filling up the great chasm with it. They dug the bones out of the body and they piled them up into mountains; they took the teeth out and they made them into rocks; they took the hair of Ymir and they made it into grasses and forests of trees; out of his hollow skull they made the sky.

Oithin with his brothers and sons did more than this. They took the sparks and the clouds of flame that blew from Muspellsheim and they made them into the sun and moon and all the stars that are in the sky. The sun and the moon were drawn by horses: the sun by Arvak and Alsvith, the Early-waking One and the Fleet One. When Oithin lighted up the world with the sun and the moon, the Giants who were born of Bergelmir and his wife were very wroth: they found two of the fleetest and fiercest of the mighty wolves of Jotunheim, and they set them to follow Sol and Mani, the sun and the moon. And ever afterwards Sol and Mani were pursued by the wolves out of Jotunheim, the place of the Giants.

Oithin, Hönir, and Lothur then made the race of men: Ask and Embla were the names of the first pair made; the Gods made them out of the ash and the elm-tree. Oithin gave them soul and motion, Hönir gave them sense and feeling, Lothur gave them warmth and colour. The Gods made a world for themselves and a world for men. Asgarth was the name of the world they made for themselves; Mithgarth was the name of the world they made for men. And, lest the Giants should come out of Jotunheim and destroy Mithgarth, the Gods set as a fence around it an eyebrow of Ymir's. Out of the flesh of Ymir Dwarfs had come. The Gods made a world for them also: Svartalfaheim, a world that is under Mithgarth.

There was a tree that spread its branches through all the worlds and that had its roots in three of the worlds. That tree was named Yggdrasil. One of its roots was in Asgarth, one was in Jotunheim, and one was in Niflheim that was the World of the Dead. The root that was in Niflheim was beside a well. Therein was the dreadful serpent, Nithogg: Nithogg gnawed for ever at the root of the World Tree, wanting to destroy it. And Ratatosk, the squirrel, ran up and down Yggdrasil making trouble between the eagle that was at the top of the tree and the serpent that was below. He went to tell the serpent how the eagle was bent upon tearing him to pieces, and he went back to tell the eagle how the serpent planned to devour him. Beside the root of the tree in Jotunheim was a well guarded by old Mimir the Wise. Whoever drank out of this well would know all of the things that are to come to pass. And beside the root that was in Asgarth was another well: the three sisters who are the Norns guarded it, and their names were Urth, Verthandi, and Skuld—Past, Present, and Future; they took the water of the well and watered Yggdrasil with it that the Tree of the World might be kept green and strong. This well was called Urda's well. Two swans were on the water of it; they made music that the Dwellers in Asgarth often heard. On the branches of the tree four stags grazed; they shook from their horns the water that fell as rain in Mithgarth. And on the topmost branch of Yggdrasil, the branch that was so high that the Gods themselves could hardly see it, was perched the eagle that the serpent was made to fear. Upon the beak of the eagle a hawk perched, a hawk that saw what the eyes of the eagle could not see.

In Asgarth there were many halls: there was the one that was called Glathsheim, built by the golden-leaved wood, Glasir: here Oithin and the twelve who were his peers had their high seats, and here the banquets of the Gods were held. Here Oithin, the Father of Gods and men, would seat himself, a blue mantle upon him, and a shining helmet shaped like an eagle upon his head. He would sit there, not eating at all, but drinking the wine of the Gods, and taking food from the table which he gave to Geri and Freki, the two wolves that crouched beside his seat. Then there was Vingolf, which had high seats for Frigg, the wife of Oithin, and the Goddesses. There was the hall Heithskjolf, that was roofed all over with silver: from it Oithin could look out upon all the worlds. There was Fensalir, where Frigg sat spinning with golden threads; there was Breithablik, where Baldr the Well-beloved lived with his fair wife, the young Nanna; there was Bilskirnir, where Thor and his wife, Sif, lived. And there was the hall in which those who were heroes amongst men lived and feasted when they had come to Oithin after their deaths in battle: that hall was named Valhall.

Between Asgarth and Mithgarth there was a bridge that was called Bifrost, or Rainbow. It was the strongest and the most lovely of bridges. Upon it was a ruddy gleam that came from the light of a fire that burned always to prevent the Giants from crossing it. Bifrost was to break when the Giants made their way across it and the battle ensued that was to end all things. Heimdal guarded the bridge. He never slept; he was able to hear the grass growing on the ground and the wool of sheep growing upon their backs. He had golden teeth. He could see before him or around him, night or day, for hundred of miles. His dwelling was called Himinbjorg, the Mount of Heaven. One day he would take up the horn that was under the root of Yggdrasil—the Gjallar-horn—and blow upon it. And the sound of the horn would tell the Gods and the Heroes that the Giants were crossing Bifrost and the battle between the Gods and the Giants— the battle that would mean the end of all things—was beginning.

The Aesir had settled in Asgarth and had prevented the Giants destroying Asgarth and Mithgarth. Other foes assailed them. The Wanes came against them and destroyed their seats. Oithin made peace with the Wanes. He gave hostages to them and took hostages from them: Hönir he gave to the Wanes; Njorth he took from them as a hostage. Then there was peace between the Aesir and the Wanes: they joined together; together they opposed the Giants.

THE BUILDING OF THE WALL

Before the peace between the Aesir and the Wanes was made, and before the seats of the Gods had been built up again, a strange being came before the assembly of the Gods. "I know what is in the mind of Oithin," he said. "He would make strong and splendid his city here. I cannot build halls that are beautiful. But I can build great walls that can never be overthrown. Let me build a wall around Asgarth."

"How long will it take you to build a wall that will go around Asgarth?" the Oithin All-Father asked him.

"A year, O Oithin," said the Stranger.

Now Oithin knew that if a great wall were built around it, the Gods would not have to spend all their strength defending Asgarth from the Giants. He thought that no payment that the Stranger could ask would be too much for the building of the wall. The Stranger swore that in a year he would have the great wall built. Then Oithin made oath that the Gods would give him what he asked in payment if the wall was finished to the last stone in a year from that day.

The Stranger went away and came back on the morrow. It was the first day of summer when he started work. He brought no one to help him except a great horse. Now the Gods thought that the horse would do no more than drag blocks of stone for the building of the wall. But the horse did more than this. He set the stones in their places and mortared them together. And day and night, by light and dark, the horse worked; soon a great wall was rising around the halls that the Gods themselves were building.

"What reward will the Stranger ask for the work he is doing for us?" the Gods asked one another.

Oithin went to the Stranger. "We marvel at the work you and your horse are doing for us," he said. "No one can doubt but that the great wall of Asgarth will be built up by the first day of summer. What reward do you claim? We would have it ready for you."

The Stranger turned from the work he was doing, leaving the great horse to pile up the blocks of stone. "O Oithin, Father of the Gods," he said. "The reward I shall ask for my work is the sun and the moon, and the Goddess Freyja for my wife."

When Oithin heard of this price he was terribly angered. He went amongst the other Gods who were then building their shining halls within the great wall, and he told them what reward the Stranger had asked for. The Gods said, "Without the sun and moon the world will wither away." And the Goddesses said, "Without Freyja all will be gloom in Asgarth."

They would have let the wall remain unbuilt rather than let the Stranger have the reward he claimed for the building of it. But one who was in the company of the Gods spoke. He was Loki, a being who only half belonged to the Gods; his father was the Wind Giant. "Let the Stranger build the wall around Asgarth," Loki said, "and

I will find a way to make him give up the hard bargain he has made with the Gods. Go tell him that the wall must be finished by the first day of summer, and that if it is not finished to the last stone on that day, the price he asks will not be given him."

The Gods went to the Stranger and they told him that if the last stone was not laid on the wall by the first day of summer, neither the sun nor the moon nor Freyja would be given him. And now they knew that the Stranger was one of the Giants.

The Giant and his great horse piled up the wall more quickly than before. At night, while the Giant slept, the horse worked on, hauling stones and laying them on the wall with his great forefeet. And day by day the wall around Asgarth grew higher and higher.

But the Gods had no joy in seeing that great wall rise higher and higher around their halls. The Giant and his horse would finish the work by the first day of summer; then he would take the sun and the moon away, and take, too, Freyja, who had come to them from the Wanes, and whom all in Asgarth loved.

But Loki was not disturbed. He kept telling the Gods that he would find a way to prevent him from finishing his work, and thus he would make the Giant forfeit the terrible price he had led Oithin to promise him.

It was three days to summer-time. All the wall was finished except the gateway. Over the gateway a stone was still to be placed. And the Giant, before he went to sleep, bade his horse haul up a great block of stone so that he might put it above the gateway in the morning, and so finish his work two full days before summer.

It happened to be a beautiful moonlit night. Svathilfari, the Giant's great horse, was hauling the largest stone he had ever hauled, when he saw a little mare come galloping towards him. The great horse had never seen so pretty a little mare, and he looked at her with surprise.

"Svathilfari, slave," said the little mare to him, and went frisking past.

Svathilfari put down the stone he was hauling and called to the little mare. She came back to him. "Why do you call me 'Svathilfari, slave'?" said the great horse.

"Because you have to work night and day for your master," said the little mare. "He keeps you working, working, working, and never lets you enjoy yourself. You dare not leave that stone down and come and play with me."

"Who told you I dare not do it?" said Svathilfari.

"I know you daren't do it," said the little mare, and she kicked up her heels and ran across the moonlit meadow.

Now the truth is that Svathilfari was tired of working day and night. When he saw the little mare go galloping off he became suddenly discontented. He left the stone he was hauling on the ground. He looked around and he saw the little mare looking at him. He galloped after her.

He did not catch up with the little mare. She went on swiftly. On she went over the moonlit meadow, turning and looking back now and again at the great Svathilfari, who came heavily after her. Down the mountain-side the mare went, and Svathilfari, who now rejoiced in his liberty, in the freshness of the wind and the smell of the flowers, still followed her. With the morning's light they came near a cave; the little mare went into it. They went through the cave. Then Svathilfari caught up with the little mare, and the two went wandering together, the little mare telling Svathilfari stories of the Dwarfs and the Elves.

They came to a grove and they stayed together in it, the little mare playing so nicely with him that the great horse forgot all about time passing. And while they were in the grove the Giant was going up and down, searching for his great horse.

He had come to the wall in the morning, expecting to put the stone over the gateway and so finish the work. But the stone that was to put the finish on the work was not near. He called for Svathilfari, but the great horse did not come. He went in search of him; he searched all down the mountain-side, and he searched as far across the earth as the Realm of the Giants. But he did not find Svathilfari.

The Gods saw the first day of summer come and the gateway of the wall stand unfinished. They said to each other that if it were not finished by the evening they need not give the sun and moon to the Giant, nor Freyja. The hours of the summer day went past; the Giant did not raise the stone over the gateway. In the evening he came before them.

"Your work is not finished," Oithin said to him. "You forced us to a hard bargain, and now we need not keep it with you. You shall not be given the sun and the moon; neither shall Freyja go with you."

"Only the wall I have built is so strong I would tear it down," said the Giant. He went outside the wall he had built and away from Asgarth. Then Loki returned. He told the Gods how he had transformed himself into a little mare, and how he had led away Svathilfari, the Giant's great horse. The Gods sat in their halls behind the great wall and rejoiced that no enemy could come upon their seats and destroy them. But Thor did not rejoice—Thor, the son of Oithin and Jorth, the champion of the Gods and the guardian of oaths. He spoke in rage about what had been done to cheat the Giant. Oithin did not rejoice: he knew that what had been done would make the Giants their undying enemies, and set them against the Aesir on the day of the great battle.

MIMIR

Oithin went to Mimir to get a draught from the Well of Wisdom —the well that Mimir guarded. He knew well what price Mimir would ask for a draught from his well—he would ask for Oithin's right eye. It was a terrible price; very troubled was All-Father when the price that Mimir would ask was revealed to him.

To be without the sight of his right eye! For all time to be without the sight of his right eye! Almost Oithin would have turned back to Asgarth, giving up his quest for wisdom.

But when he turned to the south he saw towards Muspellsheim: there stood Surt with the Flaming Sword, a terrible figure, who would one day join with the Giants in their war against the Gods. He turned to the north and he saw that place of darkness and dread, Niflheim. Oithin knew that the world was between Surt, who would destroy it with fire, and Niflheim, out of which would come that which would gather the world back to Darkness and Nothingness. He, the eldest of the Gods, would have to win the wisdom that would help to save the world.

And so, facing loss and pain, Oithin All-Father turned and went towards Mimir's Well. It was under the root of Yggdrasil that grew in Jotunheim. There sat Mimir, the Guardian of the Well of Wisdom, his deep eyes bent upon the deep water. Mimir, who had drunk every day from the Well of Wisdom, knew who it was that stood before him.

"Hail, Oithin, eldest of the Gods," he said.

Then Oithin made reverence to Mimir, the wisest of the world's beings. "I would drink from your well, Mimir," he said.

"There is a price to be paid. All who have come here to drink have shrunk from paying that price. Will you, eldest of the Gods, pay it?"

"I will not shrink from the price that has to be paid, Mimir," said Oithin All-Father.

"Then drink," said Mimir. He took the horn that was by the root of Yggdrasil; he filled it up, and he gave it to Oithin to drink from.

Oithin took the horn in both his hands and drank and drank from it. And as he drank all the future became clear to him. He saw all the sorrows and troubles that would fall upon men and Gods. But he saw, too, why the sorrows and troubles had to fall, and he saw how they might be borne so that Gods and men, by being noble in the days of sorrow and trouble, would leave in the world a force that one day, a day that was far off indeed, would destroy the evil that brought terror and sorrow and despair into the world.

Then, when he had drunk out of the great horn that Mimir had given him, Oithin put his hand to his face and plucked out his right eye. Terrible was the pain that he suffered. But he made no groan nor moan. He bowed his head and put his cloak before his face. Mimir took the eye and let it sink deep, deep into the water of the Well of Wisdom. The Eye of Oithin shone up through the water, a sign to all who came to that place of the price that the eldest of the Gods had paid for his wisdom. Mimir took water in the vessel that is that Eye. He watered the root of Yggdrasil from that vessel.

BALDR

In Asgarth there were two places that meant strength and joy to the Aesir and the Wanes: one was the garden where grew the apples that Ithun gathered—the apples that gave youthfulness to those who ate them, and the other was the Peace Stead, where, in a hall called Brei-thablik, Baldr the Well-beloved dwelt.

In the Peace Stead no crime had ever been committed, no blood had ever been shed, no falseness had ever been spoken. Contentment came into the minds of all in Asgarth when they thought upon this place. Baldr who dwelt there was beautiful. So beautiful was he that all white blossoms on the earth were called by his name. So happy was he that all the birds on the earth sang his name. So just and wise was he that the judgment he pronounced might never be altered.

But even into Baldr's stead foreboding came. He had a dream. He dreamt of Hel, the queen who is half living woman and half corpse. In his dream Hel had come into Asgarth, saying, "A lord of the Aesir I must have to dwell with me in my realm beneath the earth." A silence fell upon all when Baldr had told his dream. And Oithin and Frigg, the father and mother of Baldr, looked at each other with fear in their hearts.

Oithin went to his watch-tower. He waited there till Hugin and Munin, the ravens that flew through the worlds and came back to him with tidings of all that was happening, came to him. They flew back; lighting on each of his shoulders they told him that a bed was spread and a chair was left empty in Hel's habitation for some lordly comer.

And hearing this Oithin mounted Sleipnir, his eight-legged steed, and he rode down towards the abodes of the dead. For three days and three nights of silence he journeyed on. Once one of the hounds of Helheim broke loose and bayed upon Sleipnir's tracks. For a day and a night Garm, that hound, pursued them; Oithin smelled the blood that dripped from its monstrous jaws.

At last he came to where, wrapped in their shrouds, a field of the dead lay. He dismounted from Sleipnir; he called upon one to rise and speak with him. It was on a dead prophetess he called. And when he pronounced her name he uttered a rune that had the power to break the sleep of the dead.

There was a groaning in the middle of where the shrouded ones lay. Then Oithin cried out, "Arise, Volva, prophetess!" There was a stir in the middle of where the shrouded ones lay, and a head and shoulders were thrust up amongst the dead.

"Who calls upon Volva? The rains have drenched my flesh, and the storms have shaken my bones for more seasons than the living know. No living voice has the right to call me from my sleep with the dead."

"It is Vegtam the Wanderer who calls. For whom is the bed prepared and the seat left empty in Hel's habitation?"

"For Baldr, Oithin's son, is the bed prepared, the mead brewed, and the seat left empty. Now let me go back to my sleep with the dead." "Wise woman, cease not! Who shall become the destroyer of Baldr? Who shall steal the life from Oithin's son? Answer, Volva, prophetess!"

"Hoth the Blind shall be the destroyer of Baldr. Unwillingly I speak; now let me be still." "Wise woman, cease not! Who shall bring vengeance on those who do the evil deed? Who shall bring to the flames the slayer of Baldr?"

"Vali, who is not yet born, shall bring vengeance on the doer of the evil deed. His hands he shall not wash, his hair he shall not comb, till he brings to the flames the slayer of Baldr. Unwillingly I spake, and now I would be still."

"Wise woman, cease not! I fain would know who are the maidens who shall weep for Baldr?" "Vegtam thou art not; Oithin thou art. Ride home, Oithin; know that no one shall seek me till Loki is loosed from his bonds, and until to the last battle the fighters shall come." Then there was silence in the field of the dead. Oithin turned Sleipnir, his steed; for four days, through the gloom and silence, he journeyed back to Asgarth.

Frigg had felt the fear that Oithin had felt. She looked towards Baldr, and the shade of Hel came between her and her son. But then she heard the birds sing in the Peace Stead, and she knew that there was no thing in all the world that would injure Baldr.

And to make sure she went to all the things that could hurt him, and from each of them she took an oath that it would not injure Baldr the Well-beloved. She took an oath from fire and from water, from iron and from all metals, from earth and stones and great trees, from birds and beasts and creeping things, from poisons and diseases. Very readily they all gave oath that they would work no injury to Baldr.

When Frigg came back and told what she had accomplished, the gloom that had lain on Asgarth lifted. Baldr would be spared to them. Hel might have a place prepared in her dark habitation, but neither fire nor water, nor iron nor any other metal, nor earth nor stones nor great wood, nor birds nor beasts nor creeping things, nor poisons nor diseases, would help her to bring him down. "Hel has no arms to draw you to her," the Aesir and Wanes cried to Baldr.

Hope was renewed for them, and they made games to honour Baldr. They had him stand in the Peace Stead, and they brought against him all the things that had sworn to leave him hurtless. And neither the battle-axe flung at him, nor the stone out of the sling, nor the burning brand, nor the deluge of water, would injure the beloved of Asgarth. The Aesir and the Wanes laughed joyfully to see these things fall harmlessly from him while a throng came to join them in the games, Dwarfs and friendly Giants.

But Loki, who had been made outcast from Asgarth, came in with that throng. He watched the games from afar. He saw the missiles and the weapons being flung; he saw Baldr standing smiling and happy under the strokes of metal and stones and great wood. He wondered at the sight, but he knew that he might not ask the meaning of it from the ones who knew him.

He changed his shape into that of an old woman; he went amongst those who were making sport for Baldr. He spoke to Dwarfs and friendly Giants. "Go to Frigg and ask. Go to Frigg and ask," was all the answer Loki got from any of them.

Then to Frigg's hall Loki went. He told those in the hall that he was Groa, the old Enchantress who was drawing out of Thor's head the fragments of a grindstone that a Giant's throw had embedded in it. Frigg knew about Groa, and she praised the enchantress for what she had done.

"But will you not tell me, O queen, what is the meaning of the things I saw the Aesir and the Wanes doing?" Loki said. "I will tell you," said Frigg, looking kindly and happily on the pretended old woman. "They are hurling all manner of heavy and dangerous things at Baldr, my beloved son. And all Asgarth cheers to see that neither metal, nor stone, nor great wood will hurt him."

"But why will they not hurt him?" said the pretended old woman.

"Because I have drawn an oath from all dangerous and threatening things to leave Baldr hurtless," said Frigg.

"From all things, lady? Is there no thing in all the world that has not taken an oath to leave Baldr hurtless?"

"Well, indeed, there is one thing that has not taken the oath. But that thing is so small and weak that I passed it by without taking any thought of it."

"What can it be, lady?"

"The Mistletoe that is without root or strength. It grows on the eastern side of Valhall. I passed it by without drawing an oath from it."

"Surely you were not wrong to pass it by. What could the Mistletoe—the rootless Mistletoe—do against Baldr?"

Saying this the pretended enchantress hobbled off.

But not far did the pretender go hobbling. He changed his gait and hurried to the eastern side of Valhall. There a great oak-tree flourished; out of a branch of it a little bush of Mistletoe grew. Loki broke off a spray; with it in his hand he went to where the Aesir and the Wanes were still playing, giving honour to Baldr.

All were laughing as Loki drew near, for the Giants and the Dwarfs, the Wanes and the Heroes from Valhall, were all casting missiles. The Giants threw too far, and the Dwarfs could not throw far enough; others threw far and wide of the mark. In the midst of all that glee and gamesomeness it was strange to see one standing joyless. But one stood so, and he was of the Aesir—Hoth he was, Baldr's blind brother.

"Why do you not enter the game?" said Loki to him in his changed voice.

"I have no missile to throw at Baldr," said Hoth.

"Take this and throw it," said Loki. "It is a twig of the Mistletoe."

"I cannot see to throw it," said Hoth.

"I will guide your hand," said Loki. He put the twig of Mistletoe into Hoth's hand; he guided the hand for the throw. The twig flew towards Baldr. It struck him on the breast and it pierced him. Then Baldr fell down with a deep groan.

The Aesir and the Wanes, the Dwarfs and the friendly Giants, the Heroes out of Valhall, all stood in doubt and fear and amazement.

Loki slipped away. And blind Hoth, from whose hand the twig of Mistletoe had gone, stood quiet, not knowing that his throw had bereft Baldr of life.

Then a wailing sound arose around the Peace Stead. It was from the Aesir and the Wanes. Baldr was dead; they began to lament him. And while they were lamenting, Oithin came amongst them.

"Hel has won our Baldr from us," Oithin said to Frigg, as they both bent over the body of their beloved son.

"Nay, I will not say it," Frigg cried. When the Aesir and the Wanes had won their senses back, the mother of Baldr went amongst them. "Who amongst you would win my love and good-will?" she asked. "Whoever would, let him ride down to Hel's dark realm, and ask the queen to take ransom for Baldr. It may be that she will take it, and let Baldr come back to us. Who amongst you will go? Oithin's steed is ready for the journey."

Then forth stepped Hermodr the Bold, the brother of Baldr. He mounted Sleipnir, and turned the eight-legged steed towards Hel's dark realm.

For nine days and nine nights Hermodr rode on; his way was through rugged glens, one deeper and darker than the other. He came to the river that is called Gjöll and to the bridge across it that is all glittering with gold. The pale maid who guards the bridge spoke to, him.

"The hue of life is still on thee," said Modgudr, the pale maid, "why dost thou journey down to Hel's deathly realm?"

"I am Hermodr," he said, "and I go to see if Hel will take ransom for Baldr."

"Fearful is Hel's habitation for one to come to," said Modgudr, the pale maid. "All around is a steep wall that even thy steed may hardly leap. Its threshold is Precipice. The bed therein is Care. The table is Hunger. The hanging of the chamber is Burning Anguish."

"Nevertheless, I am appointed to ride to Hel," said Hermodr the Bold.

"Baldr had ridden over Gjöll's Bridge," said Modgudr. "Down and north lieth Hel-way."

Then Hermodr rode on till he came to Hel-gate; he dismounted from his steed and made the girths fast; he mounted again and pricked

Sleipnir with his spurs; the eight-legged steed leaped over the gate.
Then Hermodr rode to the hall. Hel came out from her hall and spoke
to Hermodr. And Hel said that if Baldr was so well beloved as was
said she would take ransom for him and let him return to Asgarth.
"If all things in the world, quick and dead, weep for him, then shall
Baldr go back to the Aesir. But he shall remain with me if any gain-
say it, if any will not weep."

Joyously then did Hermodr turn Sleipnir; joyously did he ride
back through the rugged glens, each one less gloomy than the other. He
reached the upper world; he saw that all things were still lamenting
for Baldr. Joyously he rode onward. And all men whom he sought
prayed that Baldr be kept from Hel's dark realm. And the earth,
and the stones, and the trees, and the metals, all made the same
prayer. But one day Hermodr came upon a crow that was sitting on a
dead branch of a tree. The crow made no lament as he came near. She
rose up, and flew away; Hermodr followed her to make sure that she
lamented for Baldr.

He lost sight of her near a cave. And then before the cave he saw
a hag with blackened teeth who raised no voice of lament. "If thou art
the crow that came flying here, make lament for Baldr," Hermodr
said.

"I, Thokk, will make no lament for Baldr," the hag said. "Let Hel
keep what she holds."

"All things weep tears for Baldr," Hermodr said.

"Thokk will weep dry tears for him; I loved him not," she said.

Then Hermodr the Bold knew that he might not ride back to Hel's
habitation. All things knew that there was one thing in the world that
would not weep for Baldr. With head bowed over Sleipnir's mane,
Hermodr rode back to Asgarth.

After that the Aesir and the Wanes knew that no ransom would
be taken, and they knew that with Baldr the joy and content of Asgarth
were gone indeed. They made ready his body for the burning. First
they covered Baldr's body with a rich robe; each of the Aesir and the
Wanes left beside it a most cherished possession. Then they all took
leave of him, kissing him on the brow. But Nanna, his gentle wife,
flung herself on his dead breast, and her heart broke, and she died of

grief. Then did the Aesir and the Wanes weep afresh. And they took the body of Nanna, and they placed it side by side with Baldr's body.

They took the body of Baldr and the body of Nanna and they brought them to the sea. *Hringhorni* was the name of Baldr's ship: it was the greatest of all ships; the Gods would have launched it and made Baldr's funeral pyre upon it, but the ship stirred not forward for all the effort that they made to move it. Then Hyrrokkinn, a Giantess, was sent for. She came mounted on a great wolf and having a viper for a bridle. Four Giants held fast the wolf when she alighted. Hyrrokkinn went to the ship; with a single push she sent it into the sea. The rollers struck out fire as the ship dashed over them, and all lands trembled.

Then were the bodies of Baldr and Nanna borne upon shipboard. Thor was there with his hammer Mjollnir; Freyr was there in his chariot that was drawn by the boar Gold-mane; Heimdallr was there on his horse called Gold-top; Freyja was there in her chariot that was drawn by cats; Oithin was there with his ravens upon his shoulders; Frigg and the rest of the Goddesses and Gods were there. There were also Giants and Dwarfs. Fire was kindled when the ship rode the water. And in the blaze of the fire one was seen bending over the body of Baldr and whispering into his ear. It was Oithin All-Father. He went off the ship and the fire rose into a mighty burning. Speechlessly the Aesir and the Wanes, the Giants and the Dwarfs, the Heroes out of Valhall, watched the burning. Tears streamed down their faces, and all things lamented, crying, "Baldr the Beautiful is dead, is dead."

And what was it that Oithin All-Father whispered to Baldr as he bent above him, the flames of the burning ship around them? He whispered of a Heaven above Asgarth that Surt's flames might not reach; he whispered of a life that would come to beauty again after the world of men and the world of the Gods had been searched through and through with fire.

LOKI'S PUNISHMENT

The crow went flying towards the North, croaking as she flew, "Let Hel keep what she holds. Let Hel keep what she holds." That crow was the hag Thokk transformed, and the hag Thokk was Loki.

He flew to the North and he came to the wastes of Jotunheim. As a crow he lived there, hiding himself from the wrath of the Gods. He told the Giants that the time had come for them to build the ship *Naglfar*, the ship that was to be built out of the nails of dead men, and was to sail to Asgarth on the day of Ragna rök, with the Giant Hrym steering it. And harkening to what he said, the Giants, then and there, began to build *Naglfar*, the ship that Gods and men wished to remain unbuilt for long.

Then Loki, tiring of the wastes of Jotunheim, flew to the burning South. As a lizard he lived amongst the rocks of Muspellsheim, and he made the Fire Giants rejoice when he told them that the Gods had lost much of their power—that Tyr, the bravest of the Aesir, had lost his right hand, and that Freyr, the foremost of the Wanes, had given up his magic sword in order to win Gerth, a Giant's daughter.

In Asgarth there was still one who wept for Loki—Sigyn, his wife. Although he had left her and had shown his hatred for her, Sigyn wept for her evil husband.

He left Muspellsheim as he had left Jotunheim, and he came to live in the world of men. He knew that he had now come into a place where the wrath of the Gods might find him; he made plans to be ever ready for escape. He built a house that had four doors to it so that he might see in every direction. And the power that he kept for himself was the power of transforming himself into a salmon.

Often as a salmon he hid in Gleaming Water. But even for the fishes that swam beside him, Loki had hatred. Out of flax and yarn he wove a net that men might have the means of taking fishes out of the water.

The Gods searched through all the world and they found at last the place where Loki had made his dwelling. He sprang into the waterfall and transformed himself into a salmon. When his pursuers entered his dwelling they found only a burnt-out fire. In the ashes were the marks of a burnt net; his pursuers knew that these were the traces of something made to catch fishes. And from the marks left in the ashes they made a net that was the same as the one Loki had burnt.

With the net in their hands his pursuers went to the waterfall. They dragged the net through the water. Loki was affrighted to find a thing of his own weaving used against him. He lay between two stones at the bottom of the water, and the net passed over him.

But his pursuers knew that the net had touched something at the bottom. They fastened weights to it, and they dragged the net again through the waterfall. Loki knew that he might not escape it this time; he rose in the water, and he swam towards the sea. His pursuers caught sight of him as he leaped down the waterfall. Thor waded behind, ready to seize him.

Loki came out at the mouth of the river, and behold! there was a great eagle hovering over the waves of the sea and ready to swoop down on the fishes. He turned back in the river. He made a leap that took him over the net that his pursuers were dragging. Thor was behind the net; he caught the salmon in his powerful hands, and for all the struggle that Loki made he held him. No fish had ever struggled so before. Loki got himself free all but his tail. Thor held on to his tail, and brought him amongst the rocks, and forced him to take on his proper form.

They brought him to a cavern and they bound him to three sharp-pointed rocks. There they would have left him bound and helpless. But Skathi, who was of the fierce Giant brood, was not content that he should be left untormented. She found a serpent that had a deadly venom; she hung the serpent above Loki's head. The drops of venom fell upon him, bringing him anguish drop by drop, minute by minute. So Loki's torture went on.

Sigyn with the pitying heart came to his relief. She exiled herself from Asgarth; she endured the darkness and the cold of the cavern that she might take away some of the torment from him who was her husband. Over Loki Sigyn stood, holding in her hands a shell into which fell the serpent's venom, thus sparing him from the full measure of anguish. But now and then Sigyn had to turn aside to spill out the flowing cup; then the drops of venom fell upon Loki, and he screamed in agony, twisting in his bonds. And in his bonds Loki stayed until Ragna rök came with the battle in which all things ended.

THE CHILDREN OF LOKI

Before all these things came to be, Loki, leaving Asgarth, went to live in Jarnvid, the Ironwood. There dwelt witches who were the most foul of all witches. And they had a queen over them who was the mother of sons who took upon themselves the shapes of wolves. Two of her sons were Skoll and Hati; it was they who pursued Sol, the sun, and Mani, the moon; she had a third son, Managarm, the wolf who was to be filled with the life-blood of men, who was to swallow up the moon, and stain the heavens and earth with blood. Loki wed one of the witches in the Ironwood, Angrbotha was her name, and they had children that took on dread shapes. Now the Dwellers in Asgarth knew that these powers of evil had been born into the world, and they thought it well that they should take on forms and appear before them in Asgarth. So they sent one to the Ironwood bidding Loki bring before the Gods the powers born of him and the witch Angrbotha. So Loki came into Asgarth once more. His offspring showed themselves to the Gods.

The first, whose greed was for destruction, showed himself as a fearful wolf. Fenrir he was named. And the second, whose greed was for slow destruction, showed itself as a serpent. Mithgarthsorm it was called. The third, whose greed was for the withering of all life, took on form also. When the Gods saw it they were affrighted. For this had the form of a woman: one side of her was that of a living woman and the other side of her was that of a corpse. Fear ran through Asgarth as this form was revealed and as the name that went with it, Hel, was made known.

Far out of sight of the Gods Hel was thrust. Oithin took her and hurled her down to the deeps that are below the world. He cast her down to Niflhel; there she took to herself power over nine regions. Thor took hold of Mithgarthsorm. He flung the serpent into the ocean that engirdles the world. But in the depths of the ocean Mithgarthsorm flourished. It grew and grew until it encircled the whole world. Fenrir the wolf might not be seized upon by any of the Aesir. Fearfully he ranged through Asgarth, and they were only able to bring him to the outer courts by promising to give him all the food he was able to eat.

The Aesir shrank from feeding Fenrir. But Tyr, the brave swordsman, was willing to bring food to the wolf's lair. Every day he brought him huge provision; he fed him with the point of his sword. The wolf grew and grew until he became monstrous and a terror in the minds of the Dwellers in Asgarth.

At last the Gods in council considered it and declared that Fenrir must be bound. In their own smithy the Gods made a chain to bind him, and the weight of it was greater than Thor's hammer. Not by force could the Gods get the fetter upon Fenrir; they sent Skirnir, the servant of Freyr, to beguile the wolf into letting it go upon him. Skirnir came to his lair and stood near him; he was dwarfed by the wolf's monstrous size.

"How great may thy strength be, Mighty One?" Skirnir asked. "Couldst thou break this chain easily? The Gods would try thee."

In scorn Fenrir looked down on the fetter Skirnir dragged. In scorn he stood still, allowing the chain to be placed upon him. Then, with an effort that was the least part of his strength, he stretched himself, and he broke the chain in two.

The Gods were dismayed. But they took more iron; with greater fires and mightier hammer-blows they forged another fetter—a fetter that was half again as strong as the former one. Skirnir the venturesome brought it to the wolf's lair, and in scorn Fenrir let the mightier chain be placed upon him.

He shook himself and the chain held. Then his eyes became fiery; he stretched himself with a growl and a snarl; the chain broke across, and Fenrir stood looking balefully at Skirnir.

The Gods saw that no chain they could forge would bind Fenrir, and they fell more and more into fear of him. They took counsel again; they bethought them of the wonder-work that the Dwarfs had made for them in the old days—the Spear Gungnir, the Ship *Skithblathnir*, the Hammer Mjollnir. Could the Dwarfs be got to make a fetter to bind Fenrir? If they would do it, the Gods promised, they would add to the Dwarfs' domain.

Skirnir went down to Svartalfaheim with the message from Asgarth. The chief of the Dwarfs swelled with pride to think that it was left to his people to make a fetter that would bind Fenrir. "We can make it," he said. "Out of six things we will make it."

"What are these six things?" Skirnir asked.

"The roots of stones, the breath of a fish, the beards of women, the noise made by the footfalls of cats, the sinews of bears, the spittle of a bird."

"I have never heard the noise made by a cat's footfall, nor have

I seen the roots of stones, nor the beards of women. But use what things you will, O helper of the Gods."

The Dwarf chief brought his six things together; the Dwarfs in their smithy worked for days and nights. They forged a fetter that was named Gleipnir. Smooth and soft as a silken string it was. Skirnir brought it to Asgarth, and put it into the hands of the Gods.

Then a day came when the Gods said, once again, that they should try to put a fetter on Fenrir. But if he was to be bound, they should bind him far from Asgarth. There was an island that they often went to make sport in; they spoke of going there. Fenrir growled that he would go with them. He came, and he sported in his own terrible way. And then, as if it were to make more sport, one of the Aesir shook out the smooth cord and showed it to Fenrir.

"It is stronger than you think, Mighty One," they said. "Will you not let it go on you that we may see you break it?"

Fenrir, out of his fiery eyes, looked scorn upon them. "What fame would there be for me," he said, "in breaking such a binding?"

They showed him that none in their company could break it, slender as it was. "Thou only art able to break it, Mighty One," they said.

"The cord is slender, but there may be an enchantment in it," Fenrir said.

"Thou canst not break it, Fenrir, and we need not dread thee any more," the Gods said.

Then was that ravenous wolf wroth, for he lived on the fear that he made in the minds of the Gods. "I am loath to have this binding upon me," he said, "but if one of the Aesir will put his hand in my mouth as a pledge that I shall be freed of it, I will let ye put it on me."

The Gods looked wistfully on one another. It would be health to them all to have Fenrir bound; but who would lose his hand to have it done? One and then another of the Aesir stepped backward. But not Tyr, the brave swordsman. He stepped to Fenrir, and he laid his left hand between those tremendous jaws.

"Not thy left hand—thy sword-hand, O Tyr," growled Fenrir, and Tyr put his sword-hand into that terrible mouth. Then the cord Gleipnir was put upon Fenrir. With fiery eyes he watched the Gods bind him.

When the binding was on he stretched himself as before. He stretched himself to a monstrous size; the binding did not break off him. In fury he snapped his jaws upon the hand, and Tyr's hand, the swordsman's hand, was torn off.

But Fenrir was bound. They fixed a mighty chain to the fetter; they passed the chain through a hole bored through a great rock. The monstrous wolf made terrible efforts to break loose, but the rock, and the chain, and the fetter held. Then, seeing him secured, and to avenge the loss of Tyr's hand, the Gods took Tyr's sword and drove it to the hilt through his under jaw. Horribly the wolf howled. Mightily the foam flowed down from his jaws. That foam flowing made a river that is called Von—a river of fury that flowed on until Ragna rök came.

RAGNA RÖK, THE FATE OF THE GODS

Snow fell on the four quarters of the world; icy winds blew from every side; the sun and the moon were hidden by storms. It was the Fimbul winter: no spring came and no summer; no autumn brought harvest or fruit; winter grew into winter again.

There was three years' winter. The first was called the Winter of Winds: storms blew, and snows drove down, and frosts were mighty. The children of men might hardly keep alive in that dread winter.

The second winter was called the Winter of the Sword: those who were left alive amongst men robbed and slew for what was left to feed on; brother fell on brother and slew him; over all the world there were mighty battles.

And the third winter was called the Winter of the Wolf. Then the ancient witch who lived in the Ironwood fed the Wolf Managarm on unburied men, and on the corpses of those who fell in battle. Mightily grew and flourished the wolf that was to be the devourer of Mani, the moon. The Heroes in Valhall would find their seats splashed with the blood that Managarm dashed from his jaws; this was a sign to the Gods that the time of the last battle was approaching.

A cock crew; far down in the bowels of the earth he was, and beside Hel's habitation; the rusty-red cock of Hel crew, and his crowing made a stir in the lower worlds. In Jotunheim a cock crew, Fjalar, the crimson cock, and at his crowing the Giants aroused themselves. High up in Asgarth a cock crew, the golden cock, Gollinkambi, and at his crowing the Heroes in Valhall bestirred themselves.

A dog barked; deep down in the earth a dog barked; it was Garm, the hound with the bloody mouth barking before Gnipa's Cave. The Dwarfs who heard groaned before their doors of stone. The tree Yggdrasil shook; it shivered and moaned in all its branches. There was a rending noise as the Giants moved their ship; there was a trampling sound as the hosts of Muspellsheim gathered their horses.

Jotunheim, and Muspellsheim, and the Realm of Hel waited tremblingly; it might be that Fenrir the Wolf could not burst the bonds wherewith the Gods had bound him. Without his being loosed the Gods might not be destroyed. Then was heard the rending of the rock as Fenrir broke loose. For the second time the hound Garm barked before Gnipa's Cave.

Then was heard the galloping of the horses of the riders of Muspellsheim; then was heard the laughter of Loki; then was heard the blowing of Heimdall's horn—fate was heard in the note of the Gjallarthorn that Heimdall blew before the abodes of the Gods; then was heard the opening of Valhall's five hundred and forty doors, as eight hundred heroes made ready to pass through each door.

Oithin took counsel with Mimir's head. Up from the waters of the Well of Wisdom he drew it, and by the power of the runes he knew he made the head speak to him. Where best might the Aesir and the Wanes and the Heroes meet with, and how best might they strive against, the forces of Muspellsheim and Jotunheim and the Realm of Hel? The head of Mimir counselled Oithin to meet them on Vigrith, and to wage there such war that the powers of evil would be destroyed for ever, even though his own world should be destroyed with them.

The riders of Muspellsheim reached Bifrost, the Rainbow Bridge. Now they would storm the City of the Gods and fill it with flame. But Bifrost broke under the weight of the riders of Muspellsheim, and they came not to the City of the Gods.

Mithgarthsorm, the serpent that encircles the world, reared itself up from the sea. The waters flooded the lands, and the remnant of the world's inhabitants was swept away. The mighty flood floated *Naglfar*, the Ship of Nails that the Giants were so long building, and floated the ship of Hel also. With Hrym the Giant steering it, *Naglfar* sailed against the Gods with all the powers of Jotunheim aboard. And Loki steered the ship of Hel with the Wolf Fenrir upon it; they steered for the place of the last battle.

Since Bifrost was broken the Aesir and the Wanes and the Heroes with the Valkyries rode downward to Vigrith through the waters of Thund. Oithin rode at the head of his Champions. His helmet was of gold, and in his hand was his spear Gungnir. Thor and Tyr were in his company.

In Mirkvid, the Dark Forest, the Wanes stood against the host of Muspellsheim. From the broken end of the Rainbow Bridge the riders came, all flashing and flaming, with fire before them and after them. Njorth was there with Skathi, his Giant wife, fierce in her war-dress; Freyja was there also, and Freyr had Gerth beside him as a battle maiden. Terribly bright flashed Surt's sword. No sword ever owned was as bright as his except the sword that Freyr had given away when he wanted to win Gerth, the Giant maiden, for his bride. Freyr and Surt fought; he perished; Freyr perished in the battle; he would not have perished had he his own sword, but he had no weapon except the horn of a stag.

And now, for the third time, Garm, the hound with blood upon his jaws, barked. He had broken loose on the world, and with fierce bounds he rushed towards the battle-field where the Gods had assembled their powers. Loud barked Garm. The eagle Hraesvelg screamed on the edge of Heaven. The skies were cloven; the tree Yggdrasil was shaken in all its roots.

To the place where the Gods had drawn up their ranks came the ship of Jotunheim and the ship of Hel, came the riders of Muspellsheim, came Garm, the hound with blood upon his jaws. And out of the sea that surrounded Vigrith the serpent Mithgarthsorm came.

What said Oithin to the Gods and to the Heroes who surrounded him? "We will give our lives and let our world be destroyed, so that these evil powers will not live after us." Out of Hel's ship sprang Fenrir the Wolf. His mouth gaped; his lower jaw hung against the earth, and his upper jaw scraped the sky. Against the Wolf Oithin

All-Father fought. Thor might not aid him, for Thor had now to encounter Mithgarthsorm, the monstrous serpent.

By Fenrir the Wolf Oithin was slain. But the younger Gods were now advancing to battle; and Vithar, the Silent God, Oithin's son, came face to face with Fenrir. He laid his foot on the wolf's lower jaw, that foot that had on it the sandal made of all the scraps of leather that shoe-makers had laid by for him; with his hands he seized the upper jaw and tore the gullet. And thus died Fenrir, the fiercest of all the enemies of the Gods.

Mithgarthsorm, the monstrous serpent, would have overwhelmed all with the venom he was ready to pour forth. Thor sprang forward and crushed him with a stroke of his hammer Mjollnir. Then Thor stepped back nine paces. But the serpent blew his venom over him; blinded, and choked, and burnt, Thor, the World's Defender, perished.

Loki sprang from his ship and strove with Heimdall, the Warder of the Rainbow Bridge and the Watcher for the Gods. Loki slew Heimdall and was slain by him.

Bravely fought Tyr, the God who had sacrificed his sword-hand for the binding of the Wolf. Bravely he fought, and many of the powers of evil perished by his strong left hand. But Garm, the hound with bloody jaws, slew Tyr.

And now the riders of Muspellsheim came down on the field. Bright and gleaming were all their weapons. Before them and behind them went wasting fires. Surt cast fire upon the earth; the tree Yggdrasil took fire and burned in all its great branches; the World Tree was wasted in the blaze. But the fearful fire that Surt brought on the earth destroyed him and all his host.

The wolf Hati caught up with Sol, the sun; the wolf Managarm seized on Mani, the moon; they devoured them; stars fell, and darkness came down upon the world.

The seas flowed over the burnt and wasted earth, and the skies were dark above the sea, for Sol and Mani were no more. But at last the seas drew back; earth appeared again, green and beautiful. A new sun and a new moon appeared in the heavens, one a daughter of Sol, the other a daughter of Mani. No grim wolves kept them in pursuit.

Four of the younger Gods stood on the highest of the world's peaks:

they were Vithar and Vali, the sons of Oithin, and Modi and Magni, the sons of Thor. Modi and Magni found Mjollnir, Thor's hammer, and with it they slew the monsters that still raged through the world, the hound Garm and the wolf Managarm.

Vithar and Vali found the runes of wisdom of the elder Gods. The runes told them of a Heaven that was above Asgarth, of Gimle, that was untouched by Surt's fire. There were righteous rulers there, Vili and Ve. Baldr and Hoth came from Hel's habitation; they sat on the peak together and held speech with each other, calling to mind the secrets and the happenings that they had known before Ragna rök. Deep in a wood two of human-kind were left; the fire of Surt did not touch them; they slept, and when they wakened the world was green and beautiful again. These two fed on the dews of the morning: a woman and a man they were, Lif and Lifthrasir. They walked abroad in the world, and from them and from their children came the men and women who spread themselves over the earth.

INDIAN

INDIAN

VEDIC

THE HEAVENLY NYMPH AND HER MORTAL HUSBAND

To Agni who is Fire, King Purūravas made offering. Agni, being messenger between the three worlds and lord of the house also, might show him where his immortal wife had gone to; but Agni did not reveal the place where her husband might come upon Urvashī. Brilliant is Agni; he has three heads and seven faces, and he is the destroyer of the demons who would defile the offerings.

Then to Indra King Purūravas made sacrifice; he supplicated the champion of the Gods to help him in his search for Urvashī. Indra slew the dragon that shut the waters in and he liberated them for the refreshment of the earth; he wields the thunderbolt, and his beard streams in the air. He is named the Stormy One, and he is the friend of kingly men. But from Indra Purūravas got no aid in the search for his immortal wife.

He prayed to the greatest of all the heavenly beings—to Varuna who treads down with his shining foot all wiles and who has in his hands the nooses that snare false-dealing men. Varuna's power is so great that neither flying birds nor flowing rivers can reach the end of his dominion; he knows all secret things—the flight of birds, the track of the wind, the path of ships on the sea. He can count the winkings of every mortal's eye, and he wields the universe as a man might wield dice. To Varuna the mortal king made sacrifice and supplication, but Varuna, who is greatest of all the Gods, did not help him to win back his immortal wife.

Then Purūravas went wandering through the world searching for Urvashī. She was an Apsaras, and was as fair as the Goddess of the

Dawn. She had said to Purūravas, a mortal who had befriended her, "None of us who move in the waters has ever dwelt with a mortal. Yet I will dwell with you, separating myself from my companions and from the Gandharva who dwells in the high region of the sky, he who has shining weapons and fragrant garments, if you promise that you will never let it happen that I shall see you naked." And Purūravas, who had longed for the love of this Apsaras, made solemn promise that he would never let her see him without his mantle on.

They dwelt in the forest as husband and wife, the king, Purūravas, and the Apsaras, Urvashī. For four seasons they dwelt together there. Then the heavenly bard, the Gandharva, who is the companion of the Apsarases, said, "Why is Urvashī no longer amongst us?" And when he heard that she was dwelling in the forest as the wife of a mortal, the Gandharva, jealous that this man should have a share in the beauty of the heavenly nymphs, and knowing the promise that had been made her, resolved to make Urvashī go from her husband.

Now the things that Urvashī loved most were two lambs that she had reared beside the dwelling in the forest. Every night she tethered them beside where she and her husband slept in the dark of the trees. Knowing that a man and a hero was near, no creature of the forest would come near these two lambs.

But the Apsarases, sent by the Gandharva, came near them; they came in the night and they pulled at the tether of one of the lambs. It bleated. But Urvashī only said to herself, "No creature can take away my pet, my lamb, while a man and a hero is beside me." But then she heard the bleat of the lamb as it was taken away into the forest. The other lamb was then taken, and Urvashī cried out, "How is it that my lamb, my pet, can be taken away while a man and a hero is beside me?" Purūravas heard her words. He sprang up. In the darkness of the night he did not wait to put his mantle on. All uncovered he ran towards where the lamb bleated. Then the Gandharva filled the sky with lightning, and Urvashī, looking towards where the bleating thing was, saw her husband naked.

Instantly she vanished. The light of the dawn came, and Purūravas knew that his Apsaras wife had gone from him. Thereafter he made offerings to the Gods that they might reveal to him where she had gone. And then he went searching for her through the world.

Once upon Himālaya he met Usas, the immortal and unchanging one who awakens all things. As she approaches, the birds stir their wings, and for her they give their first cries. Usas, the Dawn Goddess, was in a car drawn by swiftly going steeds; her bosom was bare and her garb was gleaming with colours. Purūravas besought her to give him tidings of Urvashī. But the Goddess, because once she had delayed on her journey and the sun had caught up on her and had branded her as one brands a thief, would not stay even to listen to his words.

And once he met the Horsemen, the Ashvins, coming upon their shining path. And with the twin brethren went Sūrya, the Maiden of the Sun. Them, too, Purūravas supplicated for tidings of Urvashī, but the Ashvins and the Maiden of the Sun went swiftly upon their way, and gave no heed to the mortal.

Then he prayed to Dyaus, the Sky Father, and to Prithivī, the Earth Mother, that they might show him where their child Urvashī had gone. He was on the level ground when he made this prayer. And when he had made it a beam of light came from the sky and showed him a lotus-covered lake that was near him. On the lake was a flock of gleaming swans. He saw them change themselves and become a company of Apsarases. Swiftly he went to the lake. Urvashī was there, but when he called out to her she said, "I am gone like the first of the dawns." She stayed where the lotuses encircled her, and she cried out to Purūravas, "I am as hard to catch as the winds of heaven." Then Purūravas threw himself down beside the lake and he made a vow that he would stay there until the wild beasts devoured him. Knowing that he would do this, her heart was moved. She drew near where he lay and told him that he might come to where she was on the last night of the year.

So on the last night of the year Purūravas came to where golden steps led up to where there were golden seats. And there Urvashī was and there she stayed with him. And in the morning she said to him, "The Gandharva will come to you and he will tell you that you may ask a boon from him. Whatever boon you wish for he will grant you. You will have to make a choice." Then Purūravas said, "Choose you for me." She said, "When he asks what boon you would have granted, say 'Let me be one of you.'" So his choice was made. The boon was

granted him, and Purūravas lived everlasting years with his Apsaras
wife.

EPIC

THE CHURNING OF THE OCEAN

The Asuras were older than their half-brothers the Gods. They
acquired great possessions in the three worlds, but because they did
not sacrifice to each other, because they did not visit holy places, they
did not acquire great powers within themselves. But the Gods who
did not have great possessions went on making sacrifices, went on
dealing truthfully with each other, went on visiting holy places until
they had greater and greater powers within themselves.

The Gods and the Asuras knew that they could gain the Amrit, the
Water of Life, if they churned up one of the seven oceans that, ring
beyond ring, encircles the worlds. They came down to the Ocean of
Milk. They took the Mountain Mandara for a churning-pole and the
hundred-headed serpent Vāsuki for a churning-rope. They wound the
serpent around the mountain, and pulling it this way and that way they
splashed and dashed the Ocean up and down and to and fro. And
the Ocean of Milk frothed and bubbled as they churned.

For a thousand years the Gods and the Asuras churned the Ocean
of Milk. All that time Vāsuki, the serpent, from his hundred heads
spat venom. The venom bit into the rocks and broke them up; it flowed
down, destroying the worlds of Gods and men. Then all creation
would have been destroyed in that flood of venom if it had not been
for the act of one of the Gods.

Shiva took up the venom in a cup and drank it. His throat became
blue with that draught of bitterness. But by his act, the Gods won to
more powers than the Asuras had.

Still they churned. Then out of the Ocean of Milk came the wish-
bestowing cow, Surabhi. Gods and Asuras rejoiced at the prosperity
that came with her. Then appeared the Apsarases, the heavenly
nymphs, and the Gods and the Asuras sported with them. The moon
was churned up, and Shiva took it and set it upon his forehead.

But now the Asuras wearied in their toil, and more and more

they sported with the Apsarases. The Gods, their powers increased through Shiva's deed, laboured at the churning, and the whole Ocean of Milk foamed and bubbled. Then was churned up the gem of gems, Kaustubha, and then white Uccaibhsravas, the best of steeds.

Now the Gods grew in strength as they laboured, and they laboured as they grew in strength, while the Asuras abandoned themselves more and more to pleasures, and they fought amongst themselves on account of the pleasures that all of them sought. And then, seated on a lotus and holding a lotus in her hand, a lovely Goddess appeared. She went to Vishnu; she cast herself on the breast of the God, and, reclining there, she delighted the Gods with the glances she bestowed on them. All knew her for Shrī, the Goddess of Good Fortune. And the Asuras, in despair because Good Fortune had gone to the side of the Gods, stood around, determined to seize by force the next good thing that came out of the churning.

And then, behold! there appeared the sage Dhanvantari, and in his hands was the cup that held the Amrit, the Water of Life. The Asuras strove to seize it; they would drink it all themselves, or else they would fling the Amrit where the serpent's venom was dripping on the rocks. Almost they overpowered the Gods in their efforts to seize the Amrit. Then Vishnu changed himself into a ravishing form; he seemed to be the loveliest of the nymphs of Heaven. The Asuras went towards where the seeming nymph postured for them. Even then they fought amongst each other. And the Gods took the cup, and, sharing it, they drank of the Amrit.

And now they were filled with such vigour that the Asuras could not overpower them. Many they drove down into hell where they became the Daityas or Demons. That was the beginning of the wars between the Gods and the Daityas—the wars that went on for ages.

The Gods were triumphant and the three worlds became filled with radiance and power. Indra, king of the Gods, seated upon his throne, made a hymn in praise of Shrī. She granted him his wish, which was that she should never abandon the Gods.

And so they lived upon that most holy mountain which is round like a ball and all made of gold. The birds there have golden feathers. Indra stays there. The steed which he gained at the Churning of the Ocean grazes near him. Beside him is his thunderbolt winged with a thousand plumes: Tvastir made it for him from the bones of the seer Dadhica: it is hundred-jointed, thousand-pointed. With the thunderbolt is his spear and his conch. Vishnu is near. But he broods upon the waters, resting upon a serpent, and Shrī, his bride, is beside him and over him the bird Garuda hovers. Shiva dwells in a lovely wood that is filled with flowers. Near him is the spear with which he will destroy the worlds at the end of an age. And beside him is his bow, his battle-axe, and his trident. Once, in jest, his wife Umā covered Shiva's eyes with her hands. Then was the world plunged into darkness, men trembled with fear, and all that lived came near to extinction. But to save the world a third eye appeared in Shiva's forehead: when it blazed forth the darkness vanished, men ceased to tremble, and power once more pervaded the worlds. And always Shiva's throat will be blue from the bitterness of the venom that he drank when he saved creation. Above the most holy mountain is the golden palace of the Lord of All—Brahmā—a palace that is built on nothing that is substantial.

THE BIRTH OF THE GANGES

There came a sage whose name was Bhagīratha: he stayed in a forest of Himālaya practising terrible austerities. For a thousand years he remained with arms upraised, with four fires burning around, and with the sun blazing upon him. At last Brahmā had compassion upon him. The Lord of All came to that sage and told him he could ask a boon as a reward for his austerities.

Then the sage said, "The boon I ask is that King Sagara's sixty thousand sons win to Indra's heaven. Their ashes lie far down in the earth. And until a water which is not the water of earth flows over the ashes and purifies them they cannot win to heaven." The Lord of All was pleased with what the sage asked, and the boon was granted.

And so Brahmā promised that Gangā would descend upon earth. Now Gangā was the daughter of Himālaya, the Lord of Snow, and she had held herself back from leaving the heaven-world. She would leave at Brahmā's command, but her downward rush would be so terrible that the earth would be dashed to pieces by it. Only one thing could save the earth from that tremendous stroke: if the head of Shiva received her stream the fall of Gangā upon earth would be broken.

For a year the sage worshipped Shiva. Then he was taken into Shiva's heaven and he saw the God with his four faces. Once Brahmā had created a nymph out of all that is loveliest in the world, and he had sent her to Shiva so that her beauty might distract him from his eternal meditation. As she walked around where he stayed a face appeared at each side of the God: the faces looking east and west and north are beautiful and pleasant to behold, but the face looking south is terrible. With the face looking east Shiva rules the world; with the face looking west he delights all beings; with the face looking north he rejoices in the company of his wife Umā. But the face looking south is his face of destruction.

Shiva, moved by the prayers of the great ascetic, agreed to take the fall of Gangā upon his head. He went forth with his trident, and standing upon a high peak he bade the daughter of Himālaya descend upon the world. She was made angry by his imperious call. "I shall descend, and I will sweep Shiva away," she said. And so, in a mighty fall, Gangā came down from the heaven-world.

But Shiva, knowing what Gangā would have done, smiled to himself. He would shame her for her arrogance. He made her streams wander through the locks and clusters of his hair. For seasons and seasons Gangā wandered through them as through the forests of Himālaya, and she was made ashamed by her powerlessness to reach the earth.

Then the sage, not seeing the river come down, prayed to Shiva once more, and once more went through awful austerities. Shiva, for the sake of Bhagīratha, allowed Gangā to make her way through the locks and clusters of his hair and come down upon the earth.

In seven streams she descended. The Gods came in their golden chariots to watch that descent upon earth, and the flashing of their chariots made it seem as if a thousand suns were in the sky. Fish of all kind and colours, dolphins of every shape and hue, flashed in the river. And sages and saints came and purified themselves in the water, for the stream that had wandered upon Shiva's head made even the wicked pure. The Gladdener, the Purifier, the Lotus-clad, the Fair eyed, were the names that were given to four of her seven streams. Three flowed to the east, three flowed to the west. The middle stream, the fullest, the clearest, flowed to where Bhagīratha waited in his chariot. He drove on, and where he drove, there did the bright, full, clear river flow.

On and on it flowed, following the chariot of the sage: now it was a sweeping current, and now it went on as though it was hardly able to bear on its wave the feather of the swan, and now full and calmly it flowed along. At last it came to the wide sea. There it sank down, and as it sank into the middle of the world the sage prayed that it would purify the ashes of King Sagara's sixty thousand sons.

In an age before, King Sagara and his sixty thousand sons had been on the earth. The king would have himself proclaimed a world-ruler, and that this might be done a steed was loosed and set to range the distances. All the land the steed ranged over would be proclaimed the king's domain, and when the steed returned it would be sacrificed to the Gods. But Sagara's steed was stolen and led down into the very middle of the earth. The king commanded his sixty thousand sons to find the steed and bring it back for the sacrifice.

They made their way down to the very middle of the earth. They went beyond where the Elephant of the East, the Elephant of the West, the Elephant of the South, and the great white Elephant of the North stand, bearing up the earth. These immortal ones they worshipped, and they passed on. At last they came to where Kapila, at the very centre of all things, sustains the world. There the steed was grazing. King Sagara's sixty thousand sons went to seize it, and as they did they attacked Kapila with trees and boulders, crying out that he was the robber of their father's steed.

As they came near he turned a flame upon them, and the sixty thousand sank down in heaps of ashes. Kapila went on with his meditation and thought no more upon the destruction he had brought upon King Sagara's sons. The king then sent his princely grandson to find the steed. He came down to the very middle of the earth. He passed the immortal elephants; he found the steed grazing near Kapila and he saw the heaps of ashes that were there. Then the bird Garuda that was flying there told him of what had befallen the sons of King

Sagara, and told him, too, that they could win to Indra's heaven only when Gangā was brought down and made flow over their ashes.

The prince led the steed back to Sagara. He became king after his grandfather, and when his duties as king had been fulfilled he went into a forest of Himālaya and engaged in sacrifices to bring Gangā down from the heaven-world. After him his son engaged in sacrifices. Then his son's son, the sage Bhagīratha, engaged in austerities that had never before been known, and these austerities won Brahmā's compassion, and so, with the mighty aid of Shiva, Gangā was brought down upon the earth.

There where Kapila ponders, sustaining the world, Gangā flowed. The river went over the heaps of ashes that were the sons of King Sagara. They were purified, and the sixty thousand, rejoicing, went into the heaven of great Indra.

SAVITRĪ AND THE LORD OF THE DEAD

In the Madras in the old days there lived a princess who was noted for her loveliness and her devotion to her every duty. Sāvitrī was her name. As she grew into maidenhood her father, King Ashvapati, was troubled because she remained unwedded: all his hopes for descendants were in this girl, his only child. But because her loveliness and devotion were so extraordinary none of the princes of the land dared woo her for his wife. Now on a day on which there was a festival, Sāvitrī came into her father's presence: the sacred flowers were in her hands, and when he looked on her and saw her lotus eyes, and her slender waist, and her golden looks, he resolved that he would have her wedded even if he was to permit her to make her own choice of a husband.

So he said to her, "A duty-loving daughter is glad to go from her father's house to the house of a husband. I shall grant a boon to you, Sāvitrī, and it shall be that you shall have liberty to choose a husband for yourself." And when her father said this Sāvitrī begged that he would give her permission to go to the holy places that the hermits lived in so that she might find some sage of princely rank who might become her husband. This permission her father gladly granted her. Then with her attendants the daughter of King Ashvapati went into the forests and visited hermitage after hermitage. And her beauty and her nobility of word and action made her dear to all whom she came near.

She returned, and she gave alms and fed the hungry around her father's palace, and all the people cried out to her, "May you obtain a fitting husband, and may you never know the widow's state." When she came into his presence, her father smiled on her, and a great sage who was with him smiled on her too. And as she stood with downcast eyes before the elders, the sage, whose name was Nārada, said to the king, "Why has not this maiden gone to a husband's house?" And the king, looking on Sāvitrī, said, "She has come back from making a choice for herself, and I think from her happy looks that we shall hear that she has chosen a fitting husband." Then King Ashvapati said, "Speak, maiden, and tell your father and this sage who the princely youth is whom you would marry." Sāvitrī bowed her head and said, with downcast looks but in happy tones:

"O my father, there was a king whose name and country you know of, who lost the sight of his eyes. And being a blind man he could not protect his kingdom, and a usurper seized upon it and drove him forth with his queen and his little son. Uncomplainingly that king went into the forest: as a lowly hermit he lived there; in the forest he reared a son who is known for all noble qualities. Him I have chosen for my husband. And with him I would live in a hermitage, attending on his father and mother."

And when the princess had said this her father showed that he approved of the choice that she had made. But the sage Nārada asked her in an anxious voice, "Who is this king who lost the sight of his eyes, and what is the name of this noble prince who has grown up in exile in the forest?" Sāvitrī replied, "The prince's name is Satyavant, and he is well named the Truth-speaker."

But Nārada when he heard this said cried out in sorrowful tones, "Well do I know this prince and well do I know his father. And no one living could make a more fitting husband for you, Sāvitrī, were it not for one drawback." "If you know him you cannot say that he has a single drawback. Is he not gentle-hearted? Is he not generous? Is he not versed in the sacred lore? Is he not patient? Is he not kindly? Is he not duty-loving? Is he not as handsome as one of the Ashvins, the heavenly horsemen? You have to acknowledge that he has all noble qualities." "He has all noble qualities, but you, daughter of King Ashvapati, must not marry him; there is a doom upon Prince Satyavant, and in a little over a year from this day he will be dead."

Then said King Ashvapati, "Unto a husband so short-lived this daughter of mine must not be given. Sāvitrī must make another choice." But the princess looked at her father, and her eyes were as steady as the eyes of the immortals, and she said in a sorrowful but steady voice, "O my father, for me to discover that the one I have chosen for my husband will be dead in a year is the heaviest of af-flictions—in so short a time to know widowhood! But I have chosen and I cannot make a second choice. I shall go back into the forest and wed Prince Satyavant there, and dwell with him and his parents and attend upon that old king and queen. And when I lose my husband in a twelvemonth I shall be content with what the Gods have willed."

King Ashvapati would have forbidden his daughter to do as she said, but Nārada, that great sage, would have him not forbid her, saying, "Sāvitrī's choice is made, and she can make no other choice. Let her go to her husband's dwelling, and leave what will come of it to the Gods." He blessed the maiden; her father wept over her, and then with her attendants, and riding in her shining chariot, Sāvitrī went into the forest.

And there she put on the red cloth that hermit women wear and covered her fair bosom with the rough bark, and was wedded, and lived in a hermitage with her husband, and dutifully served the blind king and his queen. Sāvitrī was happy there with Prince Satyavant, and her grief was in her knowledge that the days were going by, and that the twelvemonth that she had to live with her husband would in a while come to an end.

For always what Nārada the sage told her was in Sāvitrī's heart. And when hungry people whom she brought food to and served would say to her, "May you never know the state of widowhood," she would bow her head and her tears would flow down. When it came near the end of her twelvemonth of married life she prayed to the Gods to grant her power to protect the life of her husband, and as she prayed she fasted with such severity that the old king, her father-in-law, begged her not to let her life waste away.

But clear-eyed and quiet-spoken was Sāvitrī on the morning that finished the twelvemonth of her marriage with Prince Satyavant. She rose up and served the old king and queen, and when she saw her husband making ready to go into the deep forest she begged permission to go with him. Tenderly Satyavant told her that the ways were rough and that there was danger in the forest for those who did not know how to deal with the creatures of the wild. She begged it as a boon that she might be permitted to go with him. Then the old king and queen said, "Sāvitrī has been here for a year serving us all; never until now has she asked for any boon. Now let what she asks be granted to her." And so Satyavant consented to take Sāvitrī into the deep forest with him.

He gathered blue flowers and made a garland for her, and he showed her the antelope as it fled away from their approach. None of the creatures of the forest would Prince Satyavant kill, and the birds, knowing that no harm would be done to them, sang as the pair went through the ways of the deep forest. Prince Satyavant carried an axe, for he was to cut wood for the fires; also he was going to gather the wild fruits that grew there. He walked with the axe on his shoulder, tall and most princely looking, and beside him went Sāvitrī, strange to the ways of the deep forest, wearing the garland of blue flowers, and in her scanty dress of red cloth looking more like a child than like a bride.

They came to a glade in the deep forest. Then Satyavant began to hew at a tree with his axe; Sāvitrī sat and watched him, praying in her heart. He laid the axe down; he leaned against the tree. "A pain such as I have never had before is in my head," he moaned. She went to him and took his head upon her lap. "O Sāvitrī, pains that are like piercings of thousands of needles are in my head," he said. His eyes closed as his head was laid in her lap.

Then darkness grew around where they were. Sāvitrī saw a great figure standing near. "Who art thou?" she cried. "I am Yama." Then she knew that he who is King of the Dead was beside them. Tall is Yama, Guardian of the Fathers whose abode is in the south; dark blue is Yama like the sky of the dusk, but his eyes are red. Sāvitrī's

heart fainted as she looked upon him and saw that he held in his hand
the cord with which he draws forth the particle that is the life of
a being.

As he approached, Sāvitrī rose up and faced him. But his presence
was so dread-inspiring that she sank down on the ground again; she
saw him draw out with his cord the thumb-sized particle that was
Satyavant's life. He moved away. But Sāvitrī followed him as he
made his way towards the south. "Turn back," the King of the Dead
said to her, "your duties now are to attend to the clay that is left
on the ground." "A wife's duty is to live where her husband lives,
and you who carry the Staff of Justice cannot deny it." "That is so,
but turn back, and whatever boon you ask I will grant you." "Then
for the elders I ask a boon: grant that the blindness that has afflicted my husband's father will pass from him." "That boon I grant,
Sāvitrī."

There was greater darkness now, and Sāvitrī saw the attendants of
the King of the Dead: they wore dark apparel, their hair bristled, and
their legs, their eyes, and their noses were like the legs, eyes, and
noses of crows. "Turn back, Sāvitrī; no farther can any living creature go with Yama." "My life goes with my husband's life, and you
who carry the Staff of Justice cannot deny that." "Ask a boon and I
will grant it." "The boon must be for the elders; grant that the king,
my father-in-law, may regain his kingdom." "That boon I grant."

There was greater darkness where they had gone. And now Sāvitrī saw Yama's four-eyed dogs; they bared their teeth as they looked
upon her shadow. "Turn back, Sāvitrī; no living creature has ever
come so near to Yama's abode. Ask a boon and I will grant it." "The
boon I ask is that my husband be not left without descendants." "I will
grant that boon, too, O faithful Sāvitrī." "Then, great Yama, you
will have to return the husband to his wife." "That I will do, O faithful
one. Go back to the glade where his body is; watch over it, and the
life will come back to it."

Sāvitrī left that dark place and went back to the glade from whence
she had followed Yama. Satyavant's body lay there. She took his head
and pressed it against her breast. Then she laid her lips on his. As
she did life came back to his breast. His eyes opened and speech
came to him, "O Sāvitrī," he said, "I had a dream of a dark-blue

king who carried me off through the darkness, and I dreamt that you, most dear one, followed and drew me back." "Hush, Satyavant, forget your dream. The day has passed; dusk is coming. Your father and mother will be anxious about us. Arise; let us carry the wood and the wild fruits back to the king and the queen. Listen! there are the stirrings of wild things and soon the ways will be dangerous for us. And there is the red of forest-fires. Come, let us go back to the hermitage."

Then together Sāvitrī and Satyavant went back to the hermitage. and when they came near to it they were met by the old king. He cried out that his blindness had gone from him, and that he could see his son and his daughter-in-law—his daughter-in-law Sāvitrī, whose eyes were like the lotus, whose waist was slender, and whose looks were golden. Joyfully the old king led them to the hermitage; joyfully they ate the hermit's meal, and Sāvitrī waited upon them.

In a while messengers came from the kingdom which Satyavant's father had once ruled over. The usurper had met with his death, and the people asked that their old king take rule again. They went back to that kingdom; soon Satyavant and Sāvitrī were king and queen there. And before Yama took them they had a hundred descendants.

DAMAYANTĪ'S CHOICE

In the Middle Country there lived a king's daughter who had such loveliness that the people said of her, "She cannot be the child of a mortal pair." Damayantī the maiden was named. And, ruling over the mountain tribes near by, there was a king named Nala who had such beauty and such strength that he was likened both to the God of Love and the God of War. They heard of each other, these two, and so greatly were their minds moved by what they heard that Damayantī could think of no man but Nala, and Nala could think of no woman but Damayantī. But neither had seen, and neither had received nor had sent any message to, the other.

One day, on a lake in his domain, Nala saw a swan with golden wings, and using all his craft as a hunter and fowler he caught the strange swan. When it knew that it could not free itself the swan spoke human words to Nala: "Release me, King, and I will go to Damayantī and tell her of your beauty and your kindliness." Nala released the golden-winged swan.

It came to a lake in her father's garden, and allowed Damayantī to capture it. Then the golden-winged swan spoke to her and said, "Princess, I have come from a king who surpasses all men in beauty and valour; he is the one man in the world who is a fitting husband for you." "If he is not Nala do not speak of him." "He is Nala." "Then fly back and tell King Nala that I long to look upon him."

Then Damayantī lost all her playfulness and became burthened and mournful; all her thoughts were fixed upon Nala, but she did not know that she would ever look upon him. And her father, when he noted the change in her, considered that the time had come for her to look upon men and to choose a husband for herself.

For in those days kings' daughters made their own choice amongst men of princely rank: an assembly was held in their fathers' palaces, and from the suitors who presented themselves the princesses made a choice; that choice they signified by bestowing a garland upon one of the suitors. Now the king, Damayantī's father, proclaimed that such an assembly would be held in his palace. So great and widespread was the fame of her beauty that hundreds of kings' son and kings presented themselves as suitors. The Immortals, too, resolved to present themselves: Indra, Agni, Varuna, and Yama each wanted to have so lovely a being as Damayantī for his wife.

Nala heard of the assembly, and in his shining chariot he started out for the king's palace. While he was yet far from it he was met by four chariots, and the being in each one of them was so radiant that Nala knew him for one of the Immortals. He got down from his chariot and bowed before them. And they whom he knew to be Immortals addressed him, saying, "Go to the Princess Damayantī and say to her that Indra, Agni, Varuna, and Yama will present themselves at the assembly, and each will try to have her bestow her garland upon him." Nala's heart fainted within him when he heard this speech. But he could only do reverence to the Immortals and declare that he would deliver their message.

Immediately he said this he was within the palace. He found himself in a woman's chamber, and a woman who was as beautiful as the young moon was standing before him. "Who art thou, and how camest thou into my chamber?" she asked. And then at once she said, "Tell me that thou art Nala, that thou hast come to look upon me, that thou hast come to get my promise that on thee I will bestow my garland. Oh, indeed, upon thee I will bestow it." But Nala said, "Only by the power of the Gods have I come into thy chamber that is so carefully guarded." "It matters not how thou hast come; thou wilt be a suitor for me, and I will take thee for my husband—thee, Nala, whom I have always longed for." Then Nala, with breaking heart, told her that he had come as the envoy of the Immortals, and that Indra, Agni, Varuna, and Yama were beings so great that no maiden could make choice of a mortal when they were present.

But Damayantī said, "Be thou amongst the suitors; thee will I choose. And no blame can attach to thee, for the law to which even the Gods bow to permits me to make a free choice." Nala then returned to where the Immortals waited, and he told them of Damayantī's resolve. "Then, Nala, we five will be suitors for this mortal maiden," they said to him.

The king's court was crowded with suitors; great sages and saints were there also. And Damayantī entered with her maidens around her, and all who were there cried out in delight at her beauty. One suitor after another came before her. She looked from them and saw five Nalas. She knew that each of the Immortals had taken on the form and appearance of Nala. Then she was dismayed and she turned to leave the court where the princes and kings were assembled. But she knew that if she did this she would never again be permitted to make a free choice amongst suitors. Courageously she stayed; courageously she went to where the five stood. And going before them she bowed her head and prayed, "O great Gods, ye who hear the prayer that is humbly offered up, permit me to know which is Nala, the mortal to whom I have pledged myself." And as Damayantī said this she saw and she distinguished the four who were Immortals and the one who was a mortal man. For one stood with a shadow thrown from him, with unsteady eyes and a sweated brow and a fading garland, and four stood with their feet above the ground, with steady eyes and unsweated brows and unfading garlands. No shadows were thrown by them. And all in that assembly knew that the Immortals were amongst them.

Then did Damayantī make reverence to the Immortal Gods, bowing herself before them. But she put her garland over the one whose garland was faded, who had unsteady eyes and a sweated brow. So did the princess make her choice. The kings and princes who were rejected wept bitterly because of her choice. But the Immortals gave rich gifts to her and to Nala, and the saints and sages who were there praised Damayantī for the noble choice she had made.

BUDDHIST

GOTAMA'S ATTAINMENT

Gotama was born into a royal family; the maiden whom he married was a princess, and there were many who thought that he himself would become a world-ruler. And so Prince Siddhārtha (for that was his name in his father's palace) grew up with every circumstance of power and delight surrounding him. But even as the lotus grows in the water in which it is born, and rises above it, and ceases to be stained by it, so does the one who is born to be a Buddha, the Enlightened and the Giver of Enlightenment, rise above all that belongs to the world whether of delight or power, trouble or service. Gotama was born to be the Buddha of our age. He did not give his mind to those who urged him to make himself a world-ruler; rather, he left his wife and child and his father's palace, and he went into the forest, becoming a hermit so that he might discover how men may escape from death that is bound to birth, and old age that is bound to infancy. And after having lived for six years in the forest during which time he subsisted on the few grains of millet seed which he ate daily, he went once more towards where men lived, saying to himself, "I will nourish my body and seek Enlightenment through other means than through those severities which have brought me near to death."

He came to a village. Now in that village there was a woman whose name was Sujātā. She had been warned in a dream that the one who was to become Buddha would come that way and that she was to be ready to bestow a gift of food upon him. And so when Gotama came into that village Sujātā had milk and rice of the purest kinds ready for him, and she gave him this food in a golden bowl. Gotama rejoiced in the readiness with which the gift was offered, in the purity of the food, and the fineness of the vessel in which it was given. He blessed Sujātā. He ate the food and thereafter he bathed in the river. And when he placed it in the water the golden bowl floated up the stream. Thereupon a great joy possessed Gotama; the bowl floating up the stream was, he knew, a sign given him that he would soon attain Enlightenment.

So he went towards that Tree of Knowledge under which had sat the Buddhas of other ages; under it they had attained Enlightenment and had become Buddhas. And as he went towards that tree birds of bright colours flew around his head and beasts walked behind him. The friendly spirits hung banners upon trees to guide him to the place. As he went on he thought that these friendly spirits and the birds and the beasts would be witnesses to the victory that would give him Enlightenment, and that the spirits of evil would be witnesses of it also.

That thought went from his mind and it penetrated the mind of Māra, the chief of the spirits of evil. Hastily Māra got together his forces: Gotama must not be allowed to stay under the Tree of Knowledge, he told his followers. With the speed of the whirlwind, with his band Māra went to the place. But with composure, with the assurance of victory in his heart, with majesty, Gotama went towards the tree. He took his place where the Blessed Ones who had attained to Enlightenment had taken theirs; he seated himself on the eastern side of the Tree of Knowledge.

The earth heaved six times, and the birds and beasts that had come with Gotama were affrighted and fled away. But the friendly spirits remained near him. Then Māra, the chief of the evil spirits, taking on himself the appearance of a messenger from his father's country, went to where Gotama sat. Breathlessly he said to him, "Even while you sit here your evil-hearted cousin has taken possession of your father's kingdom, and is cruelly and rapaciously treating all the people whom you should protect. Go, go from this place. Destroy the tyrant, and give peace to your country!" But the words of Māra,

cunning though they were, had no effect: Gotama remained unmoved.
He reflected that if his cousin were acting in such way it was because
of a malice that possessed him, and if the nobles of the land permitted him to act unjustly it was because they were weak and cowardly. And then he thought upon weakness, malice, and cowardice,
and he resolved to raise himself above them by destroying in himself
the centre out of which they come; namely, desire that fixes itself
upon things of this world. He resolved, too, to show others how to
destroy that desire in themselves. So he remained unmoved. The spirit
of the tree cast perfumes upon him, and prayed him through its
leaves to continue his mighty efforts towards Enlightenment.

Then Māra flung against him his army of evil spirits. Terrible
beyond all imagination were they—footless and headless and eyeless
beings armed with all manner of weapons. So terrifying were they
in their mere appearances that the friendly spirits who had stayed
near him now fled from beside Gotama, and the spirit of the tree
groaned and withdrew itself into the depths of the earth. The army
of the evil spirits came towards Gotama howling terribly, raging
frightfully, brandishing spears and swords, clubs and lighted torches.
But Gotama remained unmoved; then did the weapons stick to their
hands, then were the hands that held the weapons paralyzed. Raging
to see his army made so powerless, Māra raised himself up on his
mighty elephant. He made that elephant rush towards Gotama. In his
hand he held the discus which, when flung, could split a mountain. He
flung the discus at Gotama. But the iron circle did not strike him; it
stayed in the air over his head as if it were a halo. Then Māra came
close to him and howled to him: "Depart from this place! Begone!
You have not the merit that would permit you to seat yourself where
Buddhas of former ages seated themselves. Depart, unworthy one!"
So Māra, the Evil One, said, hoping to create in Gotama's mind a
doubt about himself. And all who were with the Evil One cried out,
"He has not merit enough! He has not merit enough!" Their voices
were like the sound of all the waves in the ocean. "This place is
mine, not yours," cried the Evil One, "and I call on these many witnesses to declare that it is mine." "It is thine! It is thine! We are
witnesses!" the army of the Evil One cried out. But Gotama remained unmoved. He put his hand down upon the earth, asking the

earth to bear witness for him. And the earth in a thousand voices bore witness that he had merit enough to sit in the place in which the Buddhas of former ages had sat. Then the elephant on which Mārā rode bowed its knees in homage to Gotama. Then the army of the Evil One fled away, and Mārā turned and fled with them.

But even as he fled he remembered that there was one force that he had not used against Gotama. Something else he would bring against him to prevent his attaining Enlightenment. Mārā summoned his three daughters, Desire, Lust, and Pining. Lovely were they in the eyes of men. Now they came before Gotama as he sat under the Tree of Knowledge and danced and sang for him. He saw them, but his mind did not go out to them. All his thought was now upon the attainment of Enlightenment and the attainment of the power to enlighten others. And the daughters of Mārā, reaching to an understanding of the nobility of his purpose, ceased to dance, ceased to sing, ceased to posture; they knelt before him, and they prayed:

> That which your heart desires may you attain,
> And finding deliverance, deliver all.

When Mārā saw his own daughters kneeling before Gotama he fled away.

Then was Gotama left in peace. The sun went down, and still he remained under the tree. Enlightenment dawned upon his mind. In the twentieth hour all things were gathered up for him, and things in the farthest worlds and things beside him showed themselves to him in their values and their measures. Then did he know the law that binds all existences together. Then did he obtain perfect enlightenment. Then did he become Buddha.

And having become Buddha, rays of six colours went from his body and spread through all the universe. All creation rejoiced because out of myriads of beings one had become Buddha. For seven days he remained in meditation under the Tree of Knowledge and the serpent Mucalinda covered him with its coils. Then with knowledge of how to break the chain that binds together birth and death, infancy and old age, Buddha rose up and went forth to instruct mankind.

CHINESE

CHINESE

IN THE BEGINNING: THE WEAVER MAIDEN AND THE HERDSMAN

IN THE BEGINNING

In the beginning there was *Yang-yin* which is light-darkness, heat-cold, dryness-moisture. Then that which was subtle went upward, and that which was gross tended downward; the heavens were formed from the subtle, the earth from the gross. Now there was *Yang* and *Yin*, the active and the passive, the male and the female. From the operation of *Yang* upon *Yin* came the seasons in their order, and the seasons brought into existence all the products of the earth. The warm effluence of *Yang* produced fire, and the subtlest parts of fire went to form the sun; the effluence of *Yin* produced water, and the subtlest parts of water went to form the moon. The sun operating on the moon produced the stars. The heavens became adorned with sun, moon, and stars, and the earth received rivers, rain, and dust. And *Yang* combining with *Yin*, the principle that is above combining with the principle that is below, produces all creatures, all things. The power that is *Yang*, the receptivity that is *Yin*, can never be added to, never taken away from: in these two principles is the All.

So the sages relate in their perspicuous writings. But the people say that before *Yang* and *Yin* were separated, P'an Ku, a man, came into existence. He had a chisel and a mallet. He had horns projecting from his forehead and tusks projecting from his jaws. He grew in stature every day he lived—for eighteen thousand years he grew six feet every day in stature. Nothing was in place when P'an Ku came into the universe, but with his mallet and his chisel he ordered all things; he hewed out bases for the mountains, he scooped out basins for the seas, he dug courses for the rivers, and hollowed out the valleys. In this meritorious work P'an Ku was engaged for eighteen thousand years.

He was attended by the Dragon, the Unicorn, the Tortoise, and the Phœnix—the four auspicious creatures. The Dragon is the head of all the beasts because it is the one that is most filled with the principle of *Yang:* it is bigger than big, smaller than small, higher than high, lower than low; when it breathes its breath changes to a cloud on which it can ride up to Heaven. The Dragon has five colours in its body, and it is the possessor of a pearl which is the essence of the moon and a charm against fire; it can make itself visible and invisible; in the spring it mounts up to the clouds, and in the autumn it remains supine in the waters. The Unicorn is strong of body and exceptionally virtuous of mind, and it combines in itself the principles of *Yang* and *Yin.* It eats no living vegetation and it never treads upon green grass. The Tortoise is the most propitious of all created things; it possesses the secrets of life and death, and it can, with its breath, create clouds and palaces of enchantment. The Phœnix is at the head of all birds; its colour is the blending of the five colours and its call is the harmony of the five notes; it bathes in the pure water that flows down from the K'un-lun Mountains, and at night it reposes in the Cave of Tan.

But notwithstanding the fact that he was respectfully attended by the auspicious creatures, P'an Ku put the sun and moon in places that were not properly theirs. The sun and the moon went into the sea, and the world was left without luminaries. P'an Ku went out into the deep; he held out his hands to indicate where they were to go, and he repeated a powerful incantation three times. Then the sun and the moon went into the places that were properly theirs and the universe rejoiced at the ensuing harmony.

But the establishment of the universe was not completed until P'an Ku himself had perished; he died after eighteen thousand years of labour with his chisel and mallet; then his breath became the wind and clouds, and his beard became the streaming signs in the sky; his voice became the thunder, his limbs the four quarters of the earth; his head became the mountains, his flesh the soil, and his blood became the rivers of earth; his skin and hair became the herbs and trees, and his teeth, bones, and marrow became metals, rocks, and precious stones. Even then the universe was not adequately compacted: P'an Ku had built up the world in fifty-one stories, giving thirty-three stories to the heavens and eighteen stories to the hells beneath the earth. But he had left a great cavity in the bottom of the world, and, at inauspicious times, men and women fell down through it. A woman whose name was Nu-Ku found a stone which adequately covered the cavity; rightly positioning it, she covered up the emptiness, and so completed the making of the well-ordered world.

THE WEAVER MAIDEN AND
THE HERDSMAN

Her august father, the Sun, would have the accomplished Chih Nü turn her footsteps towards his bright gardens or appear in his celestial halls. But Chih Nü would not leave her loom. All day and every day the maiden sat by the River of Heaven weaving webs that were endless.

The Sun thought in his august mind that if the maiden were wedded she would not permit herself to be a slave to the loom. He thought that if she had a husband she would depart a little from her exceptional diligence. Therefore he let it be known that he would favourably consider a proposal involving the marriage of the accomplished Chih Nü. Then one whose dwelling was at the other side of the heavenly river drew his august regard. This was Niu Lang: he herded oxen, and he was a youth who was exceedingly amiable and who had accomplishments that matched the accomplishments of Chih Nü.

They were united, the Weaver Maiden and the Herdsman Youth; they were united in the palace of the august Sun. The omens were favourable, and the heavens made themselves as beautiful as a flying pheasant for the ceremony. The guests drank of that sweet heavenly dew which makes those who drink of it more quick-witted and intelligent than they were before. The Sun, the Weaver Maiden, the Herdsman Youth, and all the guests who were present sang in mutual harmony the song that says "The Sun and Moon are constant; the stars and other heavenly bodies have their courses; the four seasons observe their rule! How responsive are all things to the harmony that has been established in the heavens!" The august Sun expected that after this auspicious marriage his daughter would moderate her diligence and be more often at leisure.

But Chih Nü was as immoderate in her play as she was in her industry. No more did she work at her loom; no more did she attend to her inescapable duties; with her husband she played all day, and for him she danced and made music all night. The heavens went out of harmony because of this failure in right performance, and the earth was greatly troubled. Her august father came before Chih Nü and pointed out to her the dire consequences of her engaging in endless pastimes. But in spite of all he said to her the Weaver Maiden would not return to her loom.

Then the august Sun determined to make a separation between the pair whose union had such dire results. He commanded the blameless Niu Lang to go to the other bank of the River of Heaven, and to continue there his herdsman's duties. He commanded the accomplished Chih Nü to remain on her own side of the river. But the august Sun showed a spirit of kindliness to his daughter and his son-in-law. They could meet and be together for one day and one night of the year. On the seventh day of the seventh month of every year they could cross the River of Heaven and be with each other. And to make a bridge by which they might cross the river a myriad of magpies would come together, and each by catching the head-feathers of the bird next him would make a bridge with their backs and wings. And over that bridge the Weaver Maiden would cross over to where the Herdsman Youth waited for her.

All day the Weaver Maiden sat at her loom and worked with becoming diligence. Her father rejoiced that she fulfilled her duties. But no being in the heavens or on the earth was as lonely as she was, and all day the Herdsman Youth tended his oxen, but with a heart that was filled with loneliness and grief. The days and the nights went slowly by, and time when they might cross the River of Heaven and be together drew near. Then a great fear entered the hearts of the young wife and the young husband. They feared lest rain should fall; for the River of Heaven is always filled to its brim, and one drop would cause it to flood its banks. And if there was a flood the magpies could not bridge the space between the Weaver Maiden and the Herdsman Youth.

For many years after their separation no rain fell. The magpies came in their myriad. The one behind held the head-feathers of the one before, and with their backs and wings they made a bridge for the young wife to cross over to where the young husband waited for her.

With hearts that were shaken like the wings of the magpies she would cross the Bridge of Wings. They would hold each other in their arms and make over again their vows of love. Then Chih Nü would go back to her loom, and the magpies would fly away to come together in another year.

And the people of earth pray that no drop of rain may fall to flood the River of Heaven; they make such prayer when it comes near the seventh day of the seventh month. But they rejoice when no rain falls and they can see with their own eyes the magpies gathering in their myriad. Sometimes the inauspicious forces are in the ascendant; rain falls and the river is flooded. No magpies then go to form a bridge, and Chih Nü weeps beside her loom and Niu Lang laments as he drives his ox beside the flood of the River of Heaven.

JAPANESE

JAPANESE

THE SUN GODDESS AND THE STORM GOD AND THE STRIFE THERE WAS BETWEEN THEM

That lady, the resplendent Sun Goddess, was born out of the left eye of the august Father creator, and her brother, the powerful Storm God, was born out of his nostrils. To her was given the Plain of High Heaven for dwelling with the Earth for dominion, and to him the Sea was given for dwelling and dominion.

But between Ama-terasu, the Sun Goddess, and Susa-no-wo, the Storm God, there was strife. The resplendent Goddess was beneficently careful of things that grew upon the earth; she strove against the evil spirits that were abroad on the earth, and she was especially careful of the temples that men built for their celebrations of the harvest rites. Her powerful brother had no care for these things. He would leave his own realm and go clamorously upon the earth. He would strip off branches and level trees, and tear out of the ground the crops that his beneficent sister had cared for. He would break down all that guarded men from the evil spirits that were abroad upon the earth. He would make turmoil in the temples and prevent the harvest rites from being celebrated. All the work whose beginnings on earth were helped by Ama-terasu, that shining and beneficent lady, were destroyed by Susa-no-wo, the bearded and impetuous Storm God.

Once he ascended into High Heaven. He came before the Heavenly River, the Yasu. The Goddess cried out, "You who would destroy all I have given growth to upon earth, have you come to darken and lay waste the Plain of High Heaven?" The Storm God declared that he had come to establish peace and trust between himself and his resplendent sister.

Then on the bank of the Heavenly River, the Yasu, the powerful Storm God and the resplendent Sun Goddess exchanged tokens of their trust in one another. To the Storm God the Sun Goddess gave her jewels; to the Sun Goddess the Storm God gave his sword. Then, from the spring whence rose the Heavenly River, the Yasu, Ama-terasu, the Sun Goddess, and Susa-no-wo, the Storm God, drank. They put into their mouths the tokens they had received from each other: from the sword that the Goddess put into hers was born a beautiful and courageous boy; from the jewels that the Storm God put into his, were born shining Gods of growth and power.

Thereafter the cocks, the long-singing birds of the Eternal Land, crowed everywhere upon the earth, prophesying the flourishing of all growing things and the checking of all the evil spirits that went abroad upon the earth. Men gathered full crops in and celebrated the harvest rites in temples that were blown upon no more. The beneficent lady, Ama-terasu, had her way upon earth, and the powerful God, Susa-no-wo, stayed in his own realm, the sea.

Out of the sea he went once more. He went clamorously upon the earth, destroying growing things, and breaking down the guards put up against the evil spirits that went abroad upon the earth. He threw down the temples and scattered the people who had come to celebrate the harvest rites. Then Ama-terasu would look no more upon the earth that her brother had wasted. She went within a cavern and would not come forth. Confusion came upon the eight million Gods, and the spirits of evil wrought havoc through the whole of creation.

She came forth again. The Gods seized upon Susa-no-wo, cut off his great beard, and took from him all his possessions. Then he went wandering upon the earth, but he was no longer able to work havoc upon it. He came to the mountains by the side of the ocean; he planted the mountains with the hairs of his beard, and the hairs became the Forest of Kii. The forest was his dominion; men gave homage to him as Lord of the Forest. It was he who slew the dragon of that land. Once, with its eight heads rearing up, the dragon stood in his way. Susa-no-wo slew it and cut it to pieces. In the dragon's tail there was a sword—a sword that would be ever victorious—and that sword Susa-no-wo sent to Ama-terasu as his tribute to her and to her de-scendants.

Many were the dragons that were in the land that Susa-no-wo had come to. Once when he was on his way from his forest to the sea he came upon an old man and woman who were weeping upon the bank of a river. They told him the reason of their grief. Every year a maiden was given to the dragon of the place, and this time their daughter was being given him. The fury of the Storm God was aroused when he heard this: he went to where the dragon waited by the river, and he destroyed him, cutting him to pieces. Susa-no-wo then took the maiden for his wife. They lived in that land of Izumo, and they and their children after them had the lordship of that place.

Another God came to woo his daughter. He came within his house when Susa-no-wo was lying in slumber on his mat. He tied the hairs of his head to the beams of the roof, and he took in his hands the things that were Susa-no-wo's most cherished possessions—his sword, his bow and arrows, and his harp. He lifted the maiden up and carried her off with the treasures. But the harp cried out as it was taken in the hand of the younger God. Susa-no-wo awakened. He could not even move his head since his hair was tied to the beams of the roof, and he had to loosen each strand of hair before he could go in pursuit of the one who had carried off his daughter and his treasures. At last he freed himelf; led by the sound of the harp that still played of itself he followed that one. But when he came to where Oh-kuni-nushi was with the maiden whom he had carried off, Susa-no-wo said, "You have great craft, and because you have I will give you this maiden and all my possessions; I will take you for my son-in-law."

Together Susa-no-wo and Oh-kuni-nushi ruled the Izumo, and, through his daughter, the descendants of Susa-no-wo peopled that land. But Susa-no-wo knew, and Oh-kuni-nushi knew, that their children would have to give place to the children of the resplendent Sun Goddess who were destined to be the rulers of the Eight Islands.

When Ama-terasu, on account of the destructiveness which her brother had wrought, had hidden herself in the cavern, the Gods had come together and had consulted as to how Ama-terasu's beneficence might be brought into the world once more. They had brought the cocks, the long-singing birds of the Eternal Land, and had placed them outside the cavern; they had lighted fires that made such a brightness before the cavern that the cocks crowed perpetually. They had the Goddess Uzume dance for all their company. On an upturned tub she had danced, and her dancing and her laughter had made all the Gods laugh loudly. Their laughter and merriment and the sound of the cocks crowing had filled the air and had made the earth shake. Ama-terasu, within the cavern, had heard the merry din. She had wondered what merriment could be in the world while she was within the cavern. She had put a finger out and had made a little hole in the rock that closed her in. She had looked out at the crowd of the Gods, and she had seen the dancing and laughing Goddess. Then Ama-terasu had laughed. One of the strong-armed Gods had put his hand where the hole was in the rock and had made a wider opening. Then a long-armed God had put his hands within and had drawn the resplendent Goddess to the wide opening. Light immediately had filled the world. The cocks had crowed louder, and the evil spirits had drawn away. The Gods were made joyful, and the din of their merriment had filled all creation.

So the resplendent Sun Goddess had come back to the world. Then it was that the Storm God, banished, had gone forth and founded a new realm for himself. And the realm he had founded, he knew, was to pass to the descendants of the resplendent Goddess.

After the coming-forth of the Goddess from her cavern the growing plants flourished upon the earth, and the evil spirits were kept away. The cocks crew. The harvests were brought in, and the harvest rites celebrated. The temples stood unshaken and unbroken. The banished Storm God went back to his own realm, and his descendants bore rule in the Eight Islands. Then the resplendent Goddess willed to have her grandson take possession of the Islands. He came; he faced the rulers of the land armed with the sword that must always be victorious. They gave him the land and they gave him power over all that was visible. But they kept for themselves the hidden world and all the powers of divination and sorcery. And since that time the children of the Sun Goddess bear rule in our land.

THE FIRST PEOPLE

There were clouds and mists; there were divine generations who came and who passed away, leaving only him who was The-Lord-in-the-centre-of-the-Heavens and the august God and Goddess who stood each side of him. And then were produced Izana-gi and Izana-mi, the man and the woman. They went across the rainbow bridge. The man held his spear downwards and drops flowed from it; the drops hardened and held themselves together and they formed a place on which the Primeval Couple, Izana-gi, the man, and Izana-mi, the woman, could stay. But the mists were still all around them.

They had children there: Wind-child and Forest-child, Waterfall-child and Mountain-child, Stream-child and Field-child, Sea-child and Islands-children. They had children who became the ancestors of men and women. When Wind-child grew up he swept away the mists; the spaces became clear. Then Izana-mi bore the Fire-children. After their birth she sickened; then she was seen no more above the ground.

Izana-gi went down into Meido, Place of Gloom, to find her. He went down through a cave; he went into depths following her voice. She told him not to come farther; she told him not to look where she was. But Izana-gi disobeyed her command. He lighted a torch and looked towards where he heard her voice.

For a little while there was a light in the pale-grey land of Meido. Izana-gi saw Izana-mi. Her eyes were hollow, and her lips were fleshless, and her forehead was a bone. The torch went out, and Izana-mi cursed her husband for having looked on her in the Place of Gloom. She said she would not let him go back to the world of their children, and that she would make him remain a dweller in Meido.

Izana-gi ran back; but Izana-mi pursued him and she called upon the dread dwellers of the Place of Gloom to catch him and hold him. Izana-gi, as he ran, took the shoots of bamboo and the wild grapes that grew upon the comb that was in his hair and flung them to the dwellers in the Place of Gloom. They stopped to eat the shoots and the grapes. Then he ran on. He came to the cave through which he had entered the Place of Gloom. And here Izana-mi, angry still, nearly caught him. He ran through the cave, and he laid hold of a rock that was outside and closed the cave up. Still Izana-mi was angry; she said that on account of his looking upon her in the Place of Gloom she would draw down into Meido a thousand people every day. "Then I shall bring to birth a thousand and a half a thousand people every day," Izana-gi said.

He went out of the cave and he bathed in a stream that flowed by it. He washed off the pollution that came from what he had touched in the Place of Gloom. What he washed off became stains on the water. And these stains became beings who brought a thousand people every day down to Meido. Therefore was Izana-gi, through his folk, under the necessity of bringing into birth a thousand and a half a thousand people every day. And because, through the wilfulness of Izana-gi and the anger of Izana-mi, the Primeval Pair became separated, there has been ever since death and separation in the world.

POLYNESIAN

POLYNESIAN

IN THE BEGINNING

The Gods were born of the Sky and the Earth—of Rangi the Sky and Papa-tu-a-nuku the Earth. And in those days the Sky pressed down upon the Earth, and there was no difference between the light and the darkness. Nothing could grow up then, nothing could ripen, nothing could bear fruit. And the Gods, the seventy children born of Rangi and Papa, had no space for themselves.

They were huddled in clefts and hollows of the Earth, and the Sky overlaid them. Some were upon their backs, some upon their sides; others went crawling and stooping. They had heard of light, but they had only known darkness: they wondered what light might be. They consulted as to how light might be brought to where they stayed huddled, and how space might be given them. Tu-matauenga, the father of fierce human beings, spoke. "Let us slay our father and our mother," he said, "so that they will not press upon us."

But none of the other Gods would side with Tu-matauenga, father of fierce human beings. Then said Tane-mahuta, father of forests and all life that inhabits them and all things that are made from timbers, "Nay, let us force them apart. Let Rangi be made a stranger to us, but let Papa remain near us and be a nursing mother to us; let one be above us and the other beneath our feet." All thought well of what Tane-mahuta said, all except Ta-whiri-matea, father of winds and storms. He howled when his brothers spoke of raising the Sky above their heads and placing the Earth beneath their feet.

But the children of Rangi and Papa had agreed to sunder their parents. Then Rongo-ma-tane, the father of cultivated food-plants, tried to separate them. He tried and he failed. Tangaroa, the father of fishes and all that is in the sea, raised himself for the effort. But he was not able to do the great deed. Haumia-tikitiki, father of food-plants

253

that grow up without cultivation, now tried to make the separation, but his effort was without avail. Then the Gods called upon the father of fierce human beings to separate the Sky and the Earth. But for all his fierce endeavours, Tu-matauenga could not put them apart.

The Gods would have given up their plan, and would have stayed huddled between the Sky and the Earth where there was no space for them to move and no difference between the light and the darkness, if Tane-mahuta did not stand in the place where the others had made their effort. He pushed with his arms and his hands; but what he did was without avail. Then he put his shoulders upon Papa's middle; he put his feet against Rangi, the Sky. His feet raised up Rangi, his shoulders pushed Papa downwards; to shrieks and mighty groans the separation became more and more wide. "Wherefore slay your parents?" the Sky groaned. "Why do you, our children, commit this dreadful deed?" the Earth cried out. The Gods were made dumb and moveless as Earth and Sky moved and shrieked and groaned. Tane-mahuta did not abate his effort. Far down beneath him he pressed the Earth, far, far above him he thrust the Sky.

As the Sky and the Earth were rent farther and farther apart, light came to where the Gods were. They stood upright; they moved freely and to distances. The Sky and the Earth stayed where they were, far from each other. Now plants and trees grew up; there was maturity, there was ripening of fruit. The human race came into existence, and men moved here and there upon the Earth.

And for all time Sky and Earth were set apart. But still, from the tops of wooded mountains, the sighs of Papa-tu-a-nuku rise up to Rangi. Then Rangi drops tears upon her bosom—tears that men know as drops of dew.

NEW ZEALAND AND HAWAII

MA-UI THE FIRE-BRINGER

When Ma-ui, the last of her five sons, was born, his mother thought she would have no food for him. So she took him down to the shore of the sea; she cut off her hair and tied it around him, and she gave him to the waves. But Ma-ui was not drowned in the sea: first of all the jelly-fish came; it folded him in its softness and kept him warm while he floated on. And then the God of the Sea found the child and took charge of him: he brought him to his house and warmed and cherished him, and little Ma-ui grew up in the land where lived the God of the Sea.

But while he was still a boy he went back to his mother's country. He saw his mother and his four brothers, and he followed them into a house; it was a house that all the people of the country were going into. He sat there with his brothers. And when his mother called her children to take them home, she found this strange child with them. She did not know him, and she would not take him with the rest of the children. But Ma-ui followed them. And when his four brothers came out of their own house they found him outside, and they played with him. At first they played hide-and-seek, but then they made themselves spears from canes, and they began throwing the spears at the house.

The slight spears did not go through the thatch of grass that was at the outside of the house. And then Ma-ui made a charm over the cane that was his spear—a charm that toughened it and made it heavy. He flung it again, and a great hole was made in the grass-thatch of the house. His mother came out to chastise the boy and drive him away. But when she stood at the door and saw him standing there, looking so angry, and when she saw how he was able to break down the house with the throws of his spear, she knew in him the great power that his father had, and she called to him to come into the house. He would not come in until she had laid her hands upon him. When she did this his brothers were jealous that their mother made so much of this strange boy; they did not want to have him with them. It was then that the elder brother spoke and said, "Never mind; let him be with us and be our dear brother." And they all asked him to come within the house.

The door-posts, Short Post and Tall Post, would not let him come in (some say that these were his uncles and that they had been the masters of the household while the boys in the house were ungrown). Ma-ui lifted up his spear; he threw it at Tall Post and overthrew him. He threw his spear again and overthrew Short Post. And after that he went into his mother's house and was with his brothers.

In those days, say the people who know the stories of the old times, the birds were not seen by the men and women of the islands. They flew around the houses, and the flutter of their wings was heard, and the stirring of the branches and the leaves as they were lighted upon by the birds. Then there would be music. But the people who had never seen the birds thought that this was music made by the Gods who wanted to remain unseen by the people. Ma-ui could see the birds; he rejoiced in their brilliant colours, and when he called to them they would come and rest upon the branches around the place where he was; there they would sing their happiest songs to him.

There was a visitor who came from another land to the country that Ma-ui lived in. He boasted of all the wonderful things that were in his country, and it seemed to the people of Ma-ui's land that they had nothing that was fine or that could be spoken about with pride. Then Ma-ui called to the birds. They came and they made music on every side. The visitor who had boasted so much was made to wonder, and he said that there was nothing in his country that was as marvellous as the music made by Ma-ui's friends, the birds.

Then, that they might be honoured by all, Ma-ui said a charm by which the birds came to be seen by men—the red birds, the i-i-wi and the aha-hani, and the yellow birds, the o-o and the mamo, and all the other bright birds. The delight of seeing them was equal to the delight of hearing the music that they made. Ever afterwards the birds were seen and heard, and the people all rejoiced in them. This Ma-ui did when he was still a boy, growing up with his brothers and sisters in his mother's house.

His mother must have known about fire and the use of fire, else why should she have been called Hina-of-the-Fire, and how did it come that her birds, the alae, knew where fire was hidden and how to make it blaze up? Hina must have known about fire. But her son had to search and search for fire. The people who lived in houses on the islands did not know of it: they had to eat raw roots and raw fish, and they had to suffer the cold. It was for them that Ma-ui wanted to get fire; it was for them that he went down to the lower world, and that he went searching through the upper world for it.

In Kahiki-mo-e [1] they have a tale about Ma-ui that the Hawaiians do not know. There they tell how he went down to the lower world and sought out his great-great-grandmother, Ma-hui'a. She was glad to see Ma-ui of whom she had heard in the lower world; and when he asked her to give him fire to take to the upper world, she plucked a nail off her finger and gave it to him.

In this nail fire burned. Ma-ui went to the upper world with it. But in crossing a stream of water he let the nail drop in. And so he lost the fire that his great-great-grandmother had given him.

He went back to her again. And again Ma-hui'a plucked off a finger-nail and gave it to him. But when he went to the upper world and went to cross the stream, he let this burning nail also drop into the water. Again he went back, and his great-great-grandmother plucked off a third nail for him. And this went on, Ma-ui letting the nails fall into the water, and Ma-hui'a giving him the nails off her fingers, until at last all the nails of all her fingers were given to him.

But still he went on letting the burning nails fall into the water that he had to cross, and at last the nails of his great-great-grandmother's toes were given to him—all but the nail on the last of her toes. Then, when he came back once more, Ma-hui'a became blazing angry; she plucked the nail off, but instead of giving it to him she flung it upon the ground.

Fire poured out of the nail and took hold on everything. Ma-ui ran to the upper world, and Ma-hui'a in her anger ran after him. He dashed into the water. But now the forests were blazing, and the earth was burning, and the waters were boiling. Ma-ui ran on, and Ma-hui'a ran after him. And as he ran he chanted a magic incantation so that the rain might come, so that the burning might be put out:

> To the roaring thunder;
> To the great rain—the long rain;
> To the drizzling rain—the small rain;
> To the rain pattering on the leaves.
> These are the storms, the storms!
> Cause them to fall—
> To pour in torrents.

[1] New Zealand.

The rain came on—the long rain, the small rain, the rain that patters on the leaves; storms came, and rain in torrents. The fire that raged in the forests and burned on the ground was drowned out. And Ma-hui'a, who had followed him, was nearly drowned by the torrents of rain. She saw her fire, all the fire that was in the lower and upper worlds, being quenched by the rain.

She gathered up what fragments of fire she could, and she hid them in the barks of different trees, so that the rain could not get at them and quench them. Ma-ui's mother must have known where his great-great-grandmother hid the fire. If she did not, her sacred birds, the alae, knew it. They were able to take the barks off the trees, and, by rubbing them together, to bring out fire.

In Hawaii they tell how Ma-ui and his brothers used to go out fishing every day, and how, as soon as they got far out to sea, they would see smoke rising on the mountain-side. "Behold," they would say, "there is fire. Whose can it be?" "Let us hasten to the shore and cook our fish at that fire," another would say.

So, with the fish that they had caught, Ma-ui and his brothers would hasten to the shore. The swiftest of them would run up the mountain-side; but when he would get to where the smoke had been, all he would see would be the alae, the mud-hen, scratching clay over burnt-out sticks. The alae would leave the place where they had been seen, and Ma-ui would follow them from place to place, hoping to catch them when their fire was lighted.

He would send his brothers off fishing, and he himself would watch for the smoke from the fire that the alae would kindle. But they would kindle no fire on the days that he did not go out in the canoe with his brothers. "We cannot have our cooked bananas to-day," the old bird would say to the young birds, "for the swift son of Hina is somewhere near, and he would come upon us before we put out our fire. Remember that the guardian of the fire told us never to show a man where it is hidden, or how it is taken out of its hiding-place."

Then Ma-ui understood that the bird watched for his going, and that the alae made no fire until they saw him out at sea in his canoe. He knew that they counted the men who went out, and that if he was not in the number they did no cooking that day. Every time he went in the canoe he saw smoke rising on the mountain-side.

Then Ma-ui thought of a trick to play on them—on the stingy alae that would not give fire, but left men to eat raw roots and raw fish. He rolled up a mat, and he put it in the canoe, making it like a man. Then he hid near the shore. The brothers went fishing, and the birds counted the figures in the canoe. "The swift son of Hina has gone fishing; we can have cooked bananas to-day." "Make the fire, make the fire, until we cook our bananas," said the young alae.

So they gathered the wood together, and they rubbed the barks, and they made the fire. The smoke rose up from it, and swift Ma-ui ran up the mountain-side. He came upon the flock of birds just as the old one was dashing water on the embers. He caught her by the neck and held her.

"I will kill you," he said, "for hiding fire from men."

"If you kill me," said the old alae, "there will be no one to show you how to get fire."

"Show me how to get fire," said Ma-ui, "and I will let you go."

The cunning alae tried to deceive Ma-ui. She thought she would get him off his guard, that he would let go of her, and that she could fly away. "Go to the reeds and rub them together, and you will get fire," she said.

Ma-ui went to the reeds and rubbed them together. But still he held the bird by the neck. Nothing came out of the reeds but moisture. He squeezed her neck. "If you kill me there will be no one to tell you where to get fire," said the cunning bird, still hoping to get the son of Hina off his guard. "Go to the taro leaves and rub them together, and you will get fire."

Ma-ui held to the bird's neck. He went to the taro leaves and rubbed them together, but no fire came. He squeezed her neck harder. The bird was nearly dead now; but still she tried to deceive the man. "Go to the banana stumps and rub them together, and you will get fire," she said.

He went to the banana stumps and rubbed them together; but still no fire came. Then he gave the bird a squeeze that brought her near death. She showed him then the trees to go to—the hau-tree and the sandalwood-tree. He took the barks of the trees and rubbed them together, and they gave fire. And the sweet-smelling sandalwood he called "ili-aha"—that is, "fire-bark"—because fire came most easily from the bark of that tree. With sticks from these trees Ma-ui went to men. He showed them how to get fire by rubbing them together. And never afterwards had men to eat fish raw and roots raw. They could always have fire now.

The first stick he lighted he rubbed on the head of the bird that showed him at last where the fire was hidden. And that is the reason why the alae, the mud-hen, has a red streak on her head to this day.

HOW MA-UI STROVE TO WIN IMMORTALITY FOR ALL CREATURES

A time came when Ma-ui, returning to his home, said to his father, "Who now can vanquish me? I have won fire for men; I have made the sun go more slowly across the heavens; I have fished up the islands from the bottom of the sea. What thing in the world can vanquish me?" His father showed Ma-ui where the sky and the horizon met. Flashes were to be seen there. "They are from the teeth of the Goblin Goddess, Great-Hina-of-the-Night," he told Ma-ui. "She is your great ancestress. She vanquishes all creatures, for she brings all creatures to death. She will vanquish you, my child." Then Ma-ui said, "Let us both go to her fearlessly; let us take the heart out of her body, and so end her power of bringing death to all creatures." But his father would not go to where Great-Hina-of-the-Night was.

Ma-ui called for companions, and the little birds of every kind assembled to go with him—the robin and the lesser robin, the thrush and the yellow-hammer and the water-wagtail. With the little birds Ma-ui went towards where the sky and the horizon met. They went in the evening, and as they went they saw the flashing of the teeth of the Goblin Goddess. Her teeth were of volcanic glass. Her mouth was wide-shaped, like the mouth of a fish. Her hair floated all around her as sea-weed floats in the sea. Her eyes shone through the distances.

He saw her and was afraid; even great Ma-ui was made afraid by the Goblin Goddess, Great-Hina-of-the-Night. But he remembered that he had told his companions that he would find a way of giving ever-lasting life to men and to all creatures. He thought and thought on how he could come to her and take the heart out of her body.

She was sleeping, and Ma-ui prepared to enter her terrible open mouth and take the heart out of her body and give her heart to all the creatures of the earth to eat.

Then he said to the birds, "O my little companions, do not laugh, do not make a sound, when you see me go into the mouth of this Goblin Goddess. Laugh, make sounds if you will when you see me come out bearing the heart of my ancestress, Great-Hina-of-the-Night." The little birds that gathered around him, shivering, said, "Oh, our brave master, we will not laugh, we will not make a sound. But, oh, take care of yourself, Master."

Ma-ui twisted the string of his weapon around his waist. He stripped his clothes off. The skin of his legs and hips was mottled like that of a mackerel from the tattoo-marks that had been cut upon it by the chisel of Uetonga. He stood there naked, and then he went within the jaws of Great-Hina-of-the-Night. He passed the fearful teeth that were sharp like volcanic glass. He went down into her stomach. He seized upon her heart. He drew it out, and he came back as far as her jaws. He saw the sky beyond her jaws.

A little bird that often laughed tried hard not to laugh when it saw him go within the jaws of the Goblin Goddess. It twisted up its mouth to prevent its laughing. And then it laughed—little Ti-waka-waka, the water-wagtail—laughed its merry note. The Goblin Goddess opened her eyes. She started up. She caught Ma-ui between her fearful teeth, and she tore him across. There was darkness then, and the crying of all the birds. Thus died Ma-ui with the Meat of Immortality in his hands. And since his death no one has ventured near the lair of Hina-nui-te-po, the Goblin Goddess.

PE-LE, HAWAII'S GODDESS OF VOLCANIC FIRE

I

Pe-le, the Goddess, came up out of her pit in Ki-lau-ea. No longer would she sit on the lava-hearth below, with skin rugged and black-ened, with hair the colour of cinders, and with reddened eyes; no longer would she seem a hag whom no man would turn towards. She came up out of the pit a most lovely woman. Her many sisters were at her side, and each of them was only less lovely than was Pe-le upon that day. They stood each side of her because it was forbidden to come behind the Goddess or to lay a hand upon her burning back.

Pe-le and her sisters stood on the crater's edge. Around them was the blackened plain, but below them was Puna, with the surf breaking upon its beach, and with its lehua groves all decked with scarlet blossoms. This land was Pe-le's. She had made it and she had the power to destroy it. She had power in the heavens, too, for her flames reached up to the skies. All the Gods—even the great Gods, Ku, Ka-ne, Ka-ne-loa, and Lono—were forced to follow her when she left Kahiki, the land beyond the vastness of the ocean, and came to Hawaii. Ki-lau-ea on Hawaii's island was the home she had chosen. And now she came out of the pit, and she said to her many sisters, "Come, let us go down to the beach at Puna, and bathe, and feast, and enjoy ourselves." Her sisters rejoiced, and they went down with her to the beach.

And when they had bathed and feasted, and had sported themselves in the water and along the beach, Pe-le went into a cavern and laid herself down to sleep. She said to the sister who was always beside her, to the sister who was named Hi-i-aka-of-the-fire-bloom, "Let me sleep until I awake of my own accord. If any of you should attempt to awaken me before, it will be death to you all. But if it has to be that one of you must awaken me, call the youngest of our sisters, Hi-i-aka-of-the-bosom-of-Pele, and let her bring me out of sleep." So Pe-le said, and she lay in the cavern and slept. Her sisters said to each other, "How strange that the havoc-maker should sleep so deeply and without a bed-fellow!" By turns they kept watch over her as she slept in the cavern.

But the youngest of her sisters, the little Hi-i-aka, was not by her when she spoke before going to sleep. Little Hi-i-aka had gone to where the groves of lehua showed their scarlet blossoms. She was enchanted with the trees that she went amongst; she gathered the blossoms and wove them into wreaths. And then she saw another girl gathering blossoms and weaving them into wreaths, and she knew this other girl for the tree-spirit, Ho-po-e. And Ho-po-e, seeing Hi-i-aka, danced for her. These two became friends; they danced for each other, and they

played together, and never had Hi-i-aka, the little sister of the dread
Goddess, known a friend that was as dear and as lovely as Ho-po-e—
Ho-po-e whose life was in the grove of lehuas.

As for Pe-le, the Goddess, she slept in the cavern, and in her sleep
she heard the beating of a drum. It sounded like a drum that an-
nounces a hula. Her spirit went from where she slept; her spirit-
body followed the sound of that drum. Over the sea her spirit-body
followed that sound. Her spirit-body went to the Island of Kauai.
There she came to a hall sacred to Laka: a hula was being performed
there. As a most lovely woman Pe-le entered that hall. All the people
who were assembled for the hula turned to look upon her. And in that
hall Pe-le saw Prince Lo-hi-au.

He was seated on a dais, and his musicians were beside him. Pe-le,
advancing through the hall filled with wondering people, went to
where he was. Prince Lo-hi-au had her sit beside him; he had tables
spread to feast her. Pe-le would not eat. "And yet she must have come
from a very great distance," the people around her said, "for if a
woman so beautiful lived on this island, we would surely have heard
her spoken about." Prince Lo-hi-au would not eat either; his mind
was altogether on the beautiful woman who sat on the dais beside
him.

When the hula was over he took her into his house. But although
they were beside each other on the mat, Pe-le would not permit him
to caress her. She let him have kisses, but kisses only. She said to him,
"When I bring you to Hawaii you shall possess me and I shall possess
you." He tried to grasp her and hold her, but she rose in her spirit-
body and floated away, leaving the house, leaving the island, crossing
the sea, and coming back to where her body lay in the cavern in
Puna.

Prince Lo-hi-au sought wildly for the woman who had been with
him; he sought for her in the night, in the dark night of the ghosts.
And because it seemed to him that she was for ever gone, he went
back into his house, and took his loin-cloth off, and hanged himself
with it from the ridge-pole of the house. In the morning his sister
and his people came into the house and found the chieftain dead.
Bitterly they bewailed him; bitterly they cursed the woman who
had been with him and who had brought him to his death. Then

they wrapped the body in robes of tapa and laid it in a cavern of the mountain-side.

In Puna, in a cavern, Pe-le's body lay, seemingly in deep sleep. For a day and a night, and a night and a day it lay like this. None of her sisters dared try to awaken Pe-le. But at last they became frightened by the trance that lasted so long. They would have their youngest sister, Hi-i-aka, awaken the Woman of the Pit. At the end of another day they sent for her.

And Hi-i-aka saw the messenger coming for her as she stood in the grove of lehua trees with her dear and lovely friend, Ho-po-e, beside her. She watched the messenger coming for her, and she chanted the me-le:

> From the forest-land at Papa-lau-ahi,
> To the garlands heaped at Kua-o-ka-la,
> The lehua trees are wilted,
> Scorched, burnt up—
> Consumed are they by fire—
> By the fire of the Woman of the Pit.

But Ho-po-e, her friend, said, "It is not true what you chant. See! Our lehuas are neither wilted nor burnt up. If they were I would no longer be able to see you nor to speak with you. Why, then, do you lament? You will stay with me, and we shall gather more blossoms for garlands." But Hi-i-aka said, "Even as I saw the messenger who is coming to take me away from you, I saw our trees destroyed by Pe-le's fires."

Then the messenger came to them, and told Hi-i-aka that she was to return to where she had left her sisters. She took farewell of Ho-po-e and went to where her sisters awaited her. They brought her within the cavern, and they showed her Pe-le lying there, without colour, without stir. Then Hi-i-aka, the youngest of her sisters, went to Pe-le's body and chanted over it. And the spirit-body that had been hovering over the prostrate body entered into it. The breath entered the lungs again; Pe-le's bosom rose and fell; colour came into her face. Then the Woman of the Pit stretched her body; she rose up, and she spoke to her sisters.

They left that place; they went back into Pe-le's dwelling-place, into the pit of Ki-lau-ea. Then, after a while, Pe-le spoke to her sisters,

one after the other. She said to each of them, "Will you be my messenger and fetch our lover—yours and mine—from Kauai?" None of
the elder sisters would go; each one understood how dangerous such
a mission would be. But when Pe-le spoke to Hi-i-aka, the youngest
of her sisters, the girl said, "Yes, I will go, and I will bring back
the man."

Her sisters were dismayed to hear Hi-i-aka say this. The journey
was long, and for anyone who would go on the mission that Pe-le
spoke of the danger was great. Who could tell what fit of rage and
hatred might come over the Woman of the Pit—rage and hatred
against the one who would be with the man she would have for her
lover? And Hi-i-aka who had agreed to go upon such a mission was
the youngest and the least experienced of all of them. They tried to
warn her against going; but they dared not speak their thought out to
her. Besides, they knew that Hi-i-aka was so faithful to Pe-le, her
chieftain and her elder sister, that she would face every danger at her
request.

Then said Pe-le to Hi-i-aka, "When you have brought our lover
here, for five days and five nights he shall be mine. After that he shall
be your lover. But until I have lifted the tapu you must not touch
him, you must not caress him, you must not give him a kiss. If you
break this tapu it shall be death to you and to Prince Lo-hi-au." Her
sisters made signs to her, and Hi-i-aka delayed her departure. She
stood before Pe-le again, and Pe-le reproached her for her dilatori-
ness. But now Hi-i-aka spoke to her elder sister and chieftainess and
said, "I go to bring a lover to you while you stay at home. But, going,
I make one condition. If you must break out in fire and make raids
while I am gone, raid the land that we both own, but do not raid where
the lehua groves are; do not harm my friend Ho-po-e, whose life is
in the lehua groves." She said this, and she started on her journey. But
now the length of the journey and its dangers came before her and
made her afraid. She saw herself, alone and powerless, going upon
that long way. Once again she returned to where the Woman of the Pit
sat. She asked that she be given a companion for the journey. She
asked that a portion of Pe-le's mana, or magic power, be given her.
Pe-le did not deny her this: she called upon the Sun and the Moon, the
Stars, the Wind, the Rain, the Lightning and Thunder to give aid to

her sister and her messenger. And now that mana was bestowed on her, Hi-i-aka started on the way that led across islands and over seas to the house of the man whom her sister desired—her sister, Pe-le, the dread Fire Goddess.

II

Far did Hi-i-aka and her woman-companion journey, long were they upon the way, many dangers did they face and overcome, and at last they came to the village that had Lo-hi-au for its lord. "Why have you come?" said the people who entertained the worn travellers. "I have come to bring Prince Lo-hi-au to Pe-le, that they may be lovers." "Lo-hi-au has been dead many days. He fell under the spell of a witch, and he took his own life." Then they pointed out to her the cave in the mountain-side in which his sister had laid the body of Lo-hi-au.

Then was Hi-i-aka greatly stricken. But she drew together all the power that she had—the power that Pe-le had endowed her with—and looked towards the cave in the mountain-side. And she saw something hovering around the cave, and she knew it, thinned and wan as it was, for the ghost-body of Lo-hi-au. She knew that she had to bring that ghost-body back to the body that lay in the cave, and she knew that all the toils she had been through would be nothing to the toils that this would entail. She raised her hands towards the cave, and she uttered a chant to hold that ghost-body in the place. But as she looked she saw that the ghost-body was even more thinned and wan than she had thought. She was frightened by its shadowiness. The voice that came to her from before the cave was as thin and faint as the murmur that the land-shell gives out. She answered it back in a voice that was filled with pity:

> My man of the wind-driven mist,
> Or rain that plunges clean as a diver
> What time the mountain-stream runs cold
> Adown the steps at Ka-lalau—
> Where we shall ere long climb together,
> With you, my friend, with you.
> Companion of the pitchy night,
> When heavenward turns my face—
> Thou art, indeed, my man.

With her woman-companion she came to the mountain-side. The sun was going down; they would have barely time to climb the ladder that was there and go into the cavern before the night fell. Then the ladder was taken away by witches who bore an enmity to Hi-i-aka; and the ghost-body of Lo-hi-au wailed thinly and more faintly.

Hi-i-aka chanted an incantation that held the sun from sinking down. And while the sun stayed to give them light, she and her companion toiled up the cliff. They came to the entrance of the cave. Hi-i-aka caught in her hand Lo-hi-au's ghost-body. They went within. Hi-i-aka directed her companion to take hold of the dead feet. The fluttering ghost-body that she held in her hand she brought to the eye-socket and strove to make it pass through at that place. With spells she strove to make the soul-particle pass on. It went within; it reached the loins; it would pass no farther. Hi-i-aka forced it on. It went to the feet; the hands began to move, the eyelids quiver. Then breath came into the body. Hi-i-aka and her companion lifted it up and laid the body on a mat. With restoring herbs Hi-i-aka and her companion swathed the body from head to foot. But her companion said, "He will not recover in spite of all that you have done."

"I will make an incantation," Hi-i-aka said, "if it is rightly delivered, life will come back to him." Then she chanted:

> Ho, comrades from the sacred plateau!
> Ho, comrades from the burning gulf!
> Hither fly with art and cunning:
> Ku, who fells and guides the war-boat;
> Ku, who pilots us through dream-land;
> All ye Gods of broad Hawaii;
> Kanaloa, guard well your tapus;
> Candle-maker, candle-snuffer;
> Goddess, too, of passion's visions;
> Lightning red all heaven filling—
> Pitchy darkness turned to brightness—
> Lono, come, thou God of fire;
> Come, too, thou piercing eye of rain;
> Speed, speed, my prayer upon its quest!

More and more incantations Hi-i-aka made as the night passed and the day following passed. The people of the place were kept at a dance so that Hi-i-aka's task might not be broken in on. She made her last and her mightiest incantation; the soul-particle stayed in the body, and Prince Lo-hi-au lived again.

They brought him to the entrance of the cave. Three rainbows arched themselves from the mouth of the cave, and adown these three rainbows Prince Lo-hi-au, Hi-i-aka, and her companion went. To the beach they went. And in ocean the three performed the cleansing rite. And now that the toils of the journey and the toils of restoring the man to life were past, Hi-i-iaka thought upon the groves of lehua and upon her dear and lovely friend, Ho-po-e.

And now that the time had come for her to make the journey back she turned towards Hawaii and chanted:

> Oh, care for my parks of lehua—
> How they bloom in the upland Ka-li-'u!
> Long is my way and many a day
> Before you shall come to the bed of love,
> But, hark, the call of the lover,
> The voice of the lover, Lo-hi-au!

And when they had passed across many of the islands, and had crossed their channels, and had come at last to Hawaii, Hi-i-aka sent her companion before her to let Pe-le know that Lo-hi-au was being brought to her. When she had come with Lo-hi-au to the eastern gate of the sun, when she had come to Puna, she went swiftly ahead of Prince Lo-hi-au that she might look over her own land.

Pe-le had broken out in her fires; in spite of the agreement she had made with her sister and her messenger, she had wasted with fire the lehua groves. No tree now stood decked with blossoms. And the life of Ho-po-e, Hi-i-aka's dear and lovely friend, was ended with her lehua groves.

Blackness and ruin were everywhere Hi-i-aka looked. She stood in a place that overlooked her well-loved land, and all the bitterness of her heart went into the chant that she made then:

> On the heights of Poha-ke
> I stand, and look forth on Puna—
> Puna, pelted with bitter rain,
> Veiled with a downpour black as night!
> Gone, gone are my forests, lehuas
> Whose bloom once gave the birds nectar!
> Yet they were insured with a promise!

Then she said, "I have faithfully kept the compact between myself and my sister. I have not touched her lover, I have not let him caress me, I have not given him a kiss. Now that compact is at an end. I am free to treat this handsome man as my lover, this man who has had desire for me. And I will let Pe-le, with her own eyes, see the compact broken."

When he came to where she was, she took his hand; she made herself kind to him; she told him she had been longing for the time when her companion would have gone and they two would be together. Hand in hand they went over the blackened and wasted land. They came to where an unburnt lehua grew upon a rock. There Hi-i-aka gathered blossoms to make a wreath for Lo-hi-au.

And on the terrace of Ka-hoa-lii where they were in full view of Pe-le and her court, she had him sit beside her. She plaited wreaths of lehua blossoms for him. She put them around his neck, while he, knowing nothing of the eyes that were watching them, became ardent in love-making.

"Draw nearer," said Hi-i-aka, "draw nearer, so that I may fasten this wreath around your neck." She put her arm around the neck of Lo-hi-au; her body inclined towards his. She drew him to herself. The sisters around Pe-le cried out at that. "Hi-i-aka kisses Lo-hi-au! Look, Hi-i-aka kisses Lo-hi-au!" "Mouths were made for kissing," Pe-le said, but the flame came into her eyes.

III

Then Pe-le commanded her sisters to put on their robes of fire, and go forth and destroy Lo-hi-au. In their robes of fire they went to where he was; when they came to him they threw cinders upon his feet and went away again. But Pe-le knew that they had made only a pretence of destroying the man. The cauldron within her pit bubbled up; she called upon her helpers, upon Lono-makua, Ku-pulupulu, Ku-moku-halli, Ku-ala-na-wao. At first they would not help her to destroy Lo-hi-au; rather, with their own hands, did they roll the fires back into the pit. Then did Pe-le threaten her helpers; then did Lono-makua go forth to do her bidding.

Lo-hi-au saw the fires coming towards him, and he chanted:

> All about is flame—the rock-plain rent;
> The coco-palms that tufted the plain
> Are gone, all gone, clean down to Ka-poho.
> On rushes the dragon with flaming mouth,
> Eating its way to Oma-'o-lala.
> For tinder it has the hair of the fern.
> A ghastly rain blots out the sky;
> The sooty birds of storm whirl through the vault;
> Heaven groans, a-drip, as with dragon-blood!

The fires that rolled towards them spared Hi-i-aka. Lo-hi-au, choked by the vapour, fell down, and the lava-flow went over him.

So Hi-i-aka lost the one whom she had come to love, as she had lost her lehua groves and her dear and lovely friend, Ho-po-e, through the rage of her sister Pe-le, the dread Goddess. In her grief she would have broken up the strata of the earth, and would have let the sea rise up through and destroy the islands, if Ka-ne had not appeared before her—Ka-ne the Earth-shaper. Ka-ne soothed her mind, and she went back to the Pit, and sat amongst her sisters.

Once a man who was a great sorcerer came down into the Pit. "What is the purpose of your visit?" he was asked.

"I have come to know why Lo-hi-au, my friend, has been destroyed," he said.

"He and Hi-i-aka kissed, and the man was tapu for Pe-le," the sisters answered.

"He tasted death at Haena. Why was he made taste death again in Hawaii?"

Pe-le, seated at the back of the Pit, spoke: "What is it that you say? That Lo-hi-au tasted death at Haena?"

"Yes. Hi-i-aka brought his soul and his body together again. Then they sailed for Hawaii."

Then said Pe-le to her youngest sister: "Is this true? Is it true that you found Lo-hi-au dead and that you restored him to life?"

"It is true. And it is true that not until you had destroyed my friend Ho-po-e did I give a caress to Lo-hi-au."

So Hi-i-aka said, and Pe-le, the Woman of the Pit, became silent. Then the sorcerer, Lo-hi-au's friend, said, "I would speak to Pe-le.

But which is Pe-le? I have a test. Let me hold the hand of each of you, O Divine Women, so that I may know which of you is the Goddess."

He took the hand of each of Pe-le's sisters, and held the hand to his cheek. He held the hollow palm to his ear. Each hand that was given to him had only a natural warmth when it was put to his cheek. Then he took the hand of a hag whose skin was rugged and blackened, whose hair was the colour of cinders, whose eyes were red. The hand was burning on his cheek. From the hollow of the hand came reverberations of the sounds made by fountains of fire. "This is Pe-le," said the man, and he bent down and adored her.

Then Pe-le, loving this man who was Lo-hi-au's friend, and knowing that Hi-i-aka had been faithful in her service to her, softened, and would have Lo-hi-au brought to life again. But only one who was in far Kahiki possessed the power to restore Lo-hi-au to life. This was Kane-milo-hai, Pe-le's brother.

And Kane-milo-hai, coming over the waters in his shell-canoe, found Lo-hi-au's spirit, in the form of a bird, flitting over the waters. He took it, and he brought it to where Lo-hi-au lay. He broke up the lava in which the body was set, and he reformed the body out of the fragments, restoring to it the lineaments that Lo-hi-au had. Then he brought the spirit back into the body.

And afterwards it happened that Hi-i-aka, wandering where the lehua groves were growing again, and knowing that after dire destruction a new world had come into existence, heard the chant:

> Puna's plain takes the colour of scarlet—
> Red as heart's blood the bloom of lehua.
> The nymphs of the Pit string hearts in a wreath:
> O the pangs of the Pit, Ki-lau-ea!

Hi-i-aka went to where the chant came from; she discovered Lo-hi-au restored to life once more. With him she wandered through the land below Ki-lau-ea. Men and women were peopling the land, and the Gods of the Pit were not now so terror-inspiring.

PERUVIAN

PERUVIAN

VIRACOCHA: THE LLAMA-HERDER AND THE VIRGIN OF THE SUN

VIRACOCHA

In other days we who are of the race of the Incas worshipped the Sun; we held that he was the greatest and most benignant of all beings, and we named ourselves the children of the Sun. We had traditions that told of the pitiable ways that we and the rest of the human race lived in beiore the Sun, having had compassion upon us, decided to lead us towards better ways of living. . . . Lo, now! Our Lord, the Sun, put his two children, a son and a daughter, in a boat upon Lake Titicaca. He told them they were to float upon the water until they came to where men lived. He put his golden staff into the hands of his son. He told him he was to lead men into a place where that staff, dropped upon the earth, sank deep down into it.

So the children of our Lord the Sun went upon the waters of Lake Titicaca. They came to where our fathers lived in those far days. . . . Where we live now we see villages and cities; we see streams flowing down from the mountains, and being led this way and that way to water our crops and our trees; we see flocks of llamas feeding on good grass with their lambs—countless flocks. But in those days we lived where there were thickets and barren rocks; we had no llamas; we had no crops; we knew not how to make the waters flow this way and that way; we had no villages, no cities, no temples. We lived in clefts of the rocks and holes in the ground. The covering of our bodies was of bark or of leaves, or else we went naked in the day and without covering to put over us in the night. We ate roots that we pulled up out of the ground, or fought with the foxes for the dead things they were carrying away. No one bore rule amongst us, and we knew nothing of duty or kindness of one to another.

Out of their boat on Lake Titicaca came the children of our Lord to us. They brought us together; they had rule over us, and they showed us how to live as husband and wife and children, and how to know those who were leaders amongst us and how to obey those leaders. And having showed us these things they led us from the land they had found us in.

And often did he who was the son of our Lord the Sun drop the golden staff upon the ground as we went on. Sometimes the staff sank a little way into the earth, sometimes it sank to half its length in the earth. We came to a place where the golden staff, dropped by him who was the son of our Lord the Sun, sank into the earth until only its top was to be seen. And there we stayed, or, rather, there our fathers stayed, for we are many generations from the men and women who came into this place with the two who were the children of the Sun.

They showed us how to sow crops in that rich ground, and how to lead water down from the hills to water the crops and the trees. They showed us how to tame the llamas, and how to herd them and tend them as tamed beasts. They showed us how to take the wool from them and weave the wool into garments for ourselves; also, they showed us how to dye our garments so that we went brightly clad in the light of the sun. They showed us how to work in gold and silver, and how to make vessels of clay, and how to put shapes and figures upon these vessels. They showed us how to build houses, and how to build villages, and cities, and temples. And they showed us, too, how to obey the rule of those who were left to rule over us, the Incas.

Then the two who were the son and daughter of the Sun left us. Before they went from us they told us that the Sun, their father, would adopt us as his children. And so we of the Inca race became the children of the Sun. They said to us, too, "Our father, the Sun, does good to the whole world; he gives light that men may see and follow their pursuits; he makes men warm when they had been cold; he ripens their crops; he increases their flocks of llamas; he brings dew upon the ground. The Sun, our father, goes round the earth each day that he may know of man's necessities and help him to provide for them. Be like the Sun, then, far-seeing, regular in all your occupations. And bring the worship of the Sun amongst the tribes who live in darkness and ignorance."

And so these two, his son and daughter who were sent to us by the Sun, were seen no more by us. But we knew ourselves now as the children of the Sun. We subdued the tribes in his name, and brought the knowledge of his beneficence amongst them. We built a great temple to him. And the daughters of the Incas in hundreds served him as Virgins of the Sun.

Yes, but there were those amongst us who came to have other thoughts about Heaven and the ways of Heaven. "Does not the Sun go as another being directs him to go?" one of the Incas said to his councillors. "Is he not like an arrow shot onward by a man? Is he not like a llama tethered by the will of a man rather than like one who has freedom? Does he not let a little cloud obscure his splendour? Is it not plain that he may never take rest from his tasks?"

So men amongst us have said, and they who have said them have mentioned a name. Viracocha that name is. And then they would say words from rites that were known to the people of this land before the Incas came into it. They would say, "O conquering Viracocha! Thou gavest life and valour to men, saying, 'let this be a man,' and to women saying, 'let this be a woman.' Thou madest them and gavest them being! Watch over them that they may live in health and peace! Thou who art in the high heavens, and among the clouds of the tempest, grant this with long life, and accept this sacrifice, O Creator!" So those who were priests in the land before our fathers came into it prayed.

And they said that it was Viracocha who created the Sun, and created the Moon also. They said that at the beginning the Sun was not brighter than the Moon, and that in his jealousy he flung ashes upon the face of the Moon and dimmed the Moon's primal brightness. And they said that Viracocha could make great terraces of rock and clay rear themselves up with crops upon them, and that he could bring the water-courses to freshen terraces and gardens merely by striking with a hollow cane that he carried.

Now although Viracocha was so great, he obscured himself, and came back to live amongst the Gods in the guise of a beggar. None knew him for Viracocha, the Creator of all things. And he saw the Goddess Cavillaca as she sat amongst llama lambs under a lucma-tree, weaving the wool of the white llama. He saw her and he approached her. He left a ripe fruit beside her. She ate the fruit and she became with child by him.

And when her child was born her parents and her friends said to her, "You must find out who is the father of this child. Let all who live near come to this lucma-tree, and let the child crawl amongst them. The man he crawls to and touches with his hand we will know is his father."

So under the lucma-tree Cavillaca sat, and her child was with her. All who lived near came to that place, and amongst them came Viracocha, still in his beggar's dress. All came near to Cavillaca and her child. The child crawled where they stood. He came to Viracocha. He put his hand up and touched the man who was in the beggar's garb.

Then was Cavillaca made ashamed before all the Gods. She snatched up her child and held him to her. She fled away from that place. She fled towards the ocean with her child. Viracocha put on his robes of splendour and hastened after her. And as he went he cried out, "O Goddess, turn; look back at me! See how splendid I am!" But the Goddess, without turning, fled with her child from before him.

Viracocha went seeking them. As he crossed the peaks he met a condor, and the condor flew with him, and consoled him. Viracocha blessed the condor, and gave him long life and the power to traverse the wilderness and go over the highest peaks; also he gave him the right to prey upon creatures. Afterwards he met a fox; but the fox derided him, telling him that his quest was vain. He cursed the fox, saying to him that he would have to hunt at night, and that men would slay him. He met a puma, and the puma went with him and consoled him. He blessed the puma, saying that he would receive honour from men. As he went down the other side of the mountain, he came upon parrots flying from the trees of their forest. And the parrots cried out words that were of ill-omen. He cursed the parrots, saying that they would never have honour from men. But he blessed the falcon that flew with him down to the sea.

And when he came to the sea he found that Cavillaca and her child had plunged themselves into the water and had been transformed into rocks. Then Viracocha in his grief remained beside the sea.

Now beside the sea there were two virgins who were Urpihuachac's daughters. They were guarded by a serpent. Viracocha charmed the serpent with his wisdom, and the serpent permitted him to approach Urpihuachac's daughters. One flew away and became a dove. But the other lived there with Viracocha. And this Virgin of the Sea showed Viracocha where her mother kept all the fishes of the world. They were in a pond and they could not go through the waters of the world.

Viracocha broke down the walls of their pond, and let them go through the streams and the lakes and the sea. And thus he let men have fishes to eat.

He lived amongst men, and he taught them many arts. He it was, as the priests of those who were here before the Incas say, showed men how to bring streams of water to their crops, and taught them how to build terraces upon the mountains where crops would grow. He set up a great cross upon the mountain Caravay. And when the bird that cries out four times at dawn cried out, and the light came upon the cross he had set up, Viracocha went from amongst men. He went down to the sea, and he walked across it towards the west. But he told those whom he had left behind that he would send messengers back who would protect them and give them renewed knowledge of all he had taught them. He left them, but men still remember the chants that those whom he left on the mountain, by the cross, cried out their longing:

> Oh, hear me!
> From the sky above,
> In which thou mayst be,
> From the sea beneath,
> In which thou mayst be,
> Creator of the world,
> Maker of all men;
> Lord of all Lords,
> My eyes fail me
> For longing to see thee;
> For the sole desire to know thee.

THE LLAMA-HERDER AND THE VIRGIN OF THE SUN

There was a llama-herder, a young man who played a flute as he tended his flock; white llamas were in his flock, and many of them had their tender young lambs beside them. Near where he herded was the House of the Virgins of the Sun. Often those who were of that house walked abroad; there were two of them who often drew near and stood behind the rocks to listen to the music of that young man's flute.

One day the young herder whose name was Aroya-Napa looked up, and saw the two Virgins of the Sun standing beside two fountains that were there. And what else should that young man think but that these two most lovely Princesses were the embodiments of the two lovely fountains? He went on his knees to them. They gave him their hands to kiss. And then he knew that they were flesh and blood, albeit flesh and blood of the Inca, and that they were Virgins dedicated to the Sun.

He played upon his flute again, and one of the Princesses felt her heart torn with a love that came into it—a love for this young man who herded llamas. Her name was Chuqui-llantu, "Shadow-of-a-lance." And when her companion turned to go back to the House of the Virgins of the Sun she could hardly bring herself to turn back. Indeed she would not return until she had obtained something that belonged to Aroya-Napa. This was a silver plate that was on his forehead—a silver plate that had on it two figures eating a heart.

Then with her companion, Shadow-of-a-lance went back to the House of the Virgins. When they went within the doorway they were examined as was the custom; their clothes and all they carried were looked over, so that nothing that was unfitting might be brought into the House of the Virgins of the Sun.

In the place where Shadow-of-a-lance slept there were four fountains. Now she lay upon her bed and she thought upon the llama-herder, and she thought upon the silver plate that he had owned and that she now had upon her own forehead, and she thought that what it showed was her own condition, for her heart, too, was being eaten by two figures. She slept, and in her sleep she saw a bird flying between two trees and crying mournfully. In her dream she spoke to the bird—a checollo it was—and she told it that she, too, mourned for that for which there was no remedy—for a love that she, a Virgin of the Sun, had for a young man who herded llamas.

Then the bird told her that she was to arise and seat herself between the fountains, and there sing to herself what was most in her thought. If the fountains sang back the words that she sang to them, a remedy would come to her. Shadow-of-a-lance rose from her bed and sat between the fountains, and sang of the heart that was being eaten by two beings. The fountains sang her words back to her, but sang them in a way that lulled her. All night she sat singing and listening to the song that the fountains sang back to her.

Now he who herded the llamas had a mother who lived upon the mountain. She had skill and wisdom. She dreamed about her son, and when the dawn came she hurried down to where he kept his flock. He was sleeping when she came to where he lay; she saw that his face was covered with the marks of tears. He awakened; she asked him where was the silver plate that he wore upon his forehead; he told her he had given it away, and he told her to whom he had given it. Then the Woman of the Mountain knew that her son longed for a princess, and for a princess who had been dedicated a Virgin of the Sun.

She stood before the hut, and she saw Shadow-of-a-lance and her companion coming towards the place where the llama-flock was pasturing. She bade her son lie in his sleeping-place, and she covered him with a cloak she had brought with her—a magic cloak. Then she went amongst the rocks. She gathered herbs; she dipped the herbs in the fountains, and then she cooked them. The two princesses came to where she was; she served them upon her knees—she served them with the dish of herbs she had cooked.

They asked permission to go into the hut; they looked around it, and they looked in places beside it. Shadow-of-a-lance desired to see the young man she had dreamed about, and her companion did as she did. But they did not see the young man. They saw a cloak spread over a sleeping-place, but they knew there was no one under the cloak. Through the magic of the Woman of the Mountain, her son had passed into and was now part of that cloak.

Shadow-of-a-lance admired the texture and the colours of the cloak. The Woman of the Mountain told her that it had been given to her by a woman who had been beloved by Pachacamac, the great God. Then Shadow-of-a-lance, thinking that never again would she look upon the young man who had played on the flute, asked that she might be given the cloak—she wanted to have something that had gone upon him.

The Woman of the Mountain gave her the cloak, and Shadow-of-a-lance and her companion carried it between them. They went into the House of the Virgins of the Sun. The doorkeepers, as was the custom, stayed them and searched them so that nothing unfitting might be brought into that house. Then they went within, carrying the cloak.

Shadow-of-a-lance, as before, lay on her bed. She had laid the cloak beside her bed. In a while she rose, and she sat by the fountains, and she sang of the two beings who were eating her heart. The fountains did not sing her words back to her, and she wept, sitting there. Then she looked to where the cloak lay, and behold! the cloak filled out and became the youth whom she loved, the youth who loved her.

The two were together all through the night, and the fountains sang to them. In the morning they stole out together. But not all the guards were sleeping. One saw them and pursued them. Shadow-of-a-lance and her lover fled up the mountain. But now all the guards of the House of the Virgins of the Sun gave chase to them. They did not come to where there was safety; for the Sun turned the two of them into stones, and as stones they stand to this day between Calca and Huayllapampa.

CENTRAL AMERICAN
AND MEXICAN

CENTRAL AMERICAN
AND MEXICAN

IN THE BEGINNING: THE TWIN HEROES AND THE LORDS OF
XIBALBA: QUETZALCOATL: QUETZALCOATL'S ENEMY: THE
GODS OF THE AZTECA: THE AZTECA

IN THE BEGINNING

Alone was Tepeu, alone was Gucumatz, alone and wrapped in the
green and the azure. All was silence, all was motionlessness, all was
breathlessness. There was only the boundlessness of the sky, the quietude of the waters. No thing was joined to another thing; no thing was
poised; no thing held itself upright. Lo, all was silent and unruffled;
all was quietude and immensity. Then, wrapped in the green and the
azure, Tepeu and Gucumatz meditated, and spake together and consulted. Then they were aware of the presence of him who is Heart of
the Sky, who is Hurakan. "Let this and this be done," came the word
to Tepeu and Gucumatz. "Let the waters retire so that the earth may
exist. Let the earth harden its surface so that it be sown with seed.
Let there be human beings endowed with intelligence so that from
them we may receive glory and honour." "Earth," said the Gods, and
immediately earth was formed. Like great lobsters the mountains of
earth appeared above the waters. Forests appeared upon the mountains.
Then was Gucumatz filled with joy. He hailed Hurakan, naming the
signs of him who is Heart of the Sky—the Lightning in the Vault,
the Flash of Lightning, the Thunderbolt. The earth was formed with
its mountains, plains, and valleys; the rivers ran in their proper
courses; seeds were implanted in the earth.

Then the Gods made the creatures and gave them their places on the
land, in the waters, and in the air. "Thou, Deer, shalt sleep beside
where water runs; thou shalt be in the brushwood; there multiply;
thou shalt go upon four feet." And to the puma, the opossum, the
coyote, the porcupine, the peccary, they likewise spoke, giving these
creatures their different habitations. To the birds, to the fish, they
spoke also, giving them their places in the air and in the water. But

the creatures gave no answer to those who had created them: they screamed, or growled, or bleated, or twittered. Then the Gods said, "Those whom we have created are not able to utter our name. This is not well." Then they spoke to all the creatures and said, "Ye do not glorify us, but there shall yet be those who will call upon our name and be able to do our will. As for you, your flesh shall be broken under the tooth."

So the creatures went from before the Gods, each pair to their own habitation, and the Gods meditated upon the making of those who would be their supporters and their nourishers. And they made those who stood upright upon two feet, they made men out of the moist clay. But these Men of Clay could not turn their heads; they could not move of their own accord, and their sight was dim. Speech the Men of Clay had, but there was no sense in the words they uttered. The Gods broke them into pieces, and the Men of Clay moved no more upon the earth.

Then the Gods carved men out of wood. These had speech and they could move of their own accord. Also, the Gods gave them the power of generation, and they could reproduce their kind; they had posterity, and their posterity was also of wood and carved. And the Men of Wood began to be numerous on the earth.

But they did not raise their heads to the Gods; they had no thought and no memory; they had no hearts and they had no blood. And when the Gods looked upon them they saw that their faces were stiff and unchanging. And the Gods resolved to destroy the race of the Men of Wood.

So they caused a heavy and a sticky rain; it fell night and day, darkening the earth. Many of the Men of Wood were drowned by that rain. And great bats and owls attacked them, breaking their bodies with their great beaks. Seeing the bats and owls attack them, the animals, great and small, bit and tore at the Men of Wood. They ran into their houses for safety, and their houses fell down upon them. They tried to enter caves, but the caves closed themselves against them. Their own dogs bit them, their own fowls pecked at them; even their pots and cooking-utensils turned upon them. "You have burned us, you have pounded us," cried the pots and the cooking-utensils, "day and night it was *holi, holi, huqui, huqui,* grinding our sides because of you. Now we will pound you, now we will grind you." And pursued by their dogs and their fowls, by their pots and their cooking-utensils, the Men of Wood ran to the forest. Some were able to climb into the trees. Those who managed to do this saved themselves; they became the little monkeys who are in our forests in our day.

Once more the Gods thought upon the creation of man; once more they took counsel with each other. They sent the Crow and the Coyote for a substance that grew at the Place of the Division of the Waters. The Crow and the Coyote brought back this substance: it was the white and the yellow maize. The Gods ground the maize; they mixed it with the blood of the Tapir and the Serpent which the Crow and the Coyote also brought to them. And Xpiyacoc and Xmucane, the Father and the Mother of the Gods, made nine broths, and the broths, entering into the substance, made muscle and sinew. The Men of Maize stood upright; they saw and they understood; they moved, and they had sense and feeling. Four were made by the Gods, and the Gods gave names to them, to the First Men. They were Balam-Quitze, Balam-Agab, Mahucutah, and Iqi-Balam, and they were our fathers.

But the Gods saw that when the First Men lifted up their heads, their gaze took in all that was before them. Nothing was hidden from them; they knew all things. "This is not well," the Gods said to one another. "These are not simple creatures; they will rival us who are their creators." The Men of Maize rendered thanks to the Gods who had created them, saying, "We speak, we understand, we think, we walk; we see what is far and what is near; we understand all things great and small, and our gaze takes in the heavens and the earth." But what they said was not welcome to Tepeu, and Gucumatz, and Hurakan. Then the Heart of the Sky breathed a cloud before the First Men so that their eyes were covered as with a mist. They saw, but they did not see clearly what was far nor what was near. Their vision and their wisdom became small—small as they are with us.

The First Men slumbered, and during their slumber wives were made and brought to their sides. When they wakened they knew their wives, and the hearts of the First Men were filled with gladness. Children were born to them and the race of men increased and multiplied. They said prayers to the Maker, the Former, the Heart of the Sky. They prayed that children might be given them. They prayed, too, that

light might come into the world. In the time of the First Men there was
no sun in the sky.

In Tulan-Zuiva, the Place of the Seven Caves and the Seven
Ravines, gods were given them, a god for each clan of men. Tohil was
the god given to Balam-Quitze. Tohil gave Balam-Quitze's clan the gift
of fire, and when the first flame was extinguished by rain, he made fire
for them again by striking the ground with his sandal. Men of other
clans came to the clan that had Tohil for its god, and, with chattering
teeth, begged fire from them. But fire would not be given them, and they
went away, their hearts filled with misery. In those days there was no
sun to give warmth to the men who were upon the earth.

Men grew disheartened waiting for the sun to appear. Anxiously
they looked for the coming of the Morning Star, which should appear
before the sun's first rising. The star did not appear. Then the First
Men resolved that they would go to the place that was known to them
as "The Place of Sunrise."

As they started from Tulan-Zuiva for that place, a bird cried out
to them, "Ye shall die, ye shall be lost. I am your portent, and I
say that to you. Do you not believe me?" But the First Men went out
without heeding the wailing of that bird that was called "The guard
of the ravine." They went on and the owl prophesied to them, "Ye
shall die, ye shall be lost." They went on without heeding the owl.
The parrot cried out to them, "Ye shall die, ye shall be lost." But the
First Men answered the parrot back, saying, "Thou wailest when it is
spring; it is because the rain has ceased that thou dost wail. To us thou
art no portent." They went to the sea-shore, but the water they could not
cross. Then the staff that one had taken in his hands as they went out
of the gate of Tulan-Zuiva they put into the sands. The waters then
divided, and the First Men crossed from that place. He who is called
Zakiqoxol they met upon their way. "Who are these children who come
this way?" Zakiqoxol shouted out. "Who art thou? Why barrest thou
our road?" the First Men cried. "Do not kill me; I, who am here, I
am the burning heart of the forest." The First Men gave clothing to
him; they gave him his blood-red cuirass, his blood-red shoes, the
dying garment of Zakiqoxol.

And going past the place that Zakiqoxol guarded they came to
the Place of Sunrise. They burned incense. And they saw the

Morning Star. They watched it, its splendour growing as it rose in the sky. Then they saw the dawn coming. The sun appeared, and the animals, great and small, prostrated themselves as its light came upon them. The sun was not great and bright as it is now with us; it was small, pale, and shadowy. Nevertheless, it dried up the dampness that was upon the earth, making it more fit for men to live on.

Also at the first appearance of the sun the great First Beasts were turned into stone—the First Jaguar, the First Puma, the First Snake; also the gods of the clans were changed into stone: Tohil, Avilix, and Hacavitz felt their arms stiffen like the branches of trees; then in all their parts they became stone. Had the great First Beasts stayed upon the earth all creation would have been destroyed by them; and the gods who were turned into stone would have made life burdensome for men.

Now the First Men, the Four Brothers, had come to the mountain Hacavitz; they had seen the mountain lighted by the sun, and by the moon, and by the stars. Yet sorrow came upon them because of their memory of those whom they had left behind them. "Truly, indeed," they sang, "we have beheld the Sun, but where now are they, when at last the day of sunrising has come?" Then they sang, "Lo, we make our return; our work is done; our days are complete." And singing this the Four Brothers went into the mountain, leaving no track behind them.

THE TWIN HEROES AND THE LORDS OF XIBALBA

In Xibalba, the land that the sun goes down into, the land whose Lords are the Lords of the Dead, there grew a tree which was a forbidden tree—none were permitted to approach it. The leaves of that tree were wide and dark; the fruits of it were round and heavy, and they grew like gourds along the branches. A princess of Xibalba said, "Why should I not go to this tree? The fruits of it must be precious." Then she made her way to the tree.

Now amongst the fruits that hung from the branches was the head of a man. And when the princess (Xquiq was her name) stood before the tree and said to herself, "Should I die if I pluck a fruit?" a voice said to her, "Draw nearer." It was from the head that was amongst the wide, dark leaves. And the voice said, "The round lumps upon the branches and amongst the leaves are but skulls and death's-heads. Not as they are am I yet. Do you stretch forth your hand."

The princess stretched her hand forth amongst the branches and through the leaves. Then that head, striving greatly, spat into her hand. "This that I give thee is my posterity," said the head. "Now I shall cease to speak. As for thee, flee from this place into the Upper-world, and go where I shall tell thee." The princess sank down beneath the tree, and the voice told her what man the head had been upon, and told her, too, what place to go to upon the earth.

There had been two brothers whose names were Hunhun-Ahpu and Vukub-Hunapu; they were adepts at ball-playing. The Lords of Xibalba heard of their playing and sent their Owl-men to challenge the brothers to play a game in the Underworld. The brothers agreed to go. They went down a steep descent; they crossed a river in a deep gorge; they crossed a boiling river and a river of blood; they came to four roads that were red, black, white, and yellow. "I am the road to the king," said the black road, and it led the brothers to where two figures were seated on thrones. The brothers saluted them; they received no answer to their salutations, and they heard the scornful laughter of the Lords of Xibalba. Then they knew that the figures were of wood, and they were made ashamed. The game began; angrily the brothers played against the Lords of Xibalba. When that day's game was over they were brought to where they might seat themselves. But the seats they took were heated stones, and the brothers sprang up in pain and went away from them.

Then the Lords of Xibalba conducted them to the House of Gloom: there they were to take their night's rest. Torches were put into their hands, and they were commanded to keep them so that the sticks would not be black when the brothers appeared before the Lords of Xibalba the next day. The brothers did not know what to do to keep this command. They were but a short time in the House of Gloom when the torches burned out, and they were left with the blackened sticks in their hands.

When the brothers appeared before them next day, the Lords of

Xibalba said to them, "Your torches are not as we said they were to be." "Lords," the brothers said, "the torches burned themselves out." But the Lords of Xibalba had the brothers sacrificed; their heads were put upon the branches of the tree that it was forbidden to approach. The head of Hunhun-Ahpu had life still in it when Xquiq came to the tree.

She, being found there, was doomed to be sacrificed. The Owl-men were sent to slay her. Xquiq beguiled them. The Owl-men took back to the Lords of the Underworld the thickened sap of a weed as her heart; its smell was the smell of blood, and the Lords of Xibalba were made content.

The princess then journeyed towards the world from which the brothers had come—the Upperworld. She was long upon the way, and she was near to the time of her delivery when she came to the house of Hunhun-Ahpu's mother. She was not well treated for a time; the woman would not receive her as her daughter-in-law, and the woman's two sons who were in the house mocked at her. The woman, Hunhun-Ahpu's mother, told her that before she would be given shelter in the house she would have to gather maize in a field. Xquiq went into the field. The maize had all been cut, and it was left in one heap in the field. She was told that she would have to get maize without touching any that was in the heap. Maize sprang up as she went through the field, and she gathered what was wanted. Then, seeing that the Gods had helped her, Hunhun-Ahpu's mother took Xquiq into the house.

Children were born to her; they were twins, and they were wise from their birth. Their grandmother knew that they would become great heroes and great magicians. But their uncles mocked at them and strove to destroy them. Their uncles were Hunbatz and Hunchouen; they knew all the arts that were then in the world, for they were singers and flute-players, painters and sculptors, jewel-workers and smiths; also they were blow-gun shooters. But to the children of Xquiq they were cruel and envious uncles.

They would not have the youths grow up into men; they would not have them become heroes and magicians whose deeds would be greater than their own. They took the twins into a forest, and they would have sacrificed them there. But the youths transformed them into monkeys: in the trees they stayed. But even as monkeys, Hunbatz and Hunchouen are prayed to by the singers and flute-players, by the painters and sculptors, by the jewel-workers, smiths, and blow-gun shooters to this day.

After this the twins (Hunahpu and Xbalanque were their names) fashioned magic tools for themselves, and with these tools they cleared a field, pulling up the trees and cutting the vines away. The tools worked by themselves while the twins went hunting in the forest. When they came back at the end of the day they found the field ready for sowing. But when they went out of their house the next day they saw the trees growing and the vines flourishing as before. Again they set their magic tools to clear the field, and again they went hunting. And when they came back the field was once more cleared and ready for sowing. They did not sleep that night; they stayed outside their house and watched the field to see what would happen in it. And they saw that when darkness fell all the animals came into the field: the puma came and the jaguar; the hare, the rat, and the opossum; the deer, the coyote, the porcupine, and the peccary; also the birds came into the field. They called upon the felled trees and the cut vines to grow and flourish again. They lifted the tree-trunks and put them back upon their stumps, and they joined the cut vines together. This they did going through the whole of the field, and when the dawn came the twins found their field with trees and vines growing and flourishing in it.

Then they gave chase to the birds and the animals. The birds flew high above their heads. The animals fled swiftly away from them. They caught the deer and the rabbit by their tails. The deer and the rabbit pulled away from them leaving their tails in the brothers' hands. To this day these animals are without their tails. The rat was the only creature the brothers were able to catch and hold. The rat begged mercy from them. It declared that it would reveal a great secret to the brothers if they would spare it its life.

They spared the rat its life, and the rat told them where their grandmother had hidden the ball, the gloves, and the ring which their father and their uncle had used in the days when they played ball. Their grandmother had hidden these things away, fearing that the twins should find them, and become players, and be led to their destruction as their father and their uncle had been led to destruction. Now when they found the ball, the gloves, and the ring, the twins began to play the game; every day they played ball, and soon they forgot everything else except this game.

Now as they went over the world playing games against all sorts of people, they heard of the Earth Giants. There were three of them, and the three were proud and boastful. They gave no reverence to the Gods, for one of them would say, "It is I who am the sun," and another would say, "It is I who move the earth," and the third would say, "I can shake the sky and overturn the ground." The twins when they heard of this insolence resolved that they would leave off playing their game of ball until they had rid the earth of these Giants.

Vukub-Cakix was the first of them. Every day he would say to the whole of creation, "I am above all created beings; I am their sun; I am their dawn; I am their moon. Of silver are the balls of my eyes, and my teeth shine like the sky at noon. My nostrils are like the moon. Of silver is my throne, and the earth lives when I step upon it. I am the sun, I am the moon, I am the bringer of all pleasantness." All this he would say when he came to the tree on which grew the fruit that nourished him; at dawn he used to come to it. Wonderful was the tree that Vukub-Cakix owned.

The brothers came to the tree. They hid themselves in the branches. When the Giant came to the tree, Hunahpu blew a dart at him with his blow-gun. It pierced his jaw. Then the Giant raised up his arms and caught Hunahpu in the tree. He tore his arm off. Then carrying the arm, and roaring in pain, the Giant went back to his house.

Now the twins had to get back the arm that had been torn off one of their bodies. Also they had to destroy Vukub-Cakix. So they changed their appearance and they went to the Giant's house as physicians. They saw where Hunahpu's arm was being held before a fire; the Giant's wife was holding it there, and she was chanting spells over it, so that the arm might become withered and never join with the shoulder again. And they heard Vukub-Cakix crying because of the pain in his jaw.

They told him they could cure his pain. "It is not because of the dart shot through your jaw that you suffer," they said, "but it is because there are worms in your teeth. We will take your teeth out, and your jaw will be well again." "It is by my teeth alone that I am king," the Giant said. "All my beauty comes from my shining teeth and my shining eyeballs." "We will give you more shining teeth in their place," the brothers said. The Giant then consented, and he let the brothers tie him to the roots of trees. They drew his teeth out. They took away the gleam of his eyes. And then the Giant, Vukub-Cakix, died where he was tied.

They snatched Hunahpu's arm from the Giant's wife as she was still uttering spells over it. It was unwithered yet, and they joined it to Hunahpu's shoulder. And then they went forth to destroy the second of the Earth Giants.

This was Zipacna. He shook the earth, making men's houses fall down. The twins came upon him when they had with them a great host of youths. They beguiled Zipacna so that he went down into a great and a deep pit. Then Hunahpu and Xbalanque and all who were with them hurled trees down upon him. After a while the Giant ceased to stir in the pit. They filled it up with stones; they built a great house on it; they went within the house and made merry over the death of Zipacna, the Giant who made the earth shake. But as they were making merry Zipacna rose beneath the house; he flung it down; he took the hundreds of young men who had been the brothers' helpers and he flung them up into the sky. There they stayed; they have become the Four Hundred Stars.

But Hunahpu and Xbalanque the Giant was not able to catch. And when he went away they followed on his tracks, and once again they planned his destruction. Zipacna loved to gorge himself with great crabs that came up from the sea. The brothers formed a crab out of wood—the greatest crab that had ever been seen in the world—and they placed it in a deep ravine. They came to where the Giant was, and, saying that they were hunters, told him of a crab so great that they had been frightened by the sight of it. The Giant went to where he could see it. Deep down in the ravine he saw what seemed to him to be the world's greatest crab, and he climbed down the face of a cliff to come to it. And when he was down in the ravine the brothers hurled mountains upon him—mountains of such weight that not even he could get from under them. And so Zipacna, he who shook the earth, was destroyed by Hunahpu and Xbalanque.

Then, as the twins went through the world, playing the game of ball and challenging others to play against them, they came upon the last of the Earth Giants. This was Cabrakan. He tore through the forests and he made the skies shake. They came upon him as he was wallowing in his lair on the ground. "How strong art thou, O Cabrakan?" said the brothers to him. "We have heard it said that thou couldst shift a mountain as great as this one." "I will shift it while you watch me," said Cabrakan. "Eat first, O Cabrakan," said the brothers, "We will kill and cook a bird for thine eating." So they killed a great bird, and they put the bird in the earth to bake. But they put poison in the mud they encrusted the bird with. The Giant watched their cooking; he ate of the great bird greedily, and when he had licked up the scraps of flesh and crunched all the bones, he started to shift the mountain. But no sooner had he grasped the top of it than he fell down dead into the ravine that was near the mountain.

And so the Earth Giants who had disturbed the world, Vukub-Cakix, Zipacna, and Cabrakan, were destroyed by the hero twins, Hunahpu and Xbalanque. But the Lords of the Underworld had heard their movements as they went up and down on the earth, playing their game of ball. "Who are these who make such play with the ball?" they said to one another. "Do not the withered heads of Hunhun-Ahpu and Vukub-Hunahpu hang amongst the branches of our tree? Who, then, are these who play on the earth as they once played?" Then the Lords of the Underworld sent their Owl-men to challenge the brothers to play a game of ball in Xibalba.

They went down into Xibalba. They went down a long descent; they crossed a river in a deep gorge; they crossed a boiling torrent; they crossed a river of blood; beyond the fourth river they came upon the four roadways—the black, white, red, and yellow roadways.

They had heard from their mother and their grandmother how the Lords of Xibalba had received their father and their uncle, and the brothers resolved to use all the craft they had against them. So when the black road said, "I am the way to the king," they did not go upon it at first: they took an insect named Xan and sent it upon the road. And Xan came first to the images that were seated upon thrones: it pricked each of them; they did not move. Then Xan went where others stood: it pricked a leg of each and each gave a cry. "What is it, Hun-

Came?" one was asked. "What is it, Vukub-Came?" All the names of the Lords of Xibalba were uttered—Xiquipat, Ahalpuh, Cuchumaquiq, Chamiabak, Ahalcana, Chamiaholom, Patan, Quiqxic, Quiqrixgag, and Quiqure. And having heard the names, Xan went back to the brothers, told them the names it had heard, and described where the images of wood were seated.

Then the twins went on the black roadway and came to where the Lords of Xibalba stood beside the images of wood. The images they did not salute. They saluted the Lords of Xibalba, each according to his own name. Then were the Lords alarmed; they knew not what sort of men they had to deal with. They motioned the brothers towards the seats that were heated stones; but they would not seat themselves. "These are not our seats," they said.

Then they began to play the game of ball against the Lords of the Underworld. The night came before the game was finished. Then the brothers were brought to the House of Gloom in which they were to rest until the next day when the game would be played again. Torches were put into their hands, and they were commanded to appear before the Lords of Xibalba next day with torches that were not blackened.

When they went within the House of Gloom they quenched their torches. They covered them with red paint. When they came out of the House of Gloom their torches were unblackened. "Who are you?" cried the Lords of Xibalba. "Whence do you come?" "Who can say who we are, or whence we come?" the brothers answered. "We ourselves do not know." Again the game was started, and the brothers played against the Lords of Xibalba. And now the game was coming to its end, and they of the Underworld were becoming more and more anxious about ways of bringing to destruction the two who had come to them from the world above.

They sent them to the House of Cold; there the brothers kept the warmth of life in them by burning knots of pine which they found under the dust. They sent them into the House of the Jaguars, and there they fought off for the whole of the night the fierce beasts that snarled all round them. They sent them to get flowers from Vukub-Came's garden, a garden that was guarded by poisonous snakes; the ants aided them, for all creatures were ready to help the brothers in the game they were playing against the Lords of the Underworld;

the ants brought the flowers to them; the brothers filled four vases with flowers and presented them to the Lords of Xibalba.

The game was begun again, and at the end of the day Hunahpu and Xbalanque were sent to the most dread place of all; they were sent into the House of the Bats. All night they lay in the cave, the bats hovering over them. They lay flat upon their faces. But Hunahpu lifted his head. Then a great bat swept down and sheared his head off. And Hunahpu would have bled to death if a tortoise had not come and fixed himself to where the head had been. The tortoise held to his neck, giving him something like a head. Next morning the Lords of Xibalba came crowding around the cave, demanding that the brothers come forth and play the finish of the game. As they stood before the cave-mouth a rabbit sprang up at their feet. The Lords of Xibalba, thinking that this was the ball that the brothers had thrown, ran after the rabbit. Then Xbalanque looked around the cave that now was lighted. And on a ledge he found Hunahpu's head. He took the tortoise off and put the head upon Hunahpu's neck. It fastened itself there, and when the Lords of Xibalba came back from their chase of the rabbit, the brothers were ready to play the finish of the game with them.

They played; they won over the Lords of Xibalba. Then the brothers told them that they would show themselves to them as wonder-workers. They had themselves killed and their bones ground to powder. Then they transformed themselves into fishes and swam away. They came back as beggars and stood once more before the Lords of the Underworld. They burned down houses, and immediately they built them up again. They killed a dog belonging to one of the Lords and immediately restored it to life and movement. They killed each other, and brought each other back to life again. The Lords of Xibalba cried, "Do the like with us. Make us, too, know death, and life after death." "Can death exist for you, Lords of Xibalba?" the brothers cried. "Let us know death, and life afterwards," they continued to cry.

They had consented to death. The brothers slew them, but they did not bring them back to life again. They left them lying under the branches of their own forbidden tree. Then Hunahpu and Xbalanque declared who they were. "We are the avengers of the deaths of our father and our uncle," they cried. They took their withered heads from amongst the dark leaves, and they buried them with honours. Then to

all who were left in Xibalba they said, "Your state and your power
are gone from you. No more will you rule over any creatures. Go forth
from where you ruled, and make things of clay; make pots and maize-
grinders. The beasts that live in the wilderness shall be your prey
and your helpers, but all that is pleasant, all that is cultivated, shall
be far from you. Only the bees shall be yours to care for and to rule
over. O ye wicked, cruel, dismal ones, go forth and fulfill your
dooms." So the Twin Heroes said, and they who had lorded it in the
Underworld went forth and took up their menial tasks.

QUETZALCOATL

In Tollan dwelt Quetzalcoatl. And in Tollan all the arts and crafts
that we know of were first practised, for Quetzalcoatl taught them to
the people there. He taught them the smelting of silver and the clearing and setting of precious stones; he taught the craft of building with
stones; he taught them how to make statues, and paint signs in books,
and keep count of the moons and suns. All crafts except the craft of
war Quetzalcoatl taught the people of Tollan. And they made sacrifice
to him with bread, and flowers, and perfumes, and not as other peoples
made sacrifice to the other gods—by tearing the hearts out of the
opened breasts of men and women.

He lived in a house that was made of silver: four chambers that
house had: the chamber to the east was of gold, the chamber to the
west was set with stones of precious green—emeralds and turquoises
and nephrite stones, the chamber to the south was set with coloured
sea-shells, and the chamber to the north was set with jasper. The house
was thatched with the feathers of bright-plumaged birds. All the birds
of rich plumage and sweet song were gathered in that place. In the
fields the maize grew so big that a man could not carry more than one
stalk in his arms; pumpkins were great in their round as a man is
high; cotton grew in the fields red and yellow, blue, and black, and
white, and men did not have to dye it. All who lived where Quetzalcoatl was had everything to make them prosperous and happy.

There was a time when they did not have maize, when they lived
upon roots and on what they gained in the chase. Maize there was, but
it was hidden within a mountain, and no one could come to where it

was. Different gods had tried to rend the mountain apart that they might come to where the maize was; but this could not be done. Then Quetzalcoatl took the form of a black ant; with a red ant to guide him he went within the mountain Tonacatepetl, and he came to where the maize was: he took the grain, and laboriously he bore it back to men. Then men planted fields with maize; they had crops for the first time; they built cities, and they lived settled lives, and Quetzalcoatl showed them all the crafts that they could learn from him. They honoured him who dwelt in the shining house. And Quetzalcoatl had many servants; some of them were dwarfs, and all were swift of foot.

Then it came to pass that Tezcatlipoca, he who can go into all places, he who wanders over the earth stirring up strife and war amongst men, descended upon Tollan by means of spider-webs. And from the mountain he came down on a blast of wind of such coldness that it killed all the flowers in Quetzalcoatl's bright garden. And Quetzalcoatl, feeling that coldness, said to his servants, "One has come who will drive me hence; perhaps it were better that I went before he drives me, and drank from a fountain in the Land of the Sun, whence I may return, young as a boy." So he said, and his servants saw him burn down his house of silver with its green precious stones and its thatch of bright plumage, and its door-posts of white and red shells. And they saw him call upon his birds of sweet song and rich plumage, and they heard him bidding them to fly into the land of Anahuac.

Then Tezcatlipoca, that god and that sorcerer, went to where Quetzalcoatl stood, and took him into the ball-court that the two might play a game together. All the people of the city stood round to watch that game. The ball had to be cast through a ring that was high upon the wall. Quetzalcoatl took up the ball to cast it. As he did Tezcatlipoca changed himself into a jaguar and sprang upon him. Then Quetzalcoatl fled. And Tezcatlipoca chased him, driving him through the streets of the city, and out into the highways of the country.

His dwarfs fled after him and joined themselves to him. With them he crossed the mountains and came to a hill on which a great tree grew. Under it he rested. As he rested he looked into a mirror and he said, "I am grown to be an old man." Then he threw the mirror down and took up stones and cast them at the tree.

He went on, and his dwarfs made music for him, playing on flutes as they went before him. Once again he became weary, and he rested on a stone by the wayside; there, looking back towards Tollan, he wept, and his tears pitted the stone on which he sat, and his hands left their imprints upon it where he grasped the stone. The stone is there to this day with the pits and the imprints upon it. He rose up, and once again he went on his way. And men from Tollan met him, and he instructed them in crafts that he had not shown them before.

But he did not give them the treasure of jewels that his dwarfs and humpbacked servants carried for him. He flung this treasure into the fountain Cozcaapan; there it stays to this day—Quetzalcoatl's treasure. On his way he passed over a Fire-mountain and over a mountain of snow. On the mountain of snow his dwarfs and humpbacked servants all died from the cold. Bitterly he bewailed them in a song he made in that place.

Then Quetzalcoatl went down the other side of the mountain, and he came to the sea-shore. He made a raft of snakes, and on that raft he sailed out on the sea. Or so some say, telling Quetzalcoatl's story. And those who tell this say that he came to the land of Tlappallan in the Country of the Sun, and there he drank of the Water of Immortality. They say that he will one day return from that land young as a boy. But others say that when he reached the sea-shore he divested himself of his robe with its bright feathers, of his snake-skin mask of the colour of turquoise, and that, leaving these vestments upon the shore, he cast himself into a fire and was consumed to ashes. And they say that Quetzalcoatl's ashes changed into bright-coloured and sweet-singing birds, and that his heart went up into the sky and became the Morning Star. After he had been dead for eight days that star became visible to men, and thereafter Quetzalcoatl was named the Lord of the Dawn.

QUETZALCOATL'S ENEMY

Quetzalcoatl's enemy did not leave Tollan. Naked he went into the market-place and stayed there; where he sat was under the palace of the king. The king had but one daughter, and this girl, looking out upon the market-place, saw Tezcatlipoca. He pretended to be selling peppers. The girl, straightway, was smitten with love for him; she sickened and was like to die. When the king inquired about her the women told him that his daughter was like to die because of her love for a man whom she had seen in the market-place, a foreigner and a naked man.

The king sought out this foreigner. And when Quetzalcoatl's enemy was brought before him, the king said, "Thou must heal my daughter of her sickness." Then they clothed him, and dyed his body, and cut his hair, and brought him in to the king's daughter. And the girl was delighted with his company, and the cunning Tezcatlipoca made her sound and well.

After this Tezcatlipoca adorned himself, and he sent a crier from the king's palace to tell the youths and girls of Tollan of a feast he had prepared for them. They all gathered together in the market-place. Tezcatlipoca led them, playing upon his flute; the youths and girls followed him, singing and dancing. Up the mountain Texcalapa he led them. There he had them dance. He sang songs to them; they sang the same songs after him, verse for verse, although they had not known before the songs he sang. Then he beat upon a drum and a panic came upon the youths and girls; they ran, and their way was across a bridge. But Tezcatlipoca crossed the bridge before them, and he broke the bridge down, and the youths and girls, as they came to the place, pushed each other down. Those who fell from that place were turned into rocks and stones.

He changed himself again and he went into the garden that Quetzalcoatl had made. He called on the men and women of Tollan to come into it, that they might repair the waste of that garden. And when they came into it he fell upon them with a digging-tool, and left them lying dead amongst the blasted flowers in Quetzalcoatl's garden.

Another evil he did to the people of Tollan. Changing himself again he came into the market-place, and he showed the people a manikin that he had, a manikin the size of his finger who danced upon the palm of his hand. All crowded round him to see the wonder, and many of the people were trampled down. Then they heard a voice— it was Tezcatlipoca's voice, but he made it come from afar—that said, "Do not be befooled, people of Tollan. Take stones and slay this sorcerer and his manikin." They took up stones and flung them at the man and the manikin, and they left them on the ground, covered with heaps of stones. Then the odour from their bodies infected the place, and many people died of sickness that came from that odour. A voice was heard by them; it said, "Cast the bodies of the man and the manikin outside the town so that no more will die from the disease that comes from them." Then the people of Tollan fastened ropes to the man and the manikin and pulled at them. But such was the weight that was in the bodies that the people by no effort could move them. More ropes were fastened to the bodies and more people pulled at the ropes. But the ropes broke with sudden snaps, and those who were pulling were killed when they broke.

Then a voice came to the people, saying, "O people of Tollan, a verse of a song will do it." The corpse of the man and the corpse of the manikin sang, and the people took up the song, and pulled at the bodies. This time they dragged them outside the city. They cast the bodies down a steep place, and they returned to the city of Tollan.

They went back as if they were all drunken, and none amongst them could remember what they had been doing. As they went back they saw that the mountain that was beside Tollan was all on fire. They saw a white bird transfixed with an arrow flying over the city. And then stones rained down upon them, and their city was left waste and uninhabitable.

THE GODS OF THE AZTECA

Quetzalcoatl told the people about the Gods and about the creation of men and women. . . . At first there was Citlalatonac and Citlalicue, the Sky-father and the Earth-mother. Then Citlalicue gave birth to a knife of flint, and when this knife of flint was flung down it became the sixteen hundred Earth-gods. They had to live as men and women of to-day have to live—by labouring and searching for their food. But after a while they began to think that it was unfitting that they should have to do this—they, the children of the Sky-father and the Earth-mother. They sent Tlotli the Hawk to their mother, asking that men be made who would serve them, the sixteen hundred Earth-gods.

Now there had been an earth before the earth they lived on, and men and women had been upon it, and the earth and the men and women on it had been destroyed, not once, but many times. Once the earth and all that was on it had been destroyed by floods. Once all had been destroyed by the force of great winds, and once all had been destroyed by fire. Now when the sixteen hundred Earth-gods asked that a race of men and women be created who would serve them, the Earth-mother told them what they should do to bring about this creation.

They were to send one of their number down to Mictlampa, the place where there is no light, and the one who went down was to ask the Lord of that place for a bone—the bone of a man of the last race that had perished. The Earth-gods chose Xolotl for their messenger; they sent him down to Mictlampa, the place where there is no light.

Xolotl went where they sent him; he came before Mictlantecutli, the Lord of Mictlampa, and found him pouring fire into a vessel of blood. And Mictlantecutli, he whose head is a bare skull, thinking that he might beguile one of the Earth-gods and keep him for ever in that place where there is no light, spoke fairly to him. He would give the Earth-gods a bone, he said, a bone of one of the giants who had dwelt upon the earth; this bone should be put into a vessel when it was brought into the Upperworld, and each of the Earth-gods was to put a drop of his blood into the vessel with the bone; out of what would brew in the vessel two who would make the new race of men and women would come.

Xolotl knew that Mictlantecutli intended evil to him. He stole the bone and bore it away through that place of darkness. The bone was a great one, for it was a bone of one who belonged to the giant race. Yet the messenger of the Earth-gods was able to go swiftly with it through the darkness. But when he came near to the Upperworld the great owls that guard Mictlantecutli's realm flew at him and tore at his eyes. Xolotl stumbled and the great bone fell and broke into fragments. He gathered up the fragments and carried them into the Upperworld where the rest of the Earth-gods waited for him.

Then the sixteen hundred Earth-gods put the fragments of the great bone in a vessel, and each of them drew blood from his own body and dropped the blood into the vessel that held the fragments of the bone. For three days they watched over it, stirring what was in the vessel. Their labour, it seemed, was in vain. Then, on the fourth day, what was in the vessel simmered and bubbled. Out of the brew emerged a human child, a boy. The Earth-gods watched over the vessel for another four days. Then out of the brew emerged a human child, a girl. The Earth-gods took the children and nourished them on the juice of the maguey-plant; the children grew to be a man and a woman. They became man and wife, and from them come the men and women of our time.

The bone that Xolotl brought into the Upperworld was in fragments: for that reason the men and women whom it went to form are not great of stature like the giants who had lived on the earth before; the fragments were of different sizes, and for that reason the men and woman of to-day are not all of one size—some are very tall, and others are small, and there are dwarfs amongst them. The world that the first men and women of our race came into was without sun or moon. Then the great Gods held a council to decide how luminaries might be made for the sky.

At that council the gods declared that it was their will that luminaries should be formed by transformations of a pair of gods; they declared that the two who should enter a fire and allow themselves to be consumed should become the sun and the moon. They built two towers, one for each of the gods who would undertake to make a luminary for the day and for the night, and they strewed the ground with branches and flowers, and they made sacrifices. Two of the gods agreed to cast themselves down into the fires and make themselves into the sun and the moon. These two put on their crowns and their robes of bright feathers and they went up upon the towers. The rest of the gods sat around the fires that had been lighted for four days. Then the two who were upon the towers cast themselves into the fires beneath them; they were consumed.

Then the gods, at that sacred place, waited to witness the resurrection of the pair as the sun and the moon. Four days they waited beside the towers. Then they saw the sky grow red; they knew not what was going to come about; they were terrified. The sun appeared in the sky; it was very red, and none of the gods could look at it because of its blinding rays. Then the moon appeared at the other side of the sky; its light was no less great than the sun's. One of the gods took a rabbit and flung the rabbit in the face of the moon. The rabbit remained there to dim the moon's brightness. And so the moon was made more dim than the sun.

But the two luminaries stayed moveless in the sky. "Die, all of you," they cried down to the gods, "die all of you and create the stars." Then a great wind came. It blew upon them until the gods were destroyed by the force of it. Their remains were carried up to the sky, and in the sky they stay, having become the stars. The wind blew upon the sun; it made it hurry across the sky. It did not blow upon the moon, and so the moon remains moveless in the sky. But the moon comes into the sky at a different time from the sun.

All this Quetzalcoatl told the dwellers in Tollan.

THE AZTECA

Many times since the Azteca came into the valley had the years been tied into bundles, each bundle being fifty-two years. And many times at the Tying of the Years had the fires been quenched and a new fire lighted on the breast of a sacrificed man. Many times had that festival come round that is called the Knot of the Years, and many times had the king and the priests consulted about the portents that show themselves when the fires are quenched and a new fire lighted.

Montezuma the Conqueror was king at that Tying of the Years. And the portent that showed itself was in a pair of great sandals that were found upon the floor of the Temple of Huizilopochtli, the War God of the Azteca. Montezuma the Conqueror said, "This is a sign from Huizilopochtli; it signifies that he will never leave the Azteca." And he said to the priests, "Bear these sandals to Coatlicue, the mother of our god. She dwells in Aztlan the White Place. Out of Aztlan the Azteca went in the old days, guided by Huizilopochtli. They made themselves possessors of the valley; they conquered the tribes of the valley and the uplands; they built the great city Tenochtitlan. Go, tell Coatlicue all this. And say that by my arms they have now subdued the people farthest away, and have taken captives for the sacrifices from them. Huizilopochtli will never leave a people who have proved themselves such conquerors. Go; bear these sandals in all reverence to the mother of Huizilopochtli; they will be a sign to her that her son will not return to Aztlan the White Place."

So the priests of Huizilopochtli searched in their books and found out the ways that led back to Aztlan the White Place. It was a mountain that waters surrounded. The waters were filled with fish; flocks of ducks swam around; birds delighted those who dwelt there with the sight of their green and yellow plumage and enchanted them with their songs. And there, in the caverns of the mountain, the Azteca had dwelt for unnumbered generations. All the good things they had had been brought from there—the maize, the beans, the fruits. For on the waters there were barges, and on the barges grew all nourishing things. And when the men and women of the Azteca went out of the caverns that were filled with precious stones they would go in canoes amongst the floating gardens, and watch the ducks swimming, the cormorants diving, the herons flying overhead; they would gather the bright flowers of the gardens and listen to the enchanting songs of the birds.

But Huizilopochtli roused up many to depart from that place; they left the mountain and their floating gardens, taking with them, however, many of the plants that grew in the gardens. They went upon the land. The herbs of the ground pricked them; the stones bruised their feet. Plains that were filled with thorns spread out before them. Jaguars lay in wait for them, and sprang upon stragglers and tore their flesh. But aroused by Huizilopochtli and guided by him the Azteca went on. They went through deserts where famine wasted them. Then they reached the Place of the Seven Caves where they rested and were at ease for a while. Then they came to where there was a tree broken by lightning, and there some stayed. Others went on, Huizilopochtli still guiding them. And at last they came to the Lake Tezcuco. They beheld a high rock with a cactus growing on it. Upon the cactus was an eagle. Up he rose; he flew towards the rising sun, and in his talons he held a serpent. The omen was good; the Azteca halted their march there. Many battles did they fight there; they subdued the tribes that dwelt in the valley, and they built Tenochtitlan, the greatest of cities.

And now the priests of Huizilopochtli, the ambassadors of Montezuma the Conqueror, travelled the ways back to Aztlan the White Place. In Tollan, which is the navel of the world, they found four magicians who guided them across the deserts. Then they beheld a mountain that rose out of the midst of waters. The priests went towards it, leaving the magicians behind them. The smell of flowers came to them on the airs of night; in the morning they heard the songs of birds. On they went, and they saw the gardens upon the water; they saw the flocks of ducks swimming around, and the cormorants diving from the juttings of the mountain, and the herons fishing or flying overhead. They saw the birds of green and yellow plumage flying from garden to garden, and they heard them singing from the branches of fruitful trees.

The people who were there spoke to them in a language that the priests knew, and asked them why they had come across deserts to them. The priests said that they had come back to the ancestral place. They brought to Coatlicue, they said, the sandals of her son Huizilopochtli.

But when the priests mentioned the name of Montezuma the Conqueror and mentioned the names of his lords, the people of the waters said that those who had gone from them in the old days had borne no such names. They named the lords who were with the Azteca when they went from Aztlan the White Place. Then the ambassadors of Montezuma said, "We know not these lords; we have never seen them; they are long since dead." Then the people of the waters were surprised, and they said, "We who knew them are living yet."

The priest of Coatlicue came to bring them into the presence of the Goddess. She lived on a peak of the mountain. As they went upward the feet of the men from Tenochtitlan sank in the ground, for the mountain became like a heap of loosened sand. "What makes you so heavy?" their guide asked them. He was an ancient, but he went lightly upon the ground. "What do you eat?" he asked them. "We eat flesh, and we drink pulque," the ambassadors of Montezuma answered him. "It is the meat and drink you have consumed that prevent your reaching the place where your fathers dwelt. Here we eat but fruits, and roots, and grain; we drink only water, and so there is no clog upon us when we walk." As he said this a swift wind came and brought him and brought the ambassadors up to the peak of the mountain and into the cavern where Coatlicue dwelt.

They saw her; her dress was of serpents, and they were terrified of her. When she looked upon the sandals they laid before her she lamented, saying, "When Huizilopochtli went from Aztlan he said to me, his mother, 'When my time is accomplished I shall return to your lap; until that time I shall know nought save weariness. Therefore, give me two pairs of sandals, one for going forth, and one for returning.' And now, you say, he will not return to this lap of mine." Then the Goddess put on a garment of mourning, and the ambassadors went from the cavern where she dwelt.

They did not think that they stayed long in Aztlan the White Place. But when they returned to Tenochtitlan they found that the years were again being tied into a bundle, that the fires of the land were quenched, and that a new fire was being lighted on the breast of a sacrificed man. A king who was called the Second Montezuma ruled over the Azteca. Many and dread portents showed themselves at that Tying of the Years. A fisherman caught a strange bird: a shining stone was in the head of that bird, and when that stone was brought to him, the Second Montezuma looked into it and he saw wars being waged against the Azteca in which strange and more death-dealing weapons than he had ever known were being used. And at the time of the quenching of the fires his sister had died; she had been buried, but now she was seen seated at a fountain in a garden of the palace. Montezuma and his lords went before her. She told them that she had been brought to the Eastern Sea. She had seen great ships upon the sea, and in the ships were fair-faced and bearded men who carried more death-dealing weapons than any that had ever been seen in the land of the Azteca. And after that a pillar of fire appeared in the east, and it seemed to cast fire upon the whole land. Rejoicings were heard amongst the captives, and lamentations were heard amongst the old men: it was thought that the pillar of fire in the east presaged the destruction of the Empire of the Azteca.

ZUÑI

ZUÑI

PAÍYATUMA AND THE MAIDENS OF THE CORN

Whence came they, the Maidens who are told of in the stories and sung of in the songs of our Fathers, the seven Maidens with their magic wands and plumes who were lovelier than the seven bright stars that are above us now? Paíyatuma the Flute-player, the God of Dew and of the Dawn, brought them to our Fathers; they were his foster-children. And when he had brought them to where our Fathers were, he sang a song that warned all who were there that these were virgins and must be forever held as sacred beings. Paíyatuma sang:

> The corn that ye see growing upward
> Is the gift of my seven bright maidens:
> Look well that ye nourish their persons,
> Nor change ye the gift of their being
> As fertile of flesh for all men
> To the bearing of children for men,
> Lest ye lose them, and seek them in vain.

The mists of the morning were clearing away. Even as his voice had already gone into them, Paíyatuma the Flute-playing God went into the mists. Seven plants of corn he had left before our Fathers; seven Maidens he had left who would cause the corn to grow. "Thanks, thanks to thee, O Paíyatuma," our Fathers cried into the mists that closed round him. "Verily we will cherish the Maidens and the substance of their flesh."

Thereafter, as the season came round, our Fathers would build for the Maidens a bower of cedar-wood that was roofed with timbers brought from beyond the mountains. They would light a fire before the bower. All night, backwards and forwards, the Corn Maidens would dance to the music of drum and rattle and the songs sung by the elders. They would dance by the side of the seven growing plants of the corn, motioning them upward with their magic wands and plumes.

Then the first Maiden would embrace the first growing plant. As

311

she did this the fire would leap up, throwing out a yellow light. The second Maiden would embrace the second growing plant, and the fire would burn smokily with a fuller grasping of the brands; blue would be the light the fire would throw out. The third Maiden would embrace the third of the growing plants, and at this the fire would reach to the fulness of its mastery, and the light it would throw out would be red. Then the fourth Maiden would embrace the fourth growing plant, and the fire, flameless now, would throw out a white light. As the fifth Maiden embraced the fifth growing plant the fire would give up its breath in clouds of sparks and its light would be streaked with many colours. The sixth Maiden would embrace the sixth growing plant; the fire would be sleeping then, giving out less light than heat. And as the seventh Maiden embraced the seventh growing plant the fire would waken afresh in the wind of the morning, and, as the fire of the wanderer stays glowing with many colours, it would stay glowing. Beautiful the dance of the seven Maidens, delightful the music they would dance to. And when the mists of the morning came they would go within the bower and lay down their magic wands and plumes, and their soft and shining dresses, and thereafter they would mingle with the people.

All rejoiced in the dance of the white-robed Corn Maidens. But a time came when certain of the young men of the village began to speak of a music they heard sounding from Thunder Mountain. This music was more wonderful than the music we had for the dance of the Maidens. And the young men declared that the dance that went to it, the dance they had not seen, must be more wonderful than the dance that our Maidens were praised for. They spoke of these things so often that they made our dance seem a thing that was of little worth. Then the Fathers summoned two messengers and bade them take the trail that went up the mountain. They were to find out about the music and the dance. Perchance they might be joined with ours, and a music and a dance that would seem wonderful to all might be given between the bower and the fire.

The messengers took the trail that went up Thunder Mountain. As they climbed they heard the sound of flutes. They went within the cavern that the music was being played in—the Cavern of the Rainbow. Mists surrounded them as they went within; but they knew what being was there, and they made reverence to him. Here was Paíyatuma the Flute-player, the God of Dew and of the Dawn.

They heard the music and they saw the dance that was being given in the Cavern of the Rainbow. The music was not as our music, for the musicians were flute-players. The Maidens who danced were as beautiful as our Corn Maidens; seven were they also. They carried in their hands wands of cottonwood: from the branchlets and buds of these wands streamlets flowed. "They are like your Maidens as the House of the Seven Stars seen in water is like the House of the Seven Stars as it is in the sky. They are fertile, not of seed, but of the Water of Life wherein the seed is quickened." So said Paíyatuma, the God of Dew and of the Dawn. And when the messengers looked upon them they saw that the Maidens were taller than ours were, and that their colour was fainter.

Then did Paíyatuma lift up his flute and play upon it. A drum sounded also, and the cavern shook as with thunder. And as the music was played a white mist came from the flutes of the players. "Athirst are men ever for that which they have not," said Paíyatuma the Flute-player through the mist. "It is well that ye have come, and it shall be as ye wish," said he to the messengers. They knew then that he was aware of what errand they had been sent upon.

They went back and told the elders of the village that Paíyatuma's flute-players would come amongst them and make music for the dance of the Corn Maidens. The flute-players came down to the dancing-ground. Out of their bower came our white-clad, beautiful Corn Maidens. The flute-players lifted up their flutes and made music for the dance. And as the Maidens danced in the light of the. fire they who played the flutes looked on them in such wise that they were fain to let their hair fall down and cast down their eyes. Seeing the players of the flutes look on the Maidens amorously, our own youths looked on them amorously also. They plucked at their garments as they, in their dancing, came near them. Then the players of the flutes and our own youths sprang up and followed them, shouting and laying unseemly hands upon the beautiful, white-clad maidens.

Yet they finished their dance, and the seventh Maiden embraced the seventh growing plant. The mists came down, and unseen, the Maidens went into their bower. They laid their magic wands and their plumes upon the ground; they laid their white robes down also. Then they stole away. They were gone when Paíyatuma appeared. He came forth from the mists and stood amongst the assembled people. The flute-players, waving their flutes over the people who were there, followed Paíyatuma as he strode, wordless, through the mists that were rolling up the mountain.

The drum was beaten, the rattles were shaken, but still the Maidens did not come forth from their bower. The Elders went within and they found nought there but the wands and plumes and the garments that had been laid away. Then it was known that the Corn Maidens had gone. Grief and dismay filled the hearts of the people. "We must seek for and find our Maidens," they all cried, "for lacking them the corn-seed, which is the life of the flesh, cannot flourish." But where could one go seeking? The Maidens had left no trail behind them. "Who can find them but our great Elder Brother, the Eagle," the people said. "He is enduring of will and surpassing of sight. Let us send messengers to the Eagle and ask him to make search for our Maidens white and beautiful."

So messengers were sent to the cavern where the Eagle had his nest. The three eaglets that were there tried to hide themselves in the dark recesses of the cavern. "Pull not our feathers, O ye of hurtful touch," they cried, "pull not our pin-feathers, and when our wings have grown and we are flying high we will drop feathers down to you." "O great Elder Brother," said the messengers, when the Father Eagle came whirring down to his nest, "we have come to you to beg that you will make search for our Maidens white and beautiful." "I will search for them and I will find them," said the Eagle. "Neither blue bird nor wood-rat can hide from my eyes." He snapped his beak, and he looked aslant, and then he rose high in the air and went searching, searching.

All through the heights he circled and sailed, going towards the north and the south, towards the east and the west. Nowhere did he get sight of the maidens. Then he came back and he spoke to the elders of the village. "I have journeyed far and I have scanned all regions," he said, "but no sight of your Maidens did I get. Go to my younger brother the Falcon and ask him to make search for them. He flies nearer the ground and he takes his flight ere sunrise, and it may be that he can find your Maidens."

Messengers were sent to the Falcon. "If ye have snare-strings with you I will fly off as swift as an arrow," said the Falcon. "We have no snare-strings with us, O Great Brother," said the messengers, "we have come to beg of you to make search for the Maidens who have gone from us. Our great Elder Brother the Eagle went searching for them, but he could not find any trace of them." "Ho," said the Falcon, "the Eagle flies too high; he clambers above the clouds, and so how could he see your Maidens? But unless they are hidden more closely than the sparrow hides I will find them for you." So the Falcon spread his sharp wings and went skimming off the tops of the trees and bushes as though he were seeking for birds' nests or for field-mice. He travelled far. But one day he perched upon an ant-hill outside the village, and he spoke to those who came to him and told them that he had not been able to find the Maidens white and beautiful.

Then when the people wept because of their loss, the Falcon said to them, "There is yet one who might find the Maidens for you. He is Heavy Nose the Raven. Go to him and ask him to make search for your Maidens white and beautiful." And saying this the Falcon flew off the ant-hill and went searching for birds' nests.

Then the people went looking for Heavy Nose the Raven. They found him at the break of day as he was wandering about the edge of the town, seeking food in the dirt and rubbish-heaps. "O Grandfather," they said to him, "neither our Elder Brother the Eagle nor his Younger Brother the Falcon have been able to find our Maidens for us. We pray you to give us counsel and guidance in the search for them." "Ye want me to go search for them, do ye? But too hungry am I to go abroad on business for you and your kind," said Heavy Nose the Raven. "Ye are stingy. Here have I been since perching time, striving to win a throatful, but ye pick the bones and ye lick the bowls too clean for me to get anything." "O poor Grandfather," said the Elders, "come with us and we will give you something to eat."

Heavy Nose went with them to where the Council sat, and they made much of him, and they gave him the best of tobacco to smoke. But as soon as he drew in the smoke he gasped and he gulped and he nearly coughed his head off. He had smoke inside and outside of himself. And to this day, blueness of flesh, and blackness of dress, and tearfulness of eye mark the kin of Heavy Nose who smoked at our Fathers' Council.

They brought him the best of corn, and Heavy Nose ate standing up, looking at our fathers out of one eye and then out of another. "Ka, ka," he said, when he had finished eating all they had brought to him, "and now tell me what you want me to do for you?" "We would have you search for our maidens white and beautiful."

Heavy Nose sat and considered and then he flew away without speaking to our Fathers. He flew to a rubbish-heap, and he sat there and considered again. Then back he flew to our Fathers. "Only one can find your maidens white and beautiful," he said, "he of the Mist and the Dawn, Paíyatuma." And saying this, Heavy Nose the Raven flew past the rubbish-heaps and away from the village.

Our Fathers considered what he had said. They knew now that neither the Eagle, the Falcon, nor the Raven could find and bring back to them their Maidens white and beautiful, the Maidens who could make grow the plants without which life of flesh cannot flourish. Only Paíyatuma could find them and bring them back. They came upon him outside the village; he was where they had found Heavy Nose the Raven—beside the rubbish-heaps.

And Paíyatuma was in his daylight mood. His dress was soiled and torn, his eyes were bleared, and with uncouth mouth he was muttering uncouth words. He laughed at and joked with our Fathers when they came up to where he lolled—like a clown he laughed at and jested with them. And when they begged him to come with them he rose up and went with them as to some boys' performance. He strode rudely into where the Council was being held, and he greeted all who were there noisily and without dignity or shame. And when our Fathers, lamenting, begged him to find for them and bring back to them the Corn Maidens whom he had once brought to them, he shouted, "Why find that which is not lost nor summon those who will not come?"

Like a clown Paíyatuma behaved at the Council, and like a clown he would have gone on behaving if a certain priest who was there had not gone to him, and put his hand between his lips, and stroked away what was on his lips. "Thou hast drawn from me the breath of reversal," said Paíyatuma. "Purify yourselves now and I shall speak to you as it is becoming in me to speak to you." No longer was he a clown, talking thoughtlessly, speaking words that shamed his own sacred being. No, Paíyatuma stood before the Fathers, tall and grand as a great tree that has been shorn by lightning. Verily, again they knew him for the God of Dew and of the Dawn.

In his presence they purified themselves, putting away from them all that disgraced them in his eyes. From the youths in the village they chose four who had not sinned in their flesh. These four youths they brought to Paíyatuma.

And with the four youths he set out for Summerland. Where he paused he played upon his flute, and butterflies and birds came around him and fed upon the dew that was breathed forth from his flute. In a little while he came to Summerland. The seven Maidens of the Corn were there. They heard his flute-playing, and when they saw his tall form coming through the fields of corn that was already quickened they went to meet him. The butterflies and the birds came and fluttered over them—over the seven Maidens of the Corn, over the four youths from the village, over Paíyatuma, as he played upon his flute.

Back to the village they went, the Maidens, the four youths, and Paíyatuma. O greatly did the people rejoice at having their Maidens back once more amongst them. The bower was built and the fire was lighted as before. All night, backwards and forwards, the Corn Maidens danced to music and to songs sung by the elders. They danced by the side of the seven growing plants, motioning them upwards. And as each Maiden embraced the plant that was hers, the fire threw out its yellow light, its blue light, its red light, its white light, its streaked light, its dim light, its light of many colours.

Ah, but as each Maiden embraced her growing plant, she put into the corn and, by a mystery, the substance of her flesh. Then, as that light of many colours was thrown from the fire, the Maidens went forth as shadows. Into the deep night they went, and they were seen no more of men. The dawn came and the Fathers saw Paíyatuma standing with folded arms before the fire. Solemnly he spoke to them all; well have the solemn words he uttered then been remembered. The corn would grow because of the substance of their flesh that the Corn Maidens had put in it; in future seasons maidens chosen from amongst our own daughters would dance backwards and forwards to the music of the flute as well as the drum, and would embrace the seven growing plants in the light of the fire. And all would be well for the growth of the corn. But as for the Maidens white and beautiful whom he had twice brought to us, they were gone from us forever. "They have departed since the children of men would seek to change the sustaining blessedness of their flesh into humanity which sustains not, but is sustained. In the loving of men and the cherishing of men's children, they—even they—would forget the cherishing of their beautiful seed-growing. The Mother-maidens have gone, but their substance is in the plants of corn."

For that reason the corn that is for seed is held by us as a thing sacred. Through the nights and days of the Moon Nameless, of the Moon of Sacred Fire and Earth, of the Moon of Earth Whitening, of the Moon of Snow-broken Boughs, of the Moon of Snowless Pathways, of the Moon of Lesser Sand-driving Storms, the seed of the corn is held. Then it is put in the earth reverently; it is buried as a tribe might bury its beloved dead. The seed which has in it the substance of our Maiden-mothers becomes quick beneath the earth. Paíyatuma, the God of Dew and of the Dawn, freshens the growth with his breath; then Ténatsali, the God of Time and of the Seasons, brings the plants to maturity; then Kwélele, the God of Heat, ripens them with the touch of his Fire-brother's torch, giving them their full vitality. And our own maidens dance beside the corn-plants in the light of the fire, motioning them upwards—upwards.

INDEX

INDEX

The Universal Library

OCCUPATION: WRITER

By

ROBERT GRAVES

OCCUPATION: WRITER *is not a how-to-write manual. It is more like a roller-coaster ride through one of the most astonishing minds of our times. But the title is accurate as far as it goes: Robert Graves has established himself at the top of his profession with a solid body of achievement in all literary forms over more than three decades. The general public knows him for his best-selling novels, which, though they deal with history, bear about the same relation to the genre of the "historical novel" as the "Iliad" might to the* BOBBSEY TWINS. *Scholars know him as one of the most penetrating searchers and fecund interpreters of man's past. Graves regards himself as a poet. Lesser poets may well regard him as a magician, for he seems to have an almost eerie familiarity with the Muse herself.*

In this collection of shorter pieces are lusty humor, as in THE LOST ART OF SWEARING, *erudition combined with wit, as in* IMPERIAL INCEST, *light satire, as in* THE ANCESTORS OF COLONEL BLIMP, *and "a selected number of theatrical pieces, short stories, and other elegant trifles calculated to delight the most discriminating of ladies and gentlemen."*

UL-53

THE TASTEMAKERS

By

RUSSELL LYNES

"TASTE," *says the author of this book, "is our personal pleasure, our private dilemma and our public facade."* THE TASTEMAKERS *is the lively story of the people and pressures that have shaped American taste for the last dozen decades.*

In a serious but witty and perceptive account, Mr. Lynes gives the battles of the taste-makers the dignity or humor they deserve — battles that are sometimes solemn and full of conviction, sometimes pompous, sometimes gay and frivolous. He reanimates — with all their original intensity and excitement — the battles of taste that account for our likes and dislikes today.

"It is a highly original job, very sound in scholarship, very sagacious, and constantly amusing. ... The way he lightly transforms himself into an encyclopedia of American culture is delightful and a little breathtaking."   BERNARD DEVOTO

"It reads like the liveliest conversation of a wise friend—the sort of conversation one always wishes would find its way into a book."   HERBERT AGAR

UL-54

WITH NAPOLEON IN RUSSIA

By

ARMAND DE CAULAINCOURT

IN AUGUST, *1933, an architect looking among the ruins of General Armand de Caulaincourt's old chateau in Picardy, noticed a battered iron chest in a pile of debris. On opening the chest he discovered the long-lost original manuscript of General de Caulaincourt's fabulous memoirs. Upon study, these memoirs turned out to be the most important discovery of Napoleonic materials in our time, for in them was a complete eye-witness account of how the Emperor planned and fought his greatest and most disastrous war—his invasion of Russia.*

No book on Napoleon has more bearing on the events of today than this astounding chronicle of the struggle between the Emperor and the Czar. Here is revealed not only the thoughts and actions of the great Emperor as recorded by his most distinguished aide and confidant, but also startling insights into the enigmatic character and ways of the Russians, whom Caulaincourt knew well since he had been Ambassador to the court of St. Petersburg.

Scholars and students will find fascinating parallels in the events of then and now. They will also find within these pages the most vivid closeup of Napoleon that we possess, the picture of a man considered a deity by many, possessed of the most remarkable qualities of leadership, yet prisoner of irrational obsessions that led him to defeat. UL-55

THE COMEDIES OF
OSCAR WILDE

THE COMEDIES of *Oscar Wilde have delighted audiences for more than half a century. As examples of wit and cynicism fashioned with the most glittering insolence, they
are unsurpassed, and belong in the tradition
of English high-comedy which has come
down from Congreve through Goldsmith and
Sheridan.*

*This volume contains Wilde's four great
comedies, all of which bear a quality as personal and as striking as any in English literature. At a time when Victorian platitudes,
long the axioms of life on the stage, had begun to lose their force, Wilde seemed to be
turning them upside-down or wrong side out,
showing that they worked nearly as well
either way. Wilde's elegant dialogue, sparkling
proverbs and mordant mots are as apt today
as when they were first heard. They will delight readers for many years to come.*

UL-56

MADAME BOVARY

By

Gustave Flaubert

MADAME BOVARY *has been called the first modern novel. Its influence on subsequent writers has been profound enough to warrant that description. Flaubert's magnificent achievement was to present a perfect perception of his characters with perfect objectivity. The result in* MADAME BOVARY *was a new kind of realism that shocked its first readers to the core. It remains for readers today just as impressive an experience. The tragedy of Emma Bovary is inexorable and belongs to the grand tradition of tragedy, but it is peculiarly modern, too. There is no appeal to the gods or to fate, no suggestion of a deus ex machina, however disguised. Step by step, with every action and motivation almost frighteningly real, Emma makes her own tragedy—and every other character is equally fully conceived. It is as if Flaubert had created whole people rather than characters of fiction and had then abandoned them to work out their own lives. But a closer examination reveals that this impression is achieved only through the most exquisitely painstaking craft.*

UL-57

PRIDE AND PREJUDICE

By Jane Austen

JANE AUSTEN'S *brilliant comedy of manners has amused and delighted readers for more than a century. Its enduring qualities are those inherent in Miss Austen's great artistry as a novelist — in her superb ability to create living characters and in her skill as a social satirist of the most delicate kind.*

She treated the society in which she lived with a lightly ironic touch. She was concerned with the complex details of respectable life, the little perplexities of emotion and conduct which were the never-ending problems of her country gentlefolk. Miss Austen was of that society herself, yet she had the rare ability to see things as they were, objectively but sympathetically.

PRIDE AND PREJUDICE *is basically a love story — the chronicle of a long courtship in which the hero's pride and the heroine's prejudice are the primary obstacles to a well-suited marriage. It is Miss Austen's sense of dramatic progression that makes this romance into one of the most fascinating in all literature.*

UL-58

THE *delicate capture of a passing mood, the keen sympathy with the Hamlet in all human beings, the poignant probing of an overwhelming frustration—these are the elements which make up Chekov's dramatic vision of life. These plays of the twilight make Chekov, to the Russia of today, perhaps more alien than any other writer of the first rank, though he has been a major influence upon dramatists of the West.*

Perhaps Chekov's basic contribution to the stage can be summed up in the statement that he de-theatricalized the theatre. His plays end, as T. S. Eliot might say, not with a bang but a whimper. He demonstrates that tragedy can be as real in the slow wasting away of lives as in the great dramas of fore-destined catastrophe. He deals with human fate in a minor key.

That Chekov's dramas are of enduring appeal is proven by repeated revivals of his works. This volume, containing four of his major plays and five one-act masterpieces, also provides a valuable chronological table of the playwright's life and works. UL-59

McSorley's Wonderful Saloon

By

Joseph Mitchell

Most of the twenty stories in this book are about low-life in New York City. Mr. Mitchell presents an admiring description of the eccentricities of the owners and customers of McSorley's, the oldest and most independent saloon in the city, whose bartenders use four soup bowls instead of a cash register, and whose motto is "Good Ale, Raw Onions, and No Ladies."

A few of the citizens who figure in these stories are: MAZIE, *the blonde and slangy proprietor of a dime movie house, who roams the Bowery after midnight and is undoubtedly the greatest authority in the world on the habits of male and female bums;* PROFESSOR SEA GULL, *also known as Joe Gould, who filled 270 composition books with bawdy conversations overheard in Greenwich Village;* COMMODORE DUTCH, *a sporting man, who makes a living by giving an annual ball for the benefit of himself;* LADY OLGA, *the greatest bearded lady in the history of the American sideshow; and* PAPA HOUDINI, *a Harlem Calypso singer, among whose songs are* "Old Man You Too Old, You Too Bold, In Fact You Too Cold" *and* "I Like Bananas Because They Have No Bones."

UL-60

CRIME AND PUNISHMENT
BY
FYODOR DOSTOEVSKY

IT WOULD *probably be appalling to count the number of intelligent readers who have been put off from reading* Crime and Punishment *by its curious reputation as a classic of gloom — both classic and gloominess somehow suggest dullness. Nothing could be farther from Dostoevsky's masterpiece than the suggestion of dullness — disturbing, yes, even terrifying, but* Crime and Punishment *is more thrilling than any novel ever written to provide thrills.*

As Dorothy Brewster says in the introduction to this edition: "The plot, simple enough in outline, is full of breathless suspense and hair-raising episodes. It may be taken quite naively as one of the most thrilling of detective stories. Or just as naively — but more solemnly — as a Christian drama of sin and retribution…or into it may be read psychological, philosophical, and even metaphysical significance, to the limit of one's capacity for such speculation. On whatever levels of response it touches the reader's imagination, it is certain to be a disturbing experience." UL-63

MR. JELLY ROLL
By
ALAN LOMAX

SINCE *its first appearance in 1950, this biography of Ferdinand "Jelly Roll" Morton by Alan Lomax has become a classic of jazz literature. For not only is it the biography of one of the great jazz musicians of all time, it is also the story of a new kind of music that rose out of America's tumultuous plural character to become the music of the twentieth century.*

The Chicago Tribune *wrote: "Alan Lomax has fashioned a biography that, for utter candor and spontaneity of utterance, rivals the self-revelations of Rousseau and St. Augustine."*

And the San Francisco Chronicle *wrote: "You begin to get a fresh idea of what was behind the development of the new music that said so many things to so many people. You see that jazz was actually a 'cultural transmutation,' as Mr. Lomax puts it, 'a wordless counterpoint of protest and of pride.' No one with even the slightest feeling for the subject can afford to miss this book."*

UL-64